Supplement 1 to The ASTD Technical and Skills Training Handbook

Other McGraw-Hill Books Sponsored by the American Society for Training and Development

Piskurich
THE ASTD HANDBOOK OF INSTRUCTIONAL TECHNOLOGY

Craig
TRAINING AND DEVELOPMENT HANDBOOK

Kelly
THE ASTD TECHNICAL AND SKILLS TRAINING HANDBOOK

Supplement 1 to The ASTD Technical and Skills Training Handbook

Sponsored by the American Society for Training and Development

Leslie Kelly
Editor in Chief

McGraw-Hill
New York San Francisco Washington, D.C. Auckland Bogotá
Caracas Lisbon London Madrid Mexico City Milan
Montreal New Delhi San Juan Singapore
Sydney Tokyo Toronto

McGraw-Hill

A Division of The McGraw·Hill Companies

Copyright © 1996 by The McGraw-Hill Companies, Inc. All rights reserved. Printed in the United States of America. Except as permitted under the United States Copyright Act of 1976, no part of this publication may be reproduced or distributed in any form or by any means, or stored in a data base or retrieval system, without the prior written permission of the publisher.

2 3 4 5 6 7 8 9 0   DOC/DOC   9 0 1 0 9 8 7 6

ISBN 0-07-034073-0

The sponsoring editor for this book was Harold B. Crawford, the editing supervisor was Penny Linskey, and the production supervisor was Donald F. Schmidt. This book was set in Century Schoolbook. It was composed by Donald A. Feldman of McGraw-Hill's Professional Book Group composition unit.

Printed and bound by R. R. Donnelley & Sons Company.

 This book is printed on recycled, acid-free paper containing a minimum of 50% recycled de-inked fiber.

American Society for Training and Development Handbook Advisory Board

Dr. Victor Haburchak
Senior Associate Director
The Alliance
  (AT&T/CWA/IBEW)
Somerset, New Jersey

Johnna Howell
Corporate Director for Staffing
  and Development
Westin Hotels
Seattle, Washington

James A. Lacy
Principal
Jim Lacy Consulting
Dallas, Texas

G. A. Pall
President
Juran International, Inc.
Wilton, Connecticut

Rick Sullivan
Director of Training
Johns Hopkins University
  Program for International
  Education in Reproductive
  Health
Baltimore, Maryland

Contents

Preface   xi

1. **An Introduction to the Information Superhighway**   1
   Darlene Van Tiem, Ph.D.

   1.1 Introduction   1
   1.2 Information Superhighway Defined   2
   1.3 Impact on the Technical and Skills Workplace   4
   1.4 Impact on the Employee   6
   1.5 Employee Skill Needs   10
   1.6 Needs Assessment and Gap Analysis   13
   1.7 Employee Skill Development   14
   1.8 Conclusion   22
   1.9 Glossary   22
   1.10 On-line Services   25
   1.11 References   25

2. **Forming Alliances: The Regional Quality Network**   27
   Jan Green and Janice Martin

   2.1 Background   28
   2.2 Network Goals   30
   2.3 Network Objectives   31
   2.4 Network Operating Criteria   31
   2.5 Membership   32
   2.6 Funding   33
   2.7 Benefits of the Regional Quality Network   33
   2.8 Committees   35
   2.9 Conclusion   37
   2.10 Resources   38

viii   Contents

3. The Merging of Total Quality, Cultural Change, and Learning Organization Concepts in a High-Tech Environment 43
Michael A. Sullivan

    3.1 Introduction 44
    3.2 Chapter Review 44
    3.3 Influential Literature 46
    3.4 Chronological Events Supplement 59
    3.5 Learnings and Relearnings 65
    3.6 Recommendations 66
    3.7 References 66

4. The University of Chicago Hospitals Move toward a Managed Care Environment 67
Nancy Merriam and Victoria A. Gundrum

    4.1 Introduction 68
    4.2 An Introduction to the University of Chicago Hospitals 68
    4.3 Providing Care to the Surrounding Community 69
    4.4 Organizational Structure of the University of Chicago Hospitals 70
    4.5 Technology in Use Today in the Ambulatory Care Clinics 71
    4.6 Anticipated Technology in the Ambulatory Care Clinics 72
    4.7 The Impact of New Kinds of Insurance Coverage 73
    4.8 The Managed Care Working Group 74
    4.9 The Managed Care Working Group's Recommendations 75
    4.10 Breaking the Task Down into Short- and Long-Term Goals 78
    4.11 Creation and Charge of the Managed Care Systems and Operations Committee 79
    4.12 Where to Start: Focus on the Ambulatory Care Training Initiative 79
    4.13 Gathering Data: Work Flows and Baseline Measurements 80
    4.14 Securing Sponsorship 80
    4.15 Developing a Training Plan 81
    4.16 Selecting Pilot Sites 83
    4.17 Administering the Pretraining Assessment 83
    4.18 Developing Additional Tools to Measure Skill Transfer 83
    4.19 Pilot Sessions 84
    4.20 Measuring Pilot Results 85
    4.21 Reporting to the Sponsor Committee and Setting New Goals 85
    4.22 Certifying Employee Competency 86
    4.23 Where Are We Now and Where Are We Going? 87
    4.24 Glossary of Terms and Titles 88

5. Competency-Based Technical Training on an International Scale 91
Rick Sullivan

    5.1 Introduction 91
    5.2 What Is Competency-Based Training? 93
    5.3 International Technical Training 96
    5.4 JHPIEGO's Approach to CBT 101
    5.5 Transfer of Training 107

5.6	Summary	108
5.7	References	108

6. Vocational Education and Technical Training in the Netherlands   111
Jan Waldrus

6.1	Introduction	112
6.2	The Netherlands	112
6.3	The Educational System in the Netherlands	114
6.4	Certification Programs through Training Institutes	122
6.5	Conclusion	130
6.6	Resources	130

7. Liability and the Technical Trainer: Recent Cases and Comments   131
John Sample, Ph.D.

7.1	Introduction	131
7.2	Sex Discrimination, Technical Training, and Human Resources Management	132
7.3	Adventure-Based Training: An Example from a Corporate Utility	136
7.4	Negligent Technical Training in a Retail Store	139
7.5	Framework for Identifying High-Liability Tasks	140
7.6	Conclusion	146
7.7	Glossary	146
7.8	References	146

8. Developing Legally Defensible Tests   149
Robert Bass, Ph.D.

8.1	Introduction	149
8.2	Case Studies	150
8.3	Test Development Guidelines	153
8.4	Test Development	154
8.5	Additional Issues	161
8.6	Summary	164
8.7	References	164

9. On-the-Job Learning: A Look at the Papermaking Industry   165
P. J. Marsh

9.1	Introduction	165
9.2	Papermaking	166
9.3	Paper Mill South: Developing Training Checklists	167
9.4	Paper Mill North: Hourly Workers Develop and Deliver Training	172
9.5	Envelope Co.: Machine Adjuster's Methods Reverse Plant Results	176
9.6	Unstructured OJT Deficiencies	179
9.7	Seven Building Blocks of OJL	181
9.8	Conclusion	190
9.9	References	190

10. Putting Some Fun in Your Technical Training — 191
Annie S. W. Phoon

    10.1 Introduction — 192
    10.2 Techniques to Create a Stimulating Learning Environment — 193
    10.3 Techniques to Open the Training Session — 196
    10.4 Techniques to Replace or Modify the Lecture — 199
    10.5 Techniques to Review Learning — 204
    10.6 Conclusion — 207
    10.7 Learning Styles — 207
    10.8 List of Baroque Music — 208
    10.9 References — 209

Index 211

Preface

The success of *The ASTD Technical and Skills Training Handbook* has made the supplements which will be issued periodically critical to the technical skills trainer's total view of the field. The supplements are meant to complement the original handbook and further enhance the technical trainer's knowledge of what is really going on in technical training.

The group of authors in this first Supplement were chosen with several things in mind. There are some never published authors. Our distinguished Editorial Advisory Board worked with these individuals to insure that their stories would be told. We are very committed to giving our readers the very best programs available. Congratulations to our first-time book authors Bob Bass, Janice Davis, Jan Green, Nancy Merriam, Victoria Gundrum, and Jan Waldrus for jobs very well done!! They had wonderful stories to tell and we are very pleased with their chapters. Bob Bass covers a critical and growing area in technical training—use of evaluation and testing. Janice Davis and Jan Green talk about a Chamber of Commerce coalition that is offering affordable, top-notch technical training to 20 companies who have pooled their training dollars to bring critically needed skills training to small manufacturing businesses. Nancy Merriam and Victoria Gundrum offer some insight into the immense technical training needs that the health care industry is experiencing as technology changes rapidly, as well as the need to introduce greater efficiencies into an already enormous, ever-growing health care system. Finally, Jan Waldrus of the Netherlands talks about how interwoven the education and technical training efforts are in the Netherlands. U.S. businesses will find the system presents some models for education-company based collaborations.

Other authors featured in the supplement are Darlene Van Tiem of Ameritech, exploring the technological training implications of the Information Superhighway, John Sample, addressing the legal implications of technical training (this will be a running chapter in each book since it is such a critically important subject), Rick Sullivan talking about the challenge of doing medical training in a third world country, P. J. Marsh looking at how a paper company set up training for all its technical positions and coordinated it for maximum impact, Mike Sullivan following up on his installation of a total quality program at Delphi, a Division of General Motors Corporation, and Annie Phoon from Singapore, highlighting techniques for making technical training content easier to sit through and to learn.

Leslie Kelly

Acknowledgments

And what is a book without the help of some very important people? Many thanks to Hal Crawford, my Editor-in-Chief, at McGraw-Hill, Penny Linskey, my editing supervisor, at McGraw-Hill, Nancy Olson, head of publications at the American Society for Training and Development, and Ellen Carnavale, former editor of *Technical Skills Training*. These people have provided invaluable production help and advice.

But the group that really made this book a reality is my terrific Editorial Advisory Board. Again they offered as much help as was needed within excruciating deadlines. Vic Haburchak, Johnna Howell, Jim Lacy, Gabe Pall, and Rick Sullivan worked with people who had never been authors before so their stories could be told. This took many additional hours of work which they all gladly contributed. In addition their years of experience and excellent knowledge of technical training insured we had an outstanding Supplement 1 to complement an already successful handbook. They deserve loud applause for all the time invested. Interestingly enough, this volume took more time than the original handbook because of our commitment to getting and publishing the best chapters available, even if it meant helping new authors tell their very important stories.

Finally, a big thank you to my eighteen-year-old son who began working part-time at my firm this past year. He helped with coordination efforts and provided good back-up as well as great humor when the work was tedious and long.

To our readers, enjoy! All of us connected with the books continue to feel like sponges, soaking up new knowledge and insight into technical training.

Chapter

1

An Introduction to the Information Superhighway

Darlene Van Tiem, Ph.D.

Darlene Van Tiem, training director, Ameritech Advertising Services, is responsible for job-specific training (information technology, marketing, operations, finance, human resources, legal, and sales) and generic training (interpersonal, communications, management, quality and team-building, corporate culture, orientation, and leadership) as well as executive education. She is also responsible for training for a companywide software mechanization system.

Darlene conducts needs assessments and creates training programs on a just-in-time basis. She designs and implements a companywide curriculum delivery system, negotiates with and manages vendors, and assists in defining HRIS specifications. She also chairs the union/management training development board.

Prior to joining Ameritech, Darlene was curriculum manager for corporate-sponsored technical training at all General Motors locations through General Physics Corporation. Darlene has served as director of ASTD's Technical and Skills Professional Practice Area. She has received two National ASTD awards: Technical Skills Trainer of the Year (External Practitioner)—1992 and Outstanding Contribution to Leadership in the Automotive Industry Group—1993. Darlene was president of the Greater Detroit ASTD chapter in 1978. She co-authored the "Technical Training Suppliers" chapter in the ASTD Technical and Skills Training Handbook *(1995).*

1.1 Introduction

Information and computers are causing dramatic changes in the workplace by redefining the basic assumptions of work. Computers, connected to nearby and distant work sites through networks, are providing *instant* access to information and *instant* tracking of progress and products. Through the information superhighway, readily available on-line information will soon be the norm. Computers and communications equipment will have simpler technology and will be more intuitive and user-friendly. The challenge will be to prepare employees to adapt and function effectively with the resulting systems. New skills are required to adapt, understand, and maximize the new information-based systems.

1.2 Information Superhighway Defined

The "information superhighway" is a massive worldwide connectivity of *computers* and *communication equipment* outside or inside an organization or residence. The technology of the information superhighway relies on complex switches, fiber-optic cable networks or satellite transmitters, and simple-to-use communications equipment with undreamed-of capabilities.

1.2.1 Initial access

Getting onto the information superhighway is amazingly easy. Most companies and individuals begin by purchasing a modem and a computer software package to connect existing computers with an information network, such as America Online, Prodigy, CompuServe, or ASTD On-line. During this stage, internal and external electronic mail (E-mail) benefits the organization by reducing "telephone tag"; simplifying tasks such as scheduling, banking, or purchasing; promoting communication with suppliers and colleagues; and supporting market research that was previously accessible only through trained librarians.

Organizations and individuals are becoming comfortable with the new networked systems and are gradually coming to appreciate the convenience and easy access to information. World Wide Web pages are being generated across the Internet to provide point-and-click access to information about people, places, organizations, and products. The current "surfing" or access-by-accident method of finding these sites will evolve as revolutionary approaches in information gathering are developed. In addition, electronic mail usage will expand to include on-line access to various sources of information, just as telephone access is universally available today. A potential downside with access is accumulating costs (per hour charges or charges beyond a flat-rate basic service). In addition, CompuServe, America Online, and Prodigy will not be able to handle the volumes required for universal access and will need to markedly expand their capacity.

1.2.2 Universal access

Hence the great concern for universal access, which means the capability of everyone's being able to use state-of-the-art on-line computer and communications equipment. If adequate planning and implementation does not occur, *haves* will come to mean "those with adequate access to information," and *have nots* will mean "those without adequate access." Communication companies [Regional Bell Operating Companies (RBOCs), MCI, AT&T, Sprint, cable television networks, and local organizations] already vie for rights to lucrative markets. The fear is that some people will have well-maintained information highways, others will have ruts in the wilderness or information ditches, and a few will have no roadway at all. The social implications are critical for maintaining the possibility of engaging in meaningful work (Carey, 1994).

In order to be competitive, businesses are going to need *more information more quickly*. In the industrial era, advances were incremental and often gradual. In the information era, changes will come very quickly, and obsolescence will also be rapid.

1.2.3 Hardware, software, and communications equipment

The information superhighway will provide interactive media capabilities to households, schools, business and industry, libraries, hospitals, and government offices. Although equipment and software are changing rapidly, the technology is expected to include

1. Fiber-optic cable—fiberglass strands bundled in plastic sheathing that are capable of carrying 500,000 conversations simultaneously
2. Integrated Services Digital Network (ISDN)—technology that allows voice, data, and video to be transmitted over a single telephone line
3. Advanced signaling systems—satellite transmission for specialized situations, such as multiple sites, remote sites, and rural users

Cabling is one of the keys to efficient information access. At present, most residential and small business neighborhoods have access only through copper wiring, which carries a limited number of transactions simultaneously. Copper will not be able to handle the communications volume that organizations will need to be competitive in the future. For example, information-oriented companies currently require computers (linked through localized networks or modems), laser or ink-jet printers, faxes, and telephones. Fiber-optic cabling, containing strands of fine spun glass, can increase simultaneous connections. Many communications companies and building owners are replacing copper with optical fiber to increase capacity, clarity, and efficiency. Fiber itself is rapidly improving in capacity potential and transmission quality.

The information superhighway is ever evolving. Rapid improvements in the technology and increasing simplicity of use will radically increase demand. Demand will confront the limitation of today's communications access and spur the development of universal access to the information superhighway.

1.3 Impact on the Technical and Skills Workplace

The value and significance of information in the workplace will be increasingly important. Already, information has influenced aspects of every American job. Growth of the information superhighway will intensify the effect by adding more users, more services, and more advanced technology.

1.3.1 Computer-aided manufacturing (CAM)

Manufacturing has created one of the more robust applications of information systems. Computers have integrated the entire process, from design (computer-aided design) to testing (computer-aided engineering) and production (computer-aided manufacturing). These systems create networks within the manufacturing organization that allow employees access to meaningful information along the entire manufacturing process.

As a consequence, manufacturing plants are establishing problem-solving teams that identify concerns, then research and analyze the situations to determine the root causes. These teams rely on sophisticated information from sensors and computers attached to the machines to monitor quality and quantity. Machine sensors and computers are connected to a networked database; the team can then use this to analyze historical and current information, make summaries, complete "what-if" analysis, and predict trends. Using the information, the team can produce bar charts and line graphs that depict trends and relationship matrices that help them anticipate future situations. This vast interconnected chain of information increases quality and efficiency.

The automotive industry has an increasing need for information throughout the entire design and manufacturing process. David Cole, director of the University of Michigan's Office for the Study of Automotive Transportation, explained that the automotive industry "has evolved noticeably into more of an intellectually based industry."

Engineering jobs are increasing, and plant-based manufacturing jobs use more thinking and analysis to monitor processes and solve problems (Lienert and Lienert, 1995).

1.3.2 Inventory control

Inventory control is a universal need of organizations. For the most part, inventory can already be tracked efficiently—meaning that supplies are ordered by selecting just the right characteristics and then estimating total costs, including shipping, handling, tariffs, and taxes, and determining routing options that minimize cost or time. The retail industry already tracks inventory through point-of-sale scanners. The scanning system is usually linked to an automatic ordering system that plans shipments from suppliers, routes incoming supplies for several stores in a vicinity to maximize space on the carrier, prices the items, and takes into account anticipated promotions or preferences of specific local customers. Manufacturing environments have been shifting to "just-in-time" inventory control to reduce costs of purchasing and storing plant floor supplies.

Eventually workers will order supplies using "virtual reality" catalogues that provide extensive information plus the computer screen resolution and auxiliary devices necessary to be certain of the appropriateness of the features as well as the specifications. For example, electricians will order wire cutters by seeming to put their fingers into the handle grips to determine if the tool will be strong enough for typical situations. The product selection process will use virtual reality, through special gloves, wires, and sensors.

1.3.3 Data entry

As noted, scanning devices already track inventory. Data entry—which is tedious and subject to error—is increasingly being minimized or eliminated. Purchasing, production control, and logistics personnel will no longer enter redundant data because information systems will lift information off bar codes or magnetic strips and archive it.

Sales representatives, for example, will no longer need to enter parts descriptions or configuration options. Acceptable system or component combinations will be defined, so that computer screen prompts will remind the salesperson of all available options while preventing noncompatible combinations. At present, sales representatives for communications companies have proprietary software that blocks out incorrect combinations of switches, networks, and equipment, thereby increasing sales effectiveness. In addition, order information for most industries can be conveniently transmitted by docking station and modem through an automated system, electronic data interchange (EDI).

1.3.4 Product-process development

Decision support systems are already available on-line through internal company networks or external linkages. These networks enable users to request and share information. Decisions may require a wide range of research services, such as Mead Data Central's Nexis and Lexis Research Services or the Dun & Bradstreet Rating Service, to name a few (Ameritech, 1994). For example, an automotive supplier established a cross-functional team to investigate and make a proposal for the purchase of a new press. The team researched the latest stamping methods and investigated press manufacturers, utilizing the resources of the information superhighway. Without leaving the stamping plant team room, the project team acquired information that narrowed the search prior to making on-site visits. Thus the information superhighway shortened the machinery purchase cycle time and enabled a more reasoned data-gathering and alternative-seeking phase.

1.3.5 Electronic performance support systems

Electronic performance support systems (EPSS) provide electronic (computer) support, enabling workers to increase speed, productivity, or accuracy through use of a series of screens and tutorials. This is just-in-time training. It is information on demand, when needed. Levin describes EPSS "as a return to on-the-job training but with the benefit of multimedia to deliver messages through diagrams, charts and graphs, video, audio, graphics, and text" (Levin, 1994). EPSS, which often leverages expert systems technology, is used to create electronic versions of reference guides and problem-solving manuals. EPSS allows employees to search quickly for information and find exactly what is needed.

With EPSS, users have information at their fingertips and need not rely on assistance from others. By pressing a computer key or a mouse, employees can find answers without consulting printed references. Employees are able to increase job performance, make better use of training dollars, and reduce training time. EPSS empowers employees (RWD, 1995).

Clearly, the information superhighway is already part of the employment way of life. Maximizing the benefits will require new employee skills and thus affect staffing and compensation practices.

1.4 Impact on the Employee

The need for information and the ability to make decisions and plans based on information will change staffing, training, career development, and compensation practices. As business requirements change, companies expect Human Resources to find employees who have the new skill requirements.

On the other hand, for many companies, change is so rapid and continuous that seeking new skills externally is no longer feasible. Companies are anticipating the emerging skill requirements and providing training and development to prepare existing workers.

In contrast to previous gradual changes in skill requirements, businesses now face a transformation in workplace skill needs. In the past, work consisted of completing physical tasks. Through automation, the computer can now regulate the process and workflow. Employees decide what tasks need to be done and manage the task completion, including troubleshooting when unusual situations occur. For example, grinders used to take cast metal and create machined parts with speed and skill. Now, the grinding machine finishes the parts and the worker changes computer instructions for various work orders or provides basic cleaning and lubrication. Sensors monitor quality, vibrations, and other maintenance factors, alerting workers of the need to change cutting tools or make adjustments. Physical skills for grinding, such as the ability to lift parts or steadiness, are not needed. Thinking skills are necessary to understand computer programs or anticipate problems, such as during failure mode effects analysis (FMEA) sessions.

1.4.1 Staffing

Employees will require a variety of special skills to meet the demands of the information era. For example, engineering staff will require greater understanding of information-oriented capabilities, such as computer-aided design, computer-aided manufacturing, and computer-aided engineering. Manufacturing personnel will need robotics, project management, programmable equipment operation and repair, and process monitoring and control. Technical marketing personnel will require more research analysis, business case development, project management, customer orientation, and problem-solving skills. Technical sales staff will require more relationship building, negotiation, collaboration, research analysis, and basic technical product and business knowledge. Many of these skills are best initially developed through a systematic educational curriculum delivered by high schools, technical schools, and colleges.

Educational relations. The relationship of business to the educational community is increasingly critical to the effort to maintain a state-of-the-art workforce in a competitive global economy. Educational systems (high schools, job-training centers, colleges, and universities) are the most efficient source of initial knowledge development for the information workforce. Major research findings can be conveyed to students, enabling them to be informed of the latest technology. Schools and training centers with a comprehensive and systematic curriculum can provide an excellent foundation. Once employees are in the work environment, however, they no longer have access to the latest knowledge and research findings and begin losing their knowledge advantage; this is known as the *knowledge maturity curve.* Retaining this advantage through continuing education is critical in the information era. Lifelong learning will be required to maintain a competitive workforce. As a result, staffing functions will need to extend beyond recruiting to working closely with schools and colleges to reinforce the need for highly skilled graduates.

Information-based systems. Human resources activities will increasingly use the information superhighway because of the need to interface and communicate efficiently and effectively with diverse external placement and temporary employment agencies. Phones and external electronic mail can be useful in enabling prospective employees to learn about available positions and request applications. Technology will enable employers to target a much broader labor pool across a wide geographic area by posting jobs, receiving credentials from colleges and universities, and conducting reference checks on-line.

Virtual workplaces. Companies will increasingly screen for employees with home office equipment. Today, employees are working from almost any location, particularly their own homes.

Alternative workplaces are developing with lightning speed, primarily because of the availability of portable and affordable communications equipment. Telecommuting is an outcome of the information superhighway, enabling employees to work at home or at another location and send and receive work assignments, use voice mail and electronic messaging, schedule, and have discussions through communications networks.

Busy employees save time by working at home before appointments and not wasting time driving to the job or by working on major projects and assignments with fewer interruptions. Employees will need dedicated space with adequate wiring for modems, faxes, computers, printers, answering machines, voice mail, and telephones.

In addition, workers such as computer programmers do not depend on regular contact with others to get their job done. They are likely to move out of the company office, with an occasional trip in for meetings or to submit work samples or work in progress.

Encouraging virtual workplaces increases productivity, customer responsiveness, and efficiency, as a result of minimal interruptions and reduced stress. Absenteeism is reduced because people can often work for a few hours around home appliance deliveries or home repairs or while recovering from illness. This flexibility enhances worker satisfaction while containing costs, such as rent and utilities.

On the other hand, virtual workplaces require workers with greater self-motivation, self-discipline, goal orientation, and self-monitoring skills because there is less structure than in the company workplace routine. In addition, workers need to socialize in new ways, since people usually miss the daily face-to-face interaction with other employees. People may communicate on-line or by using the telephone to complete entire projects without ever seeing other team members in person.

1.4.2 Compensation

Jobs in the information era will require high initiative, offer low supervision, and demand a high degree of sensitivity to customer preferences. The information-oriented job skills will be difficult to measure. As a result, it will be very difficult to establish performance standards and benchmarks for performance appraisal and compensation. However, new compensation plans will encourage broad skill development, resulting in more flexible employees. Compensation will influence cross-training, retraining, and career development efforts, primarily through *pay for knowledge* and *pay for learning* incentives.

Pay for knowledge. Knowledge—in this context, the skills and abilities required to intelligently convert data and ideas into information and beneficial plans and actions—will be increasingly valued in the workplace. Employees will need a broader range of skills and abilities in order to solve diverse problems and meet the daily challenges of an increasingly complex, communication-oriented workplace.

As lifelong learning becomes the workplace norm, organizations will set aside both the time and the financial resources needed to acquire the necessary knowledge, skills, and abilities. Continuous and efficient learning will be part of the job. There will be two types of workplace learning:

1. Job-specific requirements ("need to know")
2. Less context-specific "employability" and career development skills

Pay for knowledge is a strategy to motivate employees to continuously learn *necessary* skills. Pay structures define the needed knowledge and the pay increments. For example, self-directed team members in some compensation plans may increase their compensation by learning

1. Basic finance and accounting to create and monitor project budgets

2. Project management to allocate resources, create workflows, and determine milestone charts
3. On-line researching to review abstracts of publications related to team projects

Required skill building will occur during work hours and will be entirely financed by the company. Necessary learning is usually just-in-time and just-enough and closely matched to job descriptions and departmental functions.

Pay for learning. Employability and career development skills are *not job-specific* but create a flexible, competitive foundation broad enough to readily apply to the ever-changing workplace. There is usually a shared commitment, with the company paying the direct financial costs (often through tuition reimbursement) and the employee providing the indirect resources, such as time and local travel.

1.5 Employee Skill Needs

During their initial years on the job, employees usually have greater technical knowledge, which they learned in school. Unfortunately, employees' knowledge quickly becomes obsolete, resulting in lower productivity. It will be necessary to maintain comprehensive and rigorous training curricula while encouraging periodic reentry into the educational arena of schools, colleges, and universities.

Workers will require a range of skill sets: personal growth, computer, and information management skills. At present, some people have some of these skills and others have very few of them. However, each worker will have to function at the highest level of expertise in each area in order to survive. Making their combination of skills unique past workplaces demanded more physical types of skills. Also, each skill area relates to computers, software, and new technology and requires team approaches.

There will also be increasing need for cross-training, as evidenced by the growing use of joint problem-solving teams. Cross-functional teams often require basic understanding of the other team members' functional areas in order to work together effectively. A taxonomy of these skills, divided into three clusters, is presented below.

1.5.1 Personal growth skills

Personal growth skills include tolerance for ambiguity, critical thinking (analysis and synthesis), self-monitoring, project management, and creativity.

Communication (reading and writing)

Reading: Is able to understand written words and sentences.

Writing: Can create language in written form that is organized, original, and understandable.

Speaking: Can understand spoken language and can speak the language in which business is conducted.

Listening: Can interpret oral language accurately, with the ability to paraphrase.

Tolerance for ambiguity. Is able to work effectively without clear direction. Is able to search out answers and take prudent risks necessary to make progress without complete information.

Critical thinking (analysis and synthesis). Has a broad perspective; can anticipate future consequences and trends. Is able to divide complex situations into component aspects and also draw together factors into an overall picture.

Self-monitoring (meta-analysis). Is aware of own behavior and can analyze it accurately, both successes and failures, for clues for improvement. Experiments and then analyzes consequences and outcomes. Open to change.

Project management. Has the ability to manage multiple activities simultaneously, which may involve a number of priorities with pressure to accomplish results in short timeframes. Organizes resources and tasks into smooth work flows, measures progress realistically, and continuously evaluates and recognizes when to make adjustments.

Flexibility. Is able to consider many options and move from one direction to another readily. Is able to adapt his or her role and tactics to fit the situation in the context of an operative code of ethics.

Creativity and innovation. Is able to generate new ideas and unique solutions; easily makes connections among previously unrelated notions; effective in brainstorming techniques. Constructively questions reasons why and seeks ways to make changes to improve products, processes, or services.

1.5.2 Computer skills

As a given, each worker will require a basic proficiency in computer skills. Basic keyboarding skills are prerequisite, which may be a tremendous learning challenge for those who have not been exposed to terminals and keyboards previously.

With prices falling, there is a significant increase in the use of computers. Most people are just getting comfortable with computers but are not using the full capacity of their computer system. Because of a lack of training, they are working at the introductory or intermediate levels of software. It is predicted that advanced skill levels will not be commonplace for two to three more years (Maurer, 1994).

Computer literacy. Has an awareness of hardware, software, and data communications.

Keyboard agility and accuracy. Is able to type accurately and quickly using all fingers and typing conventions.

Word processing. Is able to use software to produce printed work effectively and efficiently.

Database management. Is able to use software to manage data, create spreadsheets, and illustrate trends and comparisons with charts and graphs. Is able to download information from other sources to integrate with "own" data.

Equipment troubleshooting. Is able to discuss computer situations with help desks and jointly determine a remedy.

1.5.3 Self-management skills

Information-oriented work performance will be difficult to define as behaviors, a fact complicating performance evaluation. Information workers will rely more on intrinsic attitudes and problem-solving capabilities. Many employees will have remote assignments or choose to work at home. These conditions will require trust, independence, and internal locus of control for the at-home worker. Those not assigned to a company-based workplace will also need tolerance for isolation.

Trustworthiness. Has great integrity; is seen as a direct, truthful individual. Provides accurate, complete information. Completes job duties according to organization's values and code of conduct.

Independence. Is able to work alone, with limited assistance. Is able to set direction and monitor own progress. Is able to solve own problems through problem-solving strategies.

Planning and organizing. Is able to see patterns in situations and prioritize tasks. Creates plans to complete goals, assignments, and expectations. Is able to maintain own schedule.

Problem solving and decision making. Has the ability to utilize a broad set of activities to determine and implement solutions to alleviate an unsatisfactory situation. Sees beyond simplistic corrections.

Steps:

1. Identify, define, and diagnose problem.
2. Find alternative solutions.
3. Evaluate alternatives and choose solution.
4. Implement chosen solution.
5. Evaluate implementation for continuous improvement.

Self-motivation. Sets challenging, achievable goals and monitors progress toward them.

1.6 Needs Assessment and Gap Analysis*

**Needs Assessment &
Gap Analysis
Skills Related to
*Information Superhighway***

1.6.1 Contents

Directions

   Desired state

   Current state

   Prioritization

Assessment worksheets

   Personal growth skills

   Computer skills

   Self-management skills

Developmental activity worksheet

1.6.2 Directions

There are three steps in the assessment process:

   Desired state

   Current state

   Prioritization

---

*Adapted with permission from Ameritech Corporation.

Desired state. Every organization varies in terms of the skill levels necessary. Therefore, it is important to document the desired skill level for your own work group. Management or a designated individual needs to determine skill level requirements. (0 = no need, 1 = awareness, 2 = user, 3 = expert)

Current state. Describe each employee by agreeing on the actual level evidenced in the work environment. Usually the manager and the employee make judgments independently and then meet and jointly agree on final levels. This process should be done annually; more frequently would not be likely to identify substantial changes in work behaviors. (0 = no evidence, 1 = awareness, 2 = user, 3 = expert)

Prioritization. Skills need to be developed gradually and consistently. Normally, individuals, with their managers, choose one to three skills to work on formally each year. Coaching and other self-improvement efforts can enhance more skills, as well.

Skill levels

Awareness: Indicates that the job requires an awareness of the process or skill; however, the person would not be expected to perform the skill on a regular basis. This level would include introductory courses that offer a broad coverage.

User: Indicates that the person must be able to apply the skill in a competent manner. The person needs to know the steps or procedures and how to apply them in a variety of situations.

Expert: Indicates that the employee needs to know the skill well enough to instruct or consult others. This requires an advanced level of detailed knowledge and skill development in all aspects of the skill.

Assessment. Each skill category should be calculated to determine if there is a gap and the degree of the gap. The skills with the greatest gaps become the areas of greatest need.

1.6.3 Assessment worksheets

NEEDS AND GAP ANALYSIS
SKILLS RELATED TO THE INFORMATION SUPERHIGHWAY
Personal Growth Skills

Category	Desired State (0 - 3)			Current State (0 - 3)			Gap	Prioitize, Select One	Comments
	Self	Manager	Agreement	Self	Manager	Agreement			
Listening									
Reading									
Speaking									
Writing									
Tolerance for Ambiguity									
Critical Thinking									
Self-Monitoring									
Project Management									
Flexibility									
Creativity / Innovation									

Legend:
Skill Level: 0 = no evidence, 1 = Awareness, 2 = User, 3 = Expert
Gap: Desired State minus Current State

Adapted with permission from Ameritech Corporation

Figure 1.1 Needs assessment and gap analysis—personal growth skills.

NEEDS ASSESSMENT AND GAP ANALYSIS
SKILLS RELATED TO THE INFORMATION SUPERHIGHWAY
Computer Skills

Category	Desired State (0 - 3)			Current State (0 - 3)			Gap	Priotize; Select One	Comments
	Self	Manager	Agreement	Self	Manager	Agreement			
Literacy									
Keyboard Agility /Accuracy									
Word Processing									
Database Management									
Equipment Trouble-shooting									

Legend:
Skill Level: 0 = no evidence, 1 = awareness, 2 = user, 3 = expert
Gap: Desired State minus Current State

Adapted with permission from Ameritech Corporation

Figure 1.2 Needs assessment and gap analysis—computer skills.

NEEDS ASSESSMENT AND GAP ANALYSIS
SKILLS RELATED TO THE INFORMATION SUPERHIGHWAY
Information Management Skills

Category	Desired State (0 - 3)			Current State (0 - 3)			Gap	Priotize; Select One	Comments
	Self	Management	Agreement	Self	Management	Agreement			
Trustworthy									
Independent									
Planning / Organizing									
Problem-Solving & Decision-Making									
Self Motivation									

Legend:
Skill Level: 0 = no evident, 1 = awareness, 2 = user, 3 = expert
Gap: Desired State minus Current State

Adapted with permission from Ameritech Corporation

Figure 1.3 Needs assessment and gap analysis—information management skills.

1.6.4 Developmental activity worksheet

DEVELOPMENTAL ACTIVITY WORKSHEET

Name_____	Date_____

Directions: Use this worksheet when beginning a developmental activity such as participating on a task force. Start by writing a description agreed to by supervisor and reportee. Write learning objectives that are measurable. Include due dates and anticipated rating (0-3). When the assignment has been completed, evaluate the experience in terms of objectives and measures of success. Finally, rate the experience using the scale at the bottom of the page.

Description of the Developmental Assignment:

Learning Objective 1:

Anticipated Rating*____ Due Date_____

Learning Objective 2:

Anticipated Rating*____ Due Date_____

Anticipated Measures of Success:

Complete this section at end of development activity.

Evidence of Learning as Described by Employee:

Rating*____

Evidence of Learning as Described by Supervisor:

Rating*____

* Rating Scale:
0 = no evidence, 1 = Awareness, 2 = User, 3 = Expert

Figure 1.4 Developmental activity worksheet.

1.7 Employee Skill Development

Continuous learning will be key to maintaining competitive employability skills. Workers will learn daily as a regular aspect of their jobs. Compensation plans will support lifelong learning, and benefit plans will support off-hours tuition assistance. Efficient methods will be necessary to accommodate time pressures. Otherwise, information requirements will cause incredible stress.

Distance learning and on-line computer learning will create efficiencies by eliminating travel time to the course location and classroom overhead costs for equipment and space, but these approaches will also increase the costs of course development and media transmission.

Information skill needs may become so universal that access to skill development may become almost a *right* for all citizens. Because of socioeconomic inequities, local, state, and federal programs may need to encourage and make available continuous learning to promote continuous employment in order to have a consistent taxpayer base and a strong national economy.

1.7.1 Learning organizations

Clearly, as the world moves to a global economy, increasingly complex forces are driving organizations to change at a rapid pace. Businesses and industry must find new ways to remain flexible and competitive. Employees must learn quickly. However, since information changes daily, learning more detail than is necessary for any given project or assignment is often not helpful. Accessing detailed data quickly becomes critical. In short, new information needs to be continuous, readily available on demand, and simple to obtain.

Learning organizations are not easy to define. ASTD's *Infoline* (Younger, 1993) describes a learning organization as a

1. "Setting where people are constantly, spontaneously learning and applying their knowledge in order to improve the quality of goods, services, work, and life itself"
2. "Environment where learning is valued as the best, perhaps the only, source of competitive advantage"
3. "Place, ultimately, where learning has become synonymous with working"

Learning framework. Organizations need to adopt a common vision and a commitment to learning. With marketplace pressures to maintain a knowledgeable workforce, organizations cannot wait to build on the experiences of others. *Each* organization must try to develop its own strategies.

Just-in-time. To meet the ever-emerging learning demands, employees must be willing to learn in a variety of ways:

- *On-line and electronic performance support systems (EPSS).* Computer-based independent learning at the employee's workstation, desk, or remote location (such as a repair facility). Learning varies from college classes, such as courses in engineering or statistics, to computerized help, such as equipment maintenance instructions.

- *Self-study media-oriented approaches (audio, video, CD ROM, and virtual reality—self-paced and self-managed).* This is a rich source of learning, especially if it is computer-managed, with self-checks and practice for errors. The examples are usually very realistic and are frequently updated. Media applications can have high impact, especially when conveying a message or influencing attitudes. There is no opportunity to practice people-oriented skills, such as team building, leadership, supervision, or interpersonal or oral communications; however, knowledge, comprehension, and steps to a process or procedure can be checked.

1.7.2 Distance learning

Business and industry are facing time pressures, scarce resources, and globalization. Workers increasingly need knowledge; however, there is less time to learn. With increased learning needs, there are fewer resources for each learning request. Finally, with corporate globalization, learning often needs to be consistent throughout the world. Distance learning provides quick access, convenience, and consistent messages for all participants.

Distance learning refers to the situation where there is physical space between the learner and the instructor, with interactive video, fax machines, electronic markerboards, and other forms of information delivery used.

Television networks/teleconferencing. Teleconferencing is two-way communication between participant and instructor in physically separate locations. Teleconferencing equipment allows the employees to see and hear one another. As learning becomes a lifelong pursuit, the convenience and realism of teleconferencing will make it one of the media of choice. Combining the information superhighway elements of television, telephone, fax, and E-mail, teleconferencing offers interactive participation in the learning activities, including opportunities to ask questions and receive immediate feedback. There is a high degree of involvement among participants. Using teleconferencing, students or employees from different states or countries can work on the same problem or discuss current issues.

Currently, teleconferencing is usually conducted through computer/video combination equipment, such as Picturetel and Vistium Personal Video System. Many companies have broadcast and reception systems which can be used for learning. Teleconferences are often convenient and can reduce expenses for such things as travel. For example, Ford Motor Company is conducting dealership training for the sales force and service repair personnel using distance learning. Ford is also offering engineering courses through Wayne State University (Detroit, Michigan) at the engineers' own personal work stations. At Anderson Consulting, new employees log onto their desktop computers for their first corporate lessons. Ernst & Young's interactive computer-based training results in 20 to 25 percent higher achievement scores (Marx, 1995).

Multimedia, interactive, and on-line desktop learning

> Multimedia technology is creating a new paradigm in training. Unlike conventional techniques and methodologies, multimedia technology transforms the static, one-way notion of training into an interactive learning experience. In addition to offering superb training results, multimedia technology delivers a clear and measurable return on investment (ICD Publishing, 1994).

The necessary interactive equipment is commonly available, a computer with compact disc capability and audio speakers. CD-ROM discs are inserted in the compact disc player, and the learner progresses through the lessons, answering questions as required. On-line desktop learning means that the computer is linked to a network that provides feedback and monitors progress.

Interactive desktop learning means that the employee interacts with the computer training, usually by answering questions and then receiving feedback. CD-ROM and computer-based training (CBT) are the most common formats. Either format is capable of providing very cost-effective and successful training. Topics commercially available include communication, leadership, teams, marketing, customer service, diversity, quality, and computer software. The courses should be well designed using instructional design principles and developed by those with experience in CBT or CD-ROM. Learning studies consistently document that employees acquire information faster and with greater accuracy than with more conventional learning approaches.

Colleges are experimenting with on-line courses. Central Michigan University offers graduate-level statistics, carrying full credit, entirely on-line; this is convenient to students with busy schedules. There is no need to travel, and students can complete assignments whenever they wish.

1.8 Conclusion

Few people in America or in a modern global business environment are not aware of the information superhighway. The image of a roadway of computers, connections, telephones, cables, and satellites conjures up mystery and, for many people, some fear. Major telecommunications companies are committing to deals that are incomprehensible to ordinary readers and listeners. Radio, television, and newspapers carry stories involving millions of dollars for mergers and alliances. The resulting merger arrangements create alliances between seeming competitors, such as cable TV, telephone, and print media companies (Kupfer, 1994).

Computers are gradually becoming part of everyone's life, just as telephones, radios, and televisions did half a century ago; however, in the speed of acceptance there is no comparison. Fortunately, communications equipment and software are increasingly user-friendly, and so there is no panic or massive resistance. Somehow, people recognize that they must begin or advance their use of the electronic devices or be left behind.

Few people doubt the need for the information superhighway. They recognize that the growing capacity for information access and transmission through electronics and communications is critical for an effective modern economy.

The nature of information access, and the technologies that support access, will continue to evolve rapidly. The interface of technical workers with those informational technologies is expected to continue shifting rapidly. Trainers, too, are faced with increasing their skills because of the continuing challenge of state-of-the-art information superhighways.

1.9 Glossary

CAD (computer-aided design) Use of computers for designing consumer and industrial products.

CAE (computer-aided engineering) Software which analyzes designs that have been created in a computer, such as structural analysis.

CAM (computer-aided manufacturing) Automated manufacturing systems and techniques, including numerical control, process control, robotics, and materials requirements planning.

CBT (computer-based training) Use of the computer for training and instruction. CBT programs are known as courseware.

CD-ROM (compact disc read-only memory) Computer storage discs, in the same physical form as CD audio and music discs, used for digital storage of information and/or computer applications, such as catalogs, encyclopedias, education, and training.

Docking station A computer appliance into which a portable computer is inserted, enabling physical connections to remain linked to the docking station even when the laptop is removed. These connections are commonly to printers, local area networks, and other corporate information systems.

Download To transmit data from a central computer to a remote computer or from a file server to a personal computer.

EDI (electronic data interchange) Electronic communication of common business transactions, such as orders, confirmations, and invoices, between organizations.

E-mail (electronic mail) Transmission of letters, messages, and memos over a communications network; it is evolving to include voice, graphics, and video.

Employability The knowledge and skills necessary to remain employed or to acquire employment.

EPSS (electronic performance support systems) Computer programs which assist workers in job decisions and automate options to minimize errors and time. They often leverage expert systems technology.

Expert systems Highly sophisticated computer programs based on a detailed body of knowledge in a specialized area which come as close to reproducing human thought processes as is possible for a computer.

Fiber optic cable Glass wires that are separated and insulated from each other by material such as rubber or plastic, and are used to transmit radiant power.

FMEA (failure mode effects analysis) The systematic approach to predicting problems and failures, defining the consequences or effects, determining solutions, and thus avoiding the problems and failures.

Help desk Knowledgeable resource person, usually accessed by telephone, who assists computer users with questions and problems.

Information superhighway (1) Already existing communications linkages, such as corporate networks, video telephone, interactive television, on-line services, and the Internet. (2) An information transmission network with high-speed capability to connect users all over the world and allow them to transport high-quality video images, access interactive services, and tap into an infinite variety of information databases. (3) A planned system of seamless, high-speed communications networks that will be able to simultaneously deliver voice, data, and video to people anywhere, anytime. The national information infrastructure (NII) will provide widespread access to private and public networks capable of transmitting data, voice, image, and video. It will consist of user information appliances, local area networks, and regional and national networks.

Information worker Employee whose job primarily requires the collection, manipulation, classification, and storage of facts and data.

Interactive Relating with the computer program by exchanging information. The user types in a command or information, and the computer software provides a response.

Internet International network of computer networks connected via telephone lines and microwave and satellite links. This collection of networks links an estimated 25 to 35 million computer users in more than 135 countries and is growing daily.

ISDN (Integrated Services Digital Network) International communications standard that allows a communications channel to simultaneously carry voice, video, and data.

Knowledge maturity curve Recent school and college graduates have the greatest knowledge as a result of studying the latest research and journals. This knowledge advantage is quickly lost after graduation unless the employee continues to study.

Knowledge worker Employee whose job primarily requires the use of facts and rules for problem solving.

Learning organization An organization sharing a common vision and committed to continuous learning. Employees help one another learn and view workplace projects or initiatives in a holistic, systematic context.

Network Communications pathway between terminals and computers.

On-line A networked computer system with terminals in which transactions can be processed at the actual time of input and provide an immediate response.

Pay for knowledge Increased compensation based on acquiring *job-specific* skills.

Pay for learning Increased compensation based on training, education, or degree completion.

Robust Reliable, consistent, and powerfully built; able to withstand unexpected challenges.

Telecommuting Working at home or at a distant location and communicating with the office via phone, fax, and computers.

Virtual reality Storage in computer memory of complete graphic images, not just the part that is displayed on the screen.

Virtual workplace People working in diverse, distant environments, but linked by computer, fax, and phone so that they can function as if they were in a common workplace.

World Wide Web (WWW) World Wide Web pages, or on-line bulletin boards and networks, are being generated across the Internet to provide point-and-click access to information about people, places, organizations, and products. The Web relies on a set of programming techniques and a way of navigating the Internet that is simple to use. The fastest-growing subset of the Internet, the Web is used for information and commerce, such as on-line banking, periodical publication, corporate marketing, and database access.

1.10 On-line Services

America Online
8610 Westwood Center
Vienna, VA 22182
Phone: 703-448-8700

ASTD On-line
American Society for Training
  and Development
1640 King Street, PO Box 1443
Alexandria, VA 22313-2043
Phone: 703-683-8190

CompuServe Incorporated
5000 Arlington Center Blvd,
PO Box 20212
Dublin, OH 43220
Phone: 614-457-8600

The Dun & Bradstreet
Corporation
200 Nyala Farms
Westport, CT 06880
Phone: 203-222-4200

McGraw-Hill Inc.
1221 Avenue of the Americas
New York, NY 10020
Phone: 212-512-2000

Mead Data Central
(LEXIS/NEXIS)
9393 Springboro Pike, PO Box 933
Dayton, OH
Phone: 513-865-6800

Prodigy Services Company
445 Hamilton Avenue
White Plains, NY 10601
Phone: 914-003-8000

1.11 References

Ameritech RapidResource. Hoffman Estates, Ill.: Ameritech Small Business Services, 1994.
AT&T, *Making More Time for Business,* Middletown, N.J., 1994.
AT&T Center for Excellence in Distance Learning and Indiana University Center for Excellence in Education, *Distance Learning: An Introduction,* Middletown, N.J., 1994.
Carey, J., "From Internet to Infobahn," *Business Week,* May 18, 1994.
Flanagan, P., "Demystifying the Information Highway," *Management Review,* May 1994.
Greengard, S., "Making the Virtual Office a Reality," *Personnel Journal,* September 1994.
ICD Publishing, *A Cost/Benefit Analysis of Interactive Desktop Learning,* unpublished white paper, Andover, Mass., 1994.
Kupfer, A., "Parking on the Infobahn," *Fortune,* August 8, 1994.
Kupfer, A., "The Race to Rewire America," *Fortune,* April 19, 1993.
Levin, S., *Basics of EPSS (Infoline #9412).* Alexandria, Va.: American Society for Training and Development, 1994.
Lienert, A., and P. Lienert, "Reinventing the Wheel: Emphasis Is on Smarts, not Sweat," *The Detroit News,* May 28, 1995.
Marx, W., "The New High-tech Training," *Management Review,* February 1995.
Maurer, M., "PC Training, Support Remain Bottom Line," *Crain's Detroit Business,* November 28, 1994.
Metcalfe, B., "Updating Our Long-Term Road Map of the Six (Count 'em, Six) Iways," *Infoworld,* March 6, 1995.
RWD Technologies, Inc., *The Technology Report, Special Apple Edition,* Columbia, Md., 1995.

Sileo, L., *On-line Services: 1994 Review, Trends, and Forecast,* Wilton: Conn.: SIMBA Information, Inc., 1994.

Spencer, L. M., and S. M. Spencer, *Competence at Work: Models for Superior Performance.* New York: John Wiley & Sons, 1993.

T&D Toolkit, Chicago, Ill.: Ameritech, 1994.

Younger, S. M., *Learning Organizations: The Trainer's Role (Infoline #9306),* Alexandria, Va.: American Society for Training and Development, 1993.

Chapter 2

Forming Alliances: The Regional Quality Network

Jan Green and Janice Martin

Jan Green is the consultant to the Regional Quality Network. Ms. Green owns JG Facilitation Group, a firm specializing in facilitation and training. She has worked with both large and small companies, helping them incorporate facilitation skills into their quality culture. For the past several years, she has researched and developed a unique facilitation process and is presently writing a book on the subject. Jan also has an extensive background in the training arena.

Janice Martin was the Administrator for the Regional Quality Network from December 1993 to October 1995 and now holds an administrative position with a home health care provider. She is experienced in retail management and is skilled at revamping internal processes and putting new processes into place. Ms. Martin earned a degree in elementary education from Indiana University. She has worked with developmentally delayed preschool children and has been a volunteer for Big Brothers/Big Sisters.

Editor's Note: In the *ASTD Technical and Skills Training Handbook,* Chap. 5 dealt with the Alliance, which is a joint union-management alliance. This chapter deals with a different type of alliance, a multiple business alliance designed to provide technical training at affordable prices.

2.1 Background

Over the past several years, manufacturing companies have experimented with an innovative and inexpensive way to gain a competitive edge. Community, state, and industry groups, working separately and in some instances together, have identified common needs and gathered resources to meet those needs. Many of these alliances function as member-driven resources, providing assistance in basic technical skill development, problem solving, business management practices, and total quality initiatives. One common theme for any alliance is the benefit of networking with one another.

"Would companies be interested in recognizing their common needs for total quality management training and a forum in which they could share their similar experiences?" This question was posed by Wayne Reisinger, director of the (Indiana Region IV) Regional Manufacturing Extension Center (RMEC), which is sponsored by Greater Lafayette (Indiana) Progress, Inc. That was all that was necessary to build what is now known as the Regional Quality Network.

As the director of the RMEC, Reisinger's role was to work with Indiana manufacturers to identify ways in which they could improve the performance of all aspects of their businesses. As he worked with these manufacturers, Reisinger noted common issues among them—a need for training in total quality management and an opportunity to get together to share common experiences. Therefore, in May 1992, Reisinger hosted a series of breakfast meetings with local manufacturing companies to discuss the value of networking and collaborative resourcing. The response and interest from the participating companies encouraged further investigation and discussion. By July 1993, network formation meetings began and were held in three area cities with local hosts. Because more than 25 companies were interested, the decision was made to proceed with the network concept and to request state funding to do so. A developmental committee made up of representatives from interested companies established the network design criteria, budget, grant application, bylaws, and organizational structure. The developmental committee also finalized company commitments and secured sponsorship from the Greater Lafayette (Indiana) Chamber of Commerce (GLCC).

By September 1993, the developmental committee also completed the Network's vision and mission statements. The Network's vision was to increase the profit capability and the market competitiveness of area manufacturers, and its mission was to identify training needs of regional manufacturers and provide affordable total quality management training which would enhance their market competitiveness and profit capability.

Many additional milestones were attained in December 1993 as the Network concept was actually implemented:

- The Indiana Department of Commerce approved a Strategic Development Fund grant for $150,000, which was presented to the GLCC by Governor Evan Bayh.
- Eighteen manufacturers representing eight Northwest Indiana counties committed to a two-year membership. Each member committed $6400 to the two-year partnership and agreed to purchase training services from or donate training services to the Network.
- A network administrator was hired, and the member companies established their identity as the Regional Quality Network (RQN).

By January 1994, a consultant who would run the Network was hired, and the network concept was ready to unfold. At this point, the developmental committee disbanded as the official structure of the Network was formed. The initial Network structure was organized as follows (see Fig. 2.1).

The Greater Lafayette Chamber of Commerce would be the Network's sponsor and would be accountable for all state grant funds awarded to the RQN.

The *Operating Committee* would be made up of one voting representative per member company and would meet monthly to discuss issues such as admission of additional companies, applications for further grants, and curriculum adjustments.

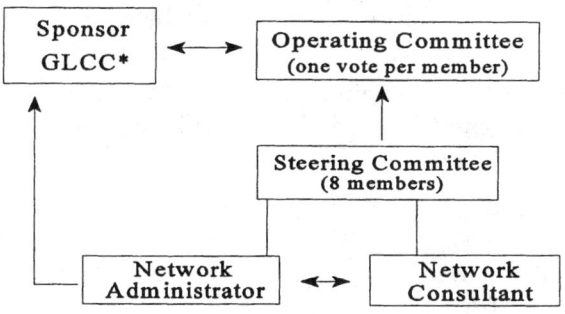

Exhibit 2.1
Initial Network Structure
* Greater Lafayette Chamber of Commerce

Figure 2.1 Initial network structure.

The *Steering Committee* would be made up of eight representatives elected from member companies. No individual representative would serve for more than two years. The steering committee would be responsible for directing the day-to-day activities of the Network and would serve as liaison between the network administrator, the network consultant, and the operating committee.

The *Network Administrator* would serve as the communication link between Network members. He or she would be responsible for tracking training fund accounts, invoicing members for training fees, coordinating training events, and publishing a Network newsletter and training alerts. The network administrator would also issue reports on grant utilization to the Network's sponsor and to the state of Indiana.

The *Network Consultant* was to be someone who both had a background in quality and total quality management training and was an expert in conducting training needs assessments. The consultant was to keep Network training focused on established criteria and have the potential to share knowledge among Network members, in part by creating a clearinghouse of information on potential outside trainers and training programs. Finally, the network consultant would be responsible for conducting benchmarking inside and outside the Network to support Network goals.

2.2 Network Goals

- To facilitate a learning network that can help manufacturers implement TQM improvement processes faster and better through leveraging of resources and dollars
- To facilitate networking among manufacturers and to enable individual manufacturers to capitalize on the synergistic benefits of networking
- To provide manufacturing organizations with access to a broader range of resources
- To provide resources that may be otherwise inaccessible to the manufacturers because of a lack of knowledge, unaffordability, or logistical impracticalities
- To provide a clearinghouse service for TQM resources and programs
- To focus learning experiences on world-class initiatives
- To facilitate the learning and implementation process for regional manufacturers for such topics as ISO 9000, benchmarking, and activity-based costing

2.3 Network Objectives

The objective of applying the TQM process within member companies is sustainable long-term profit improvement. To *achieve* a higher level of profitability, and more importantly to *sustain* it, three things must take place: a change in the corporate culture from the top to the bottom of the organization that establishes an organizational quality goal of 100 percent conformance to requirements; the installation of new quality management tools on the shop floor to achieve immediate and long-term successes; and the development of an internal delivery system to do the initial education, encourage employee involvement, and work toward continuous improvement. Based on these premises, this cooperative training network strives to improve the profitability of its members by

- Providing a core curriculum of basic study augmented with additional electives which would foster organizational culture change and sustainable improvement
- Identifying successful TQM programs within the state and capitalizing on their learning experience
- Developing a delivery system to serve regional participants
- Providing human resources and funding to administer the program in a cost-effective manner
- Identifying networking resources through synergies
- Utilizing state grant funds
- Utilizing proven "applied technology" concepts and techniques

2.4 Network Operating Criteria

As the Network developed, the members agreed that the following criteria must be followed:

- The Network was to be managed and operated by the Network members themselves.
- Each company was to be entitled to one vote.
- All companies would pay the same administrative fee, which was $3200 per year.
- All companies would be asked to commit to a 24-month period, to provide financial support through an administrative fee, and to purchase Network training services and/or provide in-kind services.
- The Network would utilize the broad umbrella approach of TQM with emphasis on technical training and training for all organizational levels.

- The membership mix would provide a broad range of company sizes, product mixes, and representation across eight counties.
- The synergies of networking would be maximized.
- The Network was to be only one of many training options for member companies.
- The RQN would achieve maximum leverage of training, resources, dollars, and people.
- Balanced participation levels among Network members would be required.

2.5 Membership

The companies which decided to join the RQN are varied, but they all agreed that the pooling of resources would be worthwhile. The members, their number of employees, and their products are:

Atapco Custom Products Division
Crawfordsville, Indiana
320 employees; loose-leaf office products

Bassett Rotary Tool
Monticello, Indiana
125 employees; carbide cutting tools

Caterpillar, Inc.
Lafayette, Indiana
1200 employees; large engine center

Delphi Body Works
Delphi, Indiana
30 employees; utility truck bodies

Donaldson Company
Frankfort, Indiana
175 employees; filtration products

Dynamic Corporation
Montmorenci, Indiana
125 employees; braking resistors for locomotives

Egyptian Lacquer Manufacturing Company
Lafayette, Indiana
70 employees; industrial coatings

Eli Lilly & Company Tippecanoe Laboratories
Lafayette, Indiana
1300 employees; pharmaceuticals and agricultural products

Fairfield Manufacturing
Lafayette, Indiana
1000 employees; gears and gear assemblies

Fluidrive, Inc.
Brookston, Indiana
115 employees; steerable wheel drive systems

Lafayette Quality Products
Lafayette, Indiana
18 employees; precision machining and metal fabrication

Landis & Gyr Energy Management Inc.
Lafayette, Indiana
500 employees; electric meters

Nor-Cote International, Inc.
Crawfordsville, Indiana
60 employees; ultraviolet screen printing inks

PowerMark Ltd.
Lafayette, Indiana
17 employees; engine repower kits

Precise Technology
West Lafayette, Indiana
80 employees; injection molding

Schwab Corporation
Lafayette, Indiana
170 employees; vault doors, safes, and file cabinets

Stalcop Cold Forming, Inc.
(joined 1/95)
Thorntown, Indiana
100 employees; cold-formed blank fasteners

Subaru-Isuzu Automotive, Inc.
Lafayette, Indiana
2000 employees; automobiles

TRW Commercial Steering Division
Lafayette, Indiana
220 employees; steering columns

Zeneca Resins (joined 1/95)
Frankfort, Indiana
21 employees; waterborne acrylic emulsions

The Network is always actively recruiting new companies. Each potential new member company receives a package of materials that helps it better understand the direction and purpose of the Network.

2.6 Funding

Fortunately, funding did not pose a significant challenge. The Indiana Department of Commerce and the member companies established a matching ratio between the grant funds and the Network's funds: The Strategic Development Fund grant was to cover 38 percent of training costs and other costs associated with operating the Network, and the companies paid the remaining 62 percent of such costs. These percentages were derived from the ratio of grant funds to funds paid and in-kind services donated by the member companies. Only charter members could participate in the initial state grant, all training costs were to be shared equally by companies participating in any given training program, administrative fees were to be invoiced up front once yearly, and training costs were to be paid as they were incurred.

2.7 Benefits of the Regional Quality Network

After much discussion, research, and analysis, the member companies had high expectations for the Network consortium. The benefits of their alliance were carefully identified. Clear benefits would help in recruiting new member companies and retaining the charter members. The obvious benefit was the *cost savings* through attending locally sponsored quality and technical training programs. The elimination of air fares and car rental and hotel charges was a tremendous advantage. Member companies would share training expenses, and with the introduction of grant funds, costs would be reduced even more.

Another benefit that blossomed immediately was the *synergy of networking*. The Network provided a forum for a regular, free exchange of ideas. Both large and small companies have been able to learn a great deal from one another, which has been a rewarding experience for all. Many of the RQN companies are now working together on projects other than RQN-sponsored activities. These opportunities developed as a result of the many networking exchanges.

Tapping into multiple resources was an additional advantage. Initially the focus was on utilizing the in-kind services provided by the larger companies. These in-kind, or donated, resources included office equipment, meeting facilities, reference materials, and training programs, which included materials and presenters. The response to requests for in-kind services has continued to be very generous, and the RQN is now seeing some of the smaller companies with no previous in-kind commitment donating personal time and additional training programs in order to offer their expertise to the Network. Other companies have labeled themselves as "coaches" for specific information sharing and are willing to work one on one to assist their comembers in meeting internal needs. In an effort to optimize networking and information sharing, the RQN has hosted networking luncheons, which have allowed members to discuss topics such as activity-based costing, cellular manufacturing, the theory of constraints, OSHA/EPA issues, and teams in the workplace, just to name a few. These luncheons are very popular, as proven by increased attendance.

By the end of 1994, the RQN offered 42 programs to its members, some of which were repeated (see Sec. 2.10, "Resources"). About half of these were technical programs offered in collaboration with Ivy Tech State College, including such topics as blueprint reading, statistical process control, geometric dimensioning and tolerancing, and computer skills. Training also included a two-day presentation on the theory of constraints by Robert Fox of the TOC Center in New Haven, Connecticut, an internationally known speaker who lectures widely to quality professionals on this topic. The theory of constraints, in brief, refers to analyzing a process within a company and determining the weakest link, or constraint, within the chain of the process. A reception followed to allow companies the opportunity to informally ask questions of Mr. Fox and his staff. Representatives expressed interest in obtaining more speakers of this caliber. Additionally, the local facility of Charter Behavioral Health System held two stress management programs for the RQN free of charge.

Pilot programs were launched during 1995. One such pilot program, Phase I/Phase II training, allowed companies to participate in classroom instruction and have a consultant assist in implementing the training concepts within the company. Training was to be held at the various company locations to facilitate attendance of production workers. The host company for any particular training session was expected to have the majority of participants, but the training would be open to all member companies.

2.8 Committees

Six months after the RQN was established Network members participated in an all-day strategic planning session. The purpose of the strategic planning session was to strengthen the Network for its members and to help member companies achieve their own specific organizational objectives. Members brainstormed answers to such questions as, "How will you know the RQN has made a difference?" and "What are the benefits of Network membership?" As a result of the planning session, the RQN committee structure was amended (see Fig. 2.2).

The steering committee, operating committee, network services/ evaluation committee, sustaining the network committee, and ISO 9000 committee had already been established before this session. Evaluation activities continued to be provided by a single group, renamed the Services Assessment Committee. Members also decided to become more proactive in attracting new members by establishing the RQN Expansion Committee. This latter committee replaced the Sustaining the Network Committee. The renamed committees reflected the evolving goals of the Network. The ISO 9000 Committee was

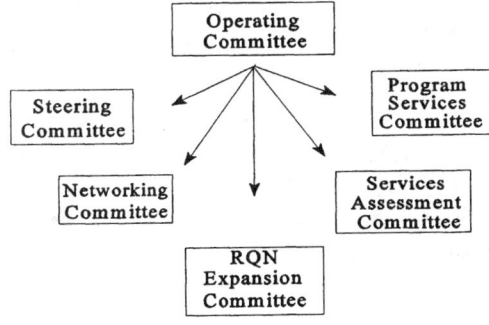

Exhibit 2.2
Amended Network Structure

Figure 2.2 Amended network structure.

disbanded, and two new committees were developed from the day's discussions: the Program Services Committee and the Networking Committee. The Network Consultant was given the task of appointing members to the latter two committees. She also chairs the Program Services Committee. In the past, the Steering and Operating Committees were two separate bodies, but under the new committee structure, the Steering Committee works for the Operating Committee, as do the four other committees.

The guidelines for the subcommittees are as follows:

- Each has a charter defined and approved by the operating committee.
- Each has an elected chairperson and secretary.
- Each is required to submit minutes of its meetings to the operating committee.
- Each is given timelines and functions as prescribed by the strategic planning session.
- Each is held accountable to the operating committee and is required to report its activities as such.

Following are the functions of the subcommittees.

2.8.1 Program services committee

This committee provides network training services based upon needs of member companies. This includes a review of the overall company assessments, clarification of network needs, and evaluation of scheduled programs. This committee also "champions" network services and periodically visits fellow member companies.

2.8.2 Networking committee

This committee facilitates intercompany networking and resource sharing. Activities may include developing a team to visit companies whose participation may be lacking, evaluating area trade shows for marketing the RQN, and developing networking and roundtable discussions.

2.8.3 Services assessment committee

This committee identifies and recommends appropriate metrics and performance assessment programs. These enable the RQN to continually evaluate and improve services to its members and to establish metrics for individual companies to use to measure progress against goals. Activities may include conducting phone surveys of nonparticipating companies that originally expressed interest in a training topic (i.e., what can we do for you?), reviewing training program evaluations, and ensuring that each member company establishes individual RQN goals and performance metrics.

2.8.4 RQN expansion committee

This committee identifies, evaluates, and recommends funding options and/or programs that will enable the RQN to be self-sustaining after state funding ceases. Activities may include pursuing alternative funding sources, expanding the network to other sectors of the community, and developing internal and external marketing programs.

2.8.5 Steering committee

At the request of the operating committee, this committee manages the Network's day-to-day operations in a manner that will ensure the network's ability to accomplish its mission. This includes "walking the talk," administering the bylaws, and providing recommendations and reviews for a functional staff and structure.

2.9 Conclusion

In summary, the Regional Quality network's first year was very successful, as noted by several milestones. The most important milestones were obtaining the $150,000 Strategic Development Fund grant from the Indiana Department of Commerce and obtaining office space, hiring the two staff persons, and designing the network's name and logo, which are now registered trademarks. Other milestones included the distribution of six newsletters, the development of the subcommittees, the completion of four quarterly progress reports as required by the Indiana Department of Commerce, two rounds of company needs assessments, and the completion of the comprehensive calendar of events for 1995. The 1995 calendar offered 57 programs, some of which were repeated, to meet the needs of the Network's members.

Today, the network's founder continues to be active with the RQN, serving on both the Operating and Steering Committees as an ex-officio, nonvoting member; he also chairs the Expansion Committee. His Expansion Committee is investigating how the network can become self-sustaining after all the grant funds are utilized, one option being to open the network to business sectors other than manufacturing. Regardless of what avenue it pursues, the network will continue to offer training and networking opportunities that will allow its members to gain the knowledge necessary to increase their profit capability and market competitiveness.

2.10 Resources

During 1994, the RQN offered 22 quality training programs and 20 technical education programs to its members.

Quality Programs

    Introduction to Quality
    TQM: Essentials for Strengthening Your Organization
    Strategic Planning Process
    Actively ISO
    Embarking on ISO 9000
    Understanding ISO 9000
    Basic Heat Treat & Metallurgy
    So You Think You Want Self-Directed Work Teams?
    Introduction to Cellular Manufacturing
    Cellular Manufacturing (3-day program)
    Coaching for RQN Success
    Competitive Benchmarking
    Problem Solving
    Theory of Constraints
    Continuous Process Improvement Bootcamp
    Customer Service and Interpersonal Skills
    Effective Listening Skills and Conflict Management
    Managing Stress Through Understanding
    Employment Law
    Productive Interviewing
    Conducting Positive Performance Appraisals
    Time and Self Management

Technical Programs

    Fundamentals of Statistical Process Control
    Advanced SPC

Basic Blueprint Reading
Advanced Blueprint Reading
Geometric Dimensioning and Tolerancing
Design of Experiments
Back Power: Sitting, Standing, and Lifting
SIT FIT: Preventing Physical Stress
CTD: Cumulative Trauma Disorders
Industrial Safety Management
Facilities Maintenance Management
OSHA Construction Safety Requirements
Hazardous Materials Operations
Hazardous Materials Refresher
Introduction to the Personal Computer
Introduction to DOS
Advanced DOS
Introduction to Spreadsheets
Introduction to Windows
Word Processing

BYLAWS of the REGIONAL QUALITY NETWORK

Article I

VISION AND MISSION

Section 1   VISION: To increase the profit capability and the market competitiveness of area manufacturers.

Section 2   MISSION: To identify training needs of regional manufacturers and provide affordable Total Quality Management training which will enhance their market competitiveness and profit capability.

Article II

MEMBERSHIP AND FEES

Section 1   ELIGIBILITY: Membership will be open to all Indiana manufacturers. Voting membership will require a manufacturer to pay an equal share of the Network administrative fee and either purchase Network training services and/or provide in-kind contributions.

Section 2   APPLICATION AND FEES: Application and fees for membership shall be prescribed by the Operating Committee.

Section 3   APPLICATION: All applications for membership in the Network shall be submitted in writing to the Operating Committee in a form prescribed for such purpose, with said application constituting an agreement on the part of the applicant to adhere to all Bylaws, policies, and procedures adopted by the Operating Committee.

Section 4 RESIGNATION: Any member of the Network may resign by delivering a written notice of resignation to the Chairperson of the Operating Committee. All prepaid administrative fees will be forfeited.

Section 5 PARTICIPATION: Network members shall be entitled to attend meetings and programs of the Network and to utilize resources established by the Network upon payment of fees, if any, as prescribed by the Network.

Section 6 STATE FUNDING: Only member companies at the specific time and date a request for funds, grants, or any financial aid is submitted will be eligible to share in such aid. Matching funds ratios for such funding will be prescribed by the Operating Committee.

Article III
OPERATING COMMITTEE

Section 1 COMPOSITION: The Operating Committee will be composed of one representative from each participating network member company. A representative from the sponsoring organization, the Greater Lafayette Chamber of Commerce (GLCC), and the Region IV Manufacturing Extension Center (RMEC) Director shall serve in an ex-officio, nonvoting capacity on the operating committee.

Section 2 RESPONSIBILITY: The operating committee will be responsible for defining and approving program services, facilitating intercompany cooperation and resource sharing, measuring program effectiveness and client satisfaction, and providing program leadership to enable the Network to accomplish its mission.

Section 3 MEETINGS: Each participating Network company will be entitled to only one vote, regardless of company size or financial commitment. The Committee will meet on a regularly scheduled frequency, but not less than quarterly. Notice of regular meetings shall be given not less than five days in advance. Such notice may be given by letter, telephone, facsimile transmission, or telegraph, and will state the meeting time, date, and place. The Operating Committee may specify which, if any, meetings are open to guests or to the public.

Section 4 SPECIAL MEETINGS: Special meetings of the Operating Committee may be held at the discretion of the Chairperson, or by request from one or more members of the Operating Committee, or by a formal request from the Network Consultant or Administrator. Notice of the special meeting must be made two days in advance. Such notice may be given by letter, telephone, facsimile transmission, or telegraph, and will state the meeting time, date, place, and the nature of the business to be discussed.

Section 5 TRANSACTIONS: Fifty percent (50%) of the Network membership, rounded up to the next whole member total, shall constitute a quorum. The majority of such quorum shall control and constitute the actions of the entire Operating Committee. These actions can be challenged by Network members; however, there must be a majority consent of the total Network membership to overturn the action.

Section 6 PROCEDURES: Meetings of the Operating Committee will be conducted by the Chairperson, facilitated by the Network Consultant, and assisted by the Network Administrator. In case of the Chairperson's absence, the Chairperson of the Steering Committee will serve as temporary

Chairperson of the Operating Committee. Minutes will be recorded during the meeting. Such minutes will be held for documentation purposes in the Network office.

Section 7 TRAINING APPROVAL: Any and all training performed for the benefit of Network members through the Network must be approved in advance by a majority of the Steering Committee members, and the opportunity for participation must be made available to all Network members.

Section 8 REPORTING: To facilitate reporting requirements to the State, all Network members must submit a quarterly report to the Network Administrator for the purpose of documentation of Network activities and benefits. Such report shall be submitted to the Network staff within fifteen days of the end of each quarter. These dates being: first-quarter report due *April 15th,* second-quarter report due *July 15th,* third-quarter report due *October 15th,* fourth-quarter report due *January 15th.*

Any and all Network member companies which perform training and/or consulting for other Network members through the Network must submit to the Network office a Workshop Summary Report, list of attendees, and supportive documentation regarding the activities performed.

Section 9 NOMINATION: Network members shall be entitled to nominate members of the Operating Committee for consideration to hold a position on the Steering Committee, a subcommittee, or a committee chairpersonship. This nomination shall require action upon the Operating Committee by nature of the motion or vote.

Article IV

STEERING COMMITTEE

Section 1 COMPOSITION: The Steering Committee shall be composed of eight (8) individual representatives from Network companies. These eight (8) individual representatives shall be appointed by and accountable to the Operating Committee. Membership will be limited to one person per company, and represent small- and large-size companies as well as be representative of the total geographic area of Region IV. The Region IV RMEC Director will be an ex-officio, nonvoting member of the Steering Committee.

Section 2 RESPONSIBILITY: The Steering Committee shall possess and may exercise only emergency powers on behalf of the Operating Committee between meetings of the Operating Committee. The Steering Committee shall furnish the Operating Committee with an accounting of such decisions and activities at its next regularly scheduled Operating Committee meeting. The Steering Committee shall be responsible for the day-to-day operation of the Network, including expenditure decisions, member assessments, Network events, and curriculum.

Section 3 TERM: Term of membership on the Steering Committee shall be for a period of all or part of one calendar year, and shall terminate on December 31 of such year. Any one company may have a representative on the Steering Committee for a maximum of three (3) years.

Section 4 MEETINGS: Regular meetings or special meetings of the Steering Committee shall be held as required, but not less than monthly. Notice of such meetings shall be given not less than five days in advance for a regular meeting and two days in advance for a special meeting. Such notice may be given by letter, telephone, facsimile transmission, or telegraph, and will state the meeting date, time, and place. The Steering Committee may specify which, if any, of the meetings are open to guests or to the public. Meetings of the Steering Committee will be conducted by a Chairperson, facilitated by the Network Consultant, and assisted by the Network Administrator.

Article V

OFFICERS

Section 1 OFFICERS: The officers shall consist of a Chairperson of the Operating Committee and any other such officers that the Operating Committee shall deem necessary for the transaction of business for the Network. The Chairperson shall be elected by the Operating Committee and shall hold office for a term of one year and/or until the respective successor has been elected.

Section 2 REMOVAL: Any officer may be removed from office for any reason by a majority vote at a duly called Operating Committee meeting. Any officer may resign by written notice to the Network Chairperson. The resignation shall be effective upon its receipt by the Network Chairperson or at a subsequent time specified in the notice of resignation. The Operating Committee members shall have the power to fill such vacancies by majority vote at a duly called Operating Committee meeting.

Article VI

SPONSOR

Section 1 RESPONSIBILITIES: For purposes of requesting State of Indiana funding for Network start-up, the Greater Lafayette Chamber of Commerce (GLCC) will serve as the sponsoring nonprofit organization. As such, the GLCC will be the recipient of the state funds granted and will have financial responsibility and accountability for administering the funds in accordance with State of Indiana reporting requirements and accepted accounting practices.

Article VII

AMENDMENTS

Section 1 PROCESS: These Bylaws may be amended or repealed or new Bylaws may be adopted in lieu thereof by the affirmative vote of a majority of the Operating Committee. The notice of the proposed alteration, repeal, or substitution shall be contained in the notice of such meeting.

---

revised 5/16/95

Chapter

3

The Merging of Total Quality, Cultural Change, and Learning Organization Concepts in a High-Tech Environment

Michael A. Sullivan

Michael A. Sullivan has been an employee of General Motors for over 34 years and has had a variety of assignments, including manufacturing, maintenance, tooling, labor relations, education and training, human resources, and salaried personnel. He has a BSIE from General Motors Institute and an MBA from Ball State University, and has submitted his proposal for dissertation for an Ed.D. at the University of Missouri—St. Louis. His current job assignment at DELPHI Energy and Engine Management Systems, GMC, Anderson, Indiana, is Manufacturing Services Manager, Plant 16. He is also an adjunct professor for Purdue University's State-Wide Technology program in Anderson.

3.1 Introduction

3.1.1 Purpose

The purpose of this chapter is to provide you with additional information about the continuing merging of total quality, cultural change, and learning organization concepts in a manufacturing, skilled-trades environment. In addition, it is this author's hope that this information, when combined with the information contained in Chap. 17 of the *ASTD Technical and Skills Training Handbook,* will provide readers with learnings and insight that they might apply to their own situation. Since, as indicated in the *Handbook* chapter, the author is a participant in the process, personal biases may still on occasion, be added.

3.1.2 Agenda

A review of Chap. 17 of the *Handbook* will be presented in an effort to establish the framework for this past year's activities. External information affecting activities will also be presented. A chronological overview of the past year's activities will follow. New learnings will be stated, followed by conclusions and recommendations.

3.2 Chapter Review

When Chap. 17 of the *Handbook* was written, Plant 16 was a part of Delco Remy Division, General Motors Corporation. It employed more than 425 salaried and hourly employees. The hourly employees were represented by Local 662 of the United Automobile Workers. The employees produced special machines, feeder systems, control systems, material handling equipment, dies, fixtures, gauges, test equipment, injection molds, and various other types of tools and equipment. Additionally, the employees provided tool grinding, maintenance, and housekeeping services. Knowing that approximately 40 percent of their business was potentially at risk as a result of divestitures, sales, or joint ventures, the then Plant Manager and Plant Superintendent made a conscious decision to pursue the UAW-GM Quality Network process as a means of involving employees and the union leadership in the leadership of the business. This quality initiative activity was the beginning of a total quality management (TQM) approach for the Plant 16 business. Learnings from Jablonski (1992) and Darnell and Hamood (1991 and 1992) were utilized. The chapter also included a chronological view of events affecting Plant 16 beginning in December 1992, when potential divestitures, sales, and joint ventures were announced, and ending in April 1994, with the Plant 16 Quality Council planning to refocus its activities. An abbreviated version of the learnings presented in the chapter is as follows:

- The nonrepresented employees fear change as much as the represented employees.
- Communication, communication, communication.
- Trust must be given to enable it to develop.
- Time becomes a precious resource.
- Facilitation skills are a precious commodity.
- Followers base their behavior on the behavior of their leaders.
- Meeting skills for all employees improve the productivity of meetings.
- Employee groups require constant nurturing.
- It takes a great amount of time for the process to provide results.
- Most people are impatient with the process.
- Myers-Briggs analyses are invaluable.
- Situational leadership training enhances the process.
- Job-specific training is absolutely necessary.
- The blending of internal and external consultants lends credibility to the process.

An abbreviated version of the conclusions and recommendations from the chapter is as follows:

- Never start the process unless the leadership is totally committed.
- Sincerity cannot be faked for very long. If you are not sincere, don't start.
- If you don't believe that people are basically good and want to do the right thing, don't start the process.
- Be prepared to spend what seems like an extraordinary amount of time.
- Consider problems as opportunities to establish desired behavior and to lead by example.
- Communicate, communicate, communicate.
- Be flexible with regard to union-management relationships. Recognize that there will be times when you are apart on issues.
- Realize that you never quite get there.

- Understand that if you are trying to implement a TQM process, you are already there.
- Some activities that are a must are
  Communication
  Union leadership participation
  Training
  Employee empowerment
  Financial freedom
  Management freedom
  Risk taking
  Facilitation/consultant skills

3.3 Influential Literature

During the past year's activities in Plant 16, four authors and their offerings had a significant impact on the TQM process. The work of Edgar Schein (1992), James Collins and Jerry Porras (1994), and Peter Senge (1990) was studied by this author, as a manager of the change process in Plant 16, and many of their concepts were utilized. The purpose of this section is to discuss some of those concepts and their relation to Plant 16 activities.

3.3.1 Edgar Schein

Edgar Schein (1992) spoke to the cultural issues. Schein stated that we must avoid superficial models of culture and build on deeper, more complex anthropological models. He went on to say that culture is a most useful concept if it helps us better understand the hidden and complex aspects of organizational life.

Two critical elements are involved in the definition of any culture, including the organizational cultural in a plant. One element is the implication of structural stability, something which is shared and is deep and stable, less conscious and therefore less tangible and visible. The second critical element is patterning or integration. This element ties together all other elements into a larger paradigm or gestalt which binds everything together into a coherent whole. According to Schein, the most useful way to think about culture is to view it as the accumulated shared learning of a given group, covering behavioral, emotional, and cognitive elements of each group member's total psychological functioning. Also, once people have a common system of communication and a language, then learning can take place at a conceptual level, and shared concepts become possible. Deeper levels of learning that guide us to the essence of culture must be thought of as concepts, or, as Schein defines them, shared basic assumptions. Shared assumptions derive their power from the fact that they begin to operate subliminally. Once formed and taken for granted, they become a defining property of the group that permits the group to differentiate itself from other groups; and in that process, value is attached to some assumptions. Schein formally defines the culture of a group as follows:

> A pattern of shared basis assumptions that the group learned as it solved its problems of external adaptation and internal integration, that has worked well enough to be considered valid and, therefore, to be taught to new members as the correct way to perceive, think, and feel in relation to those problems (Schein, 1992, p. 12).

For Schein, this definition introduces three elements which must be addressed:

1. *The problem of socialization.* How one learns and the socialization processes to which one is subjected may reveal deeper assumptions. A teaching process is always going on; if shared assumptions do not exist, there will be a more creative process of building a culture.
2. *The problem of behavior.* When we observe behavioral regularities, it is not known whether such behavior is a result of individual learnings or the shared learnings of the organization.
3. *Large organization/only one culture.* With time, any social unit will produce subcultures as a normal process of evolution.

According to Schein, there are three levels of culture in an organization:

1. *Artifacts:* Visible organizational structures and processes
2. *Espoused values:* Strategies, goals, and philosophies
3. *Basic underlying assumptions:* Unconscious, taken-for-granted beliefs, perceptions, thoughts, and feelings

It is no wonder, according to Schein, that identifying, managing, and/or changing culture is extremely difficult. Culture is an elusive, untouchable, unseeable, unfeelable concept that is, by nature, almost uncontrollable. However, culture's effect on business is so powerful and influential that it cannot be ignored. It is inherent in any "people system" and can be either a positive or a negative influence.

The recognition of the need to address cultural issues has always been present during the installation of TQM in Plant 16 over the past two years. However, the discovery of Schein's teachings made a substantial impact on direction and timing during the past year. We applied Schein's "three levels of culture" to Plant 16 as follows:

Artifacts. The visible organizational structures and processes instituted in Plant 16 during the past two-plus years include the Quality, Focus, and Action Council structure. That joint structure allowed for increased empowerment and involvement of employees at all levels in the managing of the business. The increase in the sales and engineering effort led to an increase in staff size, generating structural changes during the past year. Pursuit of internal and external customer contacts to obtain the "voice of the customer" and to tell the "Plant 16 story" to all stakeholders is a process that has been institutionalized during the past year. Cost reduction workshops for a cross section of employees were held monthly. The beginning of a Quality Assurance organization with the intentions of improving the quality of Plant 16 products and services, "delighting the customer," and beginning the journey toward obtaining various quality certifications such as ISO 9000, QS9000, TE9000, Malcolm Baldrige, Deming, etc., is certainly notable in Plant 16's attempt to provide structures and processes in its culture. Much more emphasis on measurements and feedback has also involved instituting more structure and processes. The continual emphasis on communication to and from all levels in the plant also is a testimony to the installation of structure and processes.

Espoused values. The strict adherence to the beliefs and values of the UAW-GM Quality Network; the constant use of the Plant 16 vision, "To grow the business through the quality of our people, product, and performance," to test all decisions against; and the strong desire of the plant's employees to "do the right things" are strong indicators that the espoused values are institutionalized in the plant's culture.

Basic underlying assumptions. The unconscious, taken-for-granted beliefs, perceptions, thoughts, and feelings of the employees, though difficult to determine, became more clear to this author during the past year. The majority of the Plant 16 employees are skilled tradespeople who have established "journeyperson" status, or are in the process of doing so. They consider themselves to be professionals and a part of the American middle class. They have earned substantial amounts of money throughout their careers through high wages and much overtime work. They have financed college educations for their children and, in some cases, grandchildren. They are proud of their accomplishments and skills. They take great pride in their work and react positively when afforded the opportunity to gain intrinsic rewards from their work efforts. They are extremely concerned with the potential loss of business for the plant, yet struggle against potential "fixes" that might include fewer personal financial rewards. The Myers-Briggs analysis tells us that they are primarily of "sensing-judging" temperament and react somewhat negatively to change until they become more accustomed to the new processes. This analysis is loosely based on percentages and also applies to the majority of the plant leadership. However, this temperament bias has proven to be a positive trait as the plant has moved toward a more structured environment which includes measurement, feedback, and accountability.

3.3.2 James Collins and Jerry Porras

Collins and Porras (1994) identified 12 "realities" which shatter a like number of "myths" about what it takes to make a great company. These realities and myths and how they affected this author's participation in the Plant 16 change process during the past year are listed below.

Myth 1. It takes a great idea to start a great company.

Reality 1. Few of the visionary companies studied by Collins and Porras began their life with a great idea. Many of them began without any specific idea, and many of them had early entrepreneurial failures.

Plant 16 1. There is no "great idea" behind Plant 16. Plant 16's formation actually evolved over the past few years, and now the situation that warrants action is prompted by the fact that there is not enough manufacturing activity to pay for the employees on the payroll.

Myth 2. Visionary companies require great and charismatic visionary leaders.

Reality 2. A charismatic visionary leader is not required and, in some cases, can be a detriment to the long-range survival of a company. A clock builder, rather than a time teller, is needed for success, in the view of this author.

Plant 16 2. While the charismatic leader generally gets the headlines, this author has attempted to develop a participative, empowered workforce that involves employees at all levels taking their game up a notch. All parties hope that Plant 16 will continue to pursue its vision long after the current leadership is gone.

Myth 3. The most successful companies exist first and foremost to maximize profits.

Reality 3. Visionary companies pursue a cluster of objectives, of which making money is only one—and not necessarily the primary one. Yes, they seek profits, but they're equally guided by core ideology—core values and a sense of purpose beyond just making money.

Plant 16 3. Plant 16's vision, "To grow the business through the quality of our people, products, and performance," reflects the appreciation of our organization for the people and product needs, in addition to the financial needs. The mission of the Plant 16 organization, subordinate to the vision, speaks to the following three issues:

People: To develop the full potential of all employees
Product: To be the preferred long-term supplier of tools, machines, prototypes, and services
Performance: To operate as a customer-focused, self-sufficient business, financially responsible to our stakeholders

Myth 4. Visionary companies share a common subset of "correct" core values.

Reality 4. There is no "right" set of core values for being a visionary company. The crucial variable is not the content of a company's ideology, but how deeply it believes its ideology and how consistently it lives, breathes, and expresses it.

Plant 16 4. Plant 16's acceptance of the UAW-GM Quality Network beliefs and values as its own came at the conclusion of a long, serious, introspective look by the Plant 6 Quality Council in May 1993. At that time, no thought was given to what other organizations might consider to be the "correct" core values for Plant 16 to embrace. Additionally, Plant 16 has steadfastly held to these beliefs and values without variance since that time.

Myth 5. The only constant is change.

Reality 5. A visionary company almost religiously preserves its core ideology, changing it seldom, if ever. Visionary companies, while keeping their core values tightly fixed, display a powerful drive for progress that enables them to change and adapt without compromising their cherished core ideals.

Plant 16 5. While never wavering from the core concept of growing the business, the Plant 16 organization, during the past two years, has been able to adapt and change, as necessary, to meet the ever-changing demands of customers, technology, etc.

Myth 6. Blue-chip companies play it safe.

Reality 6. Visionary companies may appear straitlaced and conservative to outsiders, but they're not afraid to make bold commitments to "Big Hairy Audacious Goals" (BHAGs). Visionary companies have judiciously used BHAGs to stimulate progress and blast past the comparison companies at crucial points in history.

Plant 16 6. Plant 16's commitment to find work for its people has led it to both internal General Motors customers and non-GM customers. No job is too large or tough for the Plant 16 organization to bid on and tackle if given the opportunity (see Fig. 3.1).

Myth 7. Visionary companies are great places to work, for everyone.

Reality 7. Only those who fit extremely well with the core ideology and demanding standards of a visionary company will find it a great place to work. If you go to work at a visionary company, either you will fit in and flourish—and probably couldn't be happier—

MANUFACTURING SERVICES OVERVIEW

- **EMPLOYEES**
  - HOURLY   636
  - SALARY   32
  - CONTRACT   6
  - **TOTAL**   **674**
- **FLOOR SPACE:**
  - PLANT 16   176,000 ft^2
  - PLANT 1, 11, 18, 19, 38   100,000 ft^2
  - **TOTAL**   **276,000 ft^2**
- **PRODUCTS AND SERVICES:**

CNC Machining	Molds
Dies-Steel and Carbide	Patternmaking
Engineering Concept & Design	Planned Maintenance
Feeder Systems	Print Tooling (Detail)
Fixtures	Prototype Samples
Gauges	Special Machine Building
Garage Repair	Tool Grinding
Heat Treat	Urethane
Housekeeping	Utilities
Material Handling Systems	

Figure 3.1 Manufacturing services overview.

or you will probably be expelled like a virus. There's no middle ground. Visionary companies can be almost cultlike. They are so clear about what they stand for and what they're trying to achieve that they simply don't have room for those who are unwilling or unable to fit their exacting standards.

Plant 16 7. During the past two years, many employees, when given the opportunity, have transferred into the Plant 16 organization. However, a few employees have just not fit into the culture. Arrangements have generally been made to transfer these non-fitting employees to other areas of the company, outside Plant 16. These transfers, while difficult to accomplish, have seemed to substantiate, for other Plant 16 personnel, the importance of being committed to the cause. This challenge is ongoing and never-ending.

Myth 8. Highly successful companies make their best moves by brilliant and complex strategic planning.

52 Chapter Three

Reality 8.   Visionary companies make some of their best moves by experimentation, trial and error, opportunism, and, quite literally, accident. What looks in retrospect like brilliant foresight and preplanning was often the result of trying a lot of stuff to see what works.

Plant 16 8.   The only complex strategic planning done by the Plant 16 leadership was related to the vision of growth. All other activities—cultural changes as well as technology changes, even to the extent of workload planning—have been primarily done by trial and error. If a reasonable concept is presented, the Plant 16 leadership embraces it; if a problem occurs, the Plant 16 leadership attempts to seize the opportunity to make a change for the better as a result of the learnings gained from trying something new and/or different.

Myth 9.   Companies should hire outside CEOs to stimulate fundamental change.

Reality 9.   In the seventeen hundred years of combined life spans of the visionary companies studied by Collins and Porras, there were only four instances in two companies in which outside CEOs were successfully hired to engender fundamental changes. Home-grown management rules at the visionary companies to a far greater degree (6:1) than at the comparison companies. Significant and fresh ideas can come from insiders.

Plant 16 9.   The entire leadership of Plant 16, union and management, including the plant manager, comes from the General Motors—Anderson family. All changes during the past two years have originated from this home-grown leadership. (The culture of this home-grown leadership is open to the ideas of others, such as external consultants.)

Myth 10.   The most successful companies focus primarily on beating the competition.

Reality 10.   Visionary companies focus primarily on beating themselves. Success comes to the visionary companies not so much as the end goal, but as a residual result of relentlessly asking the question of how to continually improve on what they did before. No matter how much they achieve, no matter how far in front of their competitors they pull, they never think they've done "well enough."

Plant 16 10.   For the Plant 16 leadership, beating the most "ruthless competitor" and being the "best under GM" are targets which are difficult to define. There are no competitors, either inside GM or outside GM, that are very similar to Plant 16. The measurements that are the most useful to Plant 16 are the ones which can be used to foster competition internally. That is to say that Plant 16 actually competes with itself by making comparisons with itself over time. Improvement trends are the gauge for whether you are beating yourself or not (see Fig. 3.2).

PLANT 16
LEAN MANUFACTURING IMPLEMENTATION SELF-ASSESSEMENT

PLANT: Plant 16

- • = Yes
- ° = No
- ∧ = High
- ∨ = Low

Awareness			Visioning/Planning			Implementation/Realization			Continuous Improvement		
Plant Staff Quality Council	•	∧	Master Plan	•	∧	Master Plan	•	∧	Throughput	•	∧
Communication Process	•	∧	Communication Model	•	∧	Communication Model	•	∧	Uptime	•	∧
BUGM Targets	•	∧	BUGM Targets	•	∧	BUGM Targets	•	∨	Inventory Turns	•	∨
Process Benchmarking	•	∧	Processes Benchmarked	•	∧	Competitive Benchmarking	•	∧	Benchmarking	•	∧
Teamwork Benefits	•	∧	Improvement Teams	•	∧	Improvement Teams	•	∨	Value Added Content	°	∧
Workplace Organization	•	∨	Workplace Organization	•	∨	Workplace Organization	•	∨	Common Systems	°	∨
Visual Controls	•	∨	Visual Controls/Boundary	°	∨	Visual Controls/Boundary	°	∨	Variation Reduction	°	∨
Waste/NVA	•	∨	Waste/NVA Elimination	•	∨	Waste/NVA Elimination	•	∨	Process Audits	°	∨
Lead Time Reduction	•	∨	Lead Time Reduction	•	∨	Lead Time Reduction	•	∨	Continuous Improvements	•	∨
Planned Maintenance	•	∧	Planned Maintenance	•	∧	Planned Maintenance	•	∨	Planned Maintenance	•	∨
Continuous Improvement	•	∨	Continuous Improvement	•	∧	Floorspace Utilization	•	∧	Floorspace Utilization	•	∧
						Common Process	•	∧			
						Continuous Improvement	•	∧			

Figure 3.2 Lean manufacturing implementation self-assessment.

Myth 11. You can't have your cake and eat it, too.

Reality 11. Visionary companies reject having to make a choice between stability or progress; cultlike cultures or individual autonomy; home-grown managers or fundamental change; conservative practices or BHAGs (Big Hairy Audacious Goals); making money or living according to values and purpose. Instead, they embrace the genius of the "and" rather than the "or," and pursue all their needs without having to make trade-offs.

Plant 16 11. Plant 16 actually has no choice on multiple fronts of this matter. The organization must continue installing a change process, changing the culture of the plant, improving product quality, improving product delivery, reducing cost, attracting new customers, improving union-management relations, maintaining a safe work environment, meeting government regulations, etc., while providing a positive profit margin. There are no "ors" in the Plant 16 vocabulary, only "ands."

Myth 12. Companies become visionary primarily through vision statements.

Reality 12. Visionary companies, according to Collins and Porras, attained success not so much because they wrote or issued visionary pronouncements, but because of hard work and by following the never-ending process of improvement.

Plant 16 12. The Plant 16 organization, while stating a vision of growth, has recognized that the steps to success are many and steep.

**FUTURE DIRECTION
PLANT 16 SKILLED TRADES**

- Continue To Lead Manufacturing Services With The Joint Quality Council And Focus Councils
- Consolidate Excess Skilled Trades From Ruthless Competitor Into Central Facility
- Reallocate Resources To Needed Trades
- Attain Profit Center Financial Status And Appropriate Systems (1995)
- Provide Secure Jobs By Focusing On Growing The Business Competitively With Delphi-E/Delphi/NAO and Non-GM Project Work
- Continue To Provide Anderson Plants With Services
- Become A Focal Point For Balance Of NAO To Study And Replicate

Figure 3.3 Future direction.

A simple vision pronouncement does not gain customers or improve quality. Much hard work and activity has taken place since the drafting of the plant's vision in 1993. Much more hard work and activity is expected in the future (see Fig. 3.3).

3.3.3 Peter Senge

Senge, in 1990, raised several key issues that affected our approach in Plant 16. On the subject of structure, he said that it does not mean the logical structure of a carefully developed argument or the reporting structure as shown by an organization chart. Rather, structure is a system of key interrelationships influencing behavior over time. These are interrelationships not necessarily among people, but among key variables, such as population, natural resources, engineers' product ideas, and/or technical and managerial know-how in a high-tech company. The reason that structural explanations are so important, according to Senge, is that they address the underlying causes of behavior at a level at which patterns of behavior can be changed. Senge's thoughts on structure, coupled with Schein's thoughts on structure, as expressed below, helped lead Plant 16 toward a more structured approach to the business. Schein's (1992) insight focused on visible parts of an organization: periodic reports, routines, procedures, forms, and recurrent tasks that have to be performed, all lending structure and predictability to an otherwise vague and ambiguous organizational world. These structures, according to Schein, help make life predictable, thereby reducing ambiguity and anxiety. Though employees sometimes complain about stifling bureaucracy, they need recurrent processes to avoid the anxiety of an uncertain and unpredictable world. Additionally, systems and procedures can formalize the process of getting the leader's attention and thus reinforce the message that the leader cares. As a result of these learnings, Plant 16 began the process of putting structure into place. From an organizational point of view, the Steering Focus Council was formed. This focus council, made up of the two UAW district committeemen, the sales and engineering manager, and the plant manager, was established to provide guidance to the other focus councils and to monitor the adherence to our vision, mission, and values. The four focus councils, each meeting weekly, report their activities to the Plant Quality Council on a monthly basis. A Quality Assurance organization was established by naming a Quality Assurance general supervisor and jointly appointing a union counterpart to work with him. Their task was, and still is, to improve product and service quality, and to prepare the plant for the attainment of ISO 9000 and/or QS9000 certification, the Baldrige Award, and, hopefully, the Deming Award. This effort requires a major effort toward structured procedures in the plant. An effort was begun to better schedule, track, and analyze work as it enters and leaves the plant. Several supervisors' roles were changed to allow them to become coordinators and customer contacts. The tracking of several critical measurements was begun. Implementation workshops, which involve key people working on continuous improvement activities, were begun. In essence, the plant leadership began the process of forming behavioral patterns by putting structured approaches and measurements in place. This activity, in addition to the cultural change effort which was begun in early 1993, has led to a more organized approach to systems and processes and is generally well accepted by the employees.

Senge also spoke to the concept that a shared vision is not an idea; rather, it is a force in people's hearts. It may be inspired by an idea, but once it goes further, it is compelling enough to acquire the support of more than one person and is no longer an abstraction. A shared vision creates a sense of commonality which permeates the organization and gives coherence to diverse activities. Shared visions, according to Senge, derive their power from a common caring. One of the reasons people seek to build shared visions is their desire to be connected in an important undertaking. Generative learning, the expansion of the ability to create, occurs only when people are striving to accomplish something that matters deeply to them. A shared vision is the first step in allowing people who mistrust each other to begin to work together. An organization's shared sense of purpose, vision, and operating values establishes the most basic level of commonality—a common identity. You cannot have a learning organization without shared vision. Vision establishes an overarching goal, and the loftiness of the target compels new ways of thinking and acting. Shared vision allows you to try and fail without giving up on the long-range vision which fosters risk taking and experimentation. The shared vision of Plant 16, "To grow the business through the quality of our people, products, and performance," has captured the majority of the employees in the plant and has helped give them a common foundation for their behavior. It has become a common understanding that the key to a beneficial future for all Plant 16 employees, and for the employees of Plant 16's internal customers, is for Plant 16 to find and keep many more internal and external customers.

Senge goes on to discuss the new view of leadership in a learning organization. In a learning organization, leaders are designers, stewards, and teachers. They are responsible for building organizations in which people continually expand their capabilities to understand complexity, clarify vision, and improve shared mental models—that is, they are responsible for learning. Lao-tzu said that a bad leader is one that people despise, a good leader is one that people praise, but a great leader is one that lets the people say, "We did it ourselves." Design is generally a neglected part of leadership because little credit goes to the designer. The functions of design are rarely visible; they take place behind the scenes. The consequences of today are the result of work done long in the past, and work today will show its benefits far into the future. The leader who does not aspire to gain fame, be in control, or be the center of attention generally finds deep satisfaction in empowering others and being part of an organization that is capable of producing results about which people truly care. The leader's task, then, in a learning organization is designing the learning processes whereby people throughout the organization can deal productively with the critical issues they face, and develop their mastery in the learning disciplines. During the past year, Plant 16 saw much upheaval: Some leaders changed positions, some left the organization, many employees were added to the plant, old customers were sold to new owners, etc. The pressure on the leadership to take a more "upfront, charismatic, controlling" approach, as opposed to the long-range "design" approach, was great. However, this author, as well as others, preferred to keep the steady, long-range design approach. As a consequence, many leaders and employees accepted the empowerment responsibilities and took their game up several notches to a new level.

Senge defines learning organizations as "organizations where people continually expand their capacity to create the results they truly desire, where expansive patterns of thinking are nurtured, where collective aspiration is set free, and where people are continually learning how to learn together." While Senge says that learning organizations help to satisfy our need for "intrinsic" benefits from work, perhaps the most salient reason for building learning organizations is the expanded capabilities such organizations possess. What fundamentally distinguishes learning organizations from traditional authoritarian "controlling organizations" is the mastery of certain basic disciplines:

- *Systems thinking:* a framework for seeing interrelationships rather than things, for seeing patterns of change rather than static "snapshots."
- *Personal mastery:* continually clarifying and deepening our personal vision, focusing our energies, developing patience, and seeing reality objectively.
- *Mental models:* deeply ingrained assumptions, generalizations, or even pictures or images that influence how we understand the world and how we take action; the thoughts that control perceptions of what can or cannot be done.
- *Shared vision:* the purpose, goal, mission, or vision that binds people together around a common identity and a sense of destiny.

- *Team learning:* when dialogue, talking and thinking together, allows the IQ of the group to be above that of anyone in the group; the whole becomes smarter than the sum of the parts.

Of these five disciplines, Plant 16 leadership and employees are fairly well advanced in their perspective and implementation of shared vision and team learning. While the organization is not yet strong at developing mental models, personal mastery, or systems thinking, much progress has been made in a relatively short period of time, and the expectation level of the plant's ability to mature rapidly is high. Positive feedback from customers and visitors around issues such as business awareness of employees, customer focus awareness of employees, concern for product quality expressed by employees, minimal complaints and grievances from employees, etc., all suggest a maturing of the organization.

Senge notes that learning disabilities can be fatal in organizations. He identifies seven myths which make organizations poor learners:

- *I am my position.* The "who you are is what you do" type of thinking leads to a myopic and nonsystemic view of the organization, where we no longer see how our actions affect the rest of the system. It produces concern for our own job only and not what effect we may have on others.
- *The enemy is out there.* With a very narrow sense of self-identification, it becomes very natural to think of people outside and around us as the "enemy" that is responsible for most problems.
- *The illusion of taking charge.* All too often, our proactiveness is actually trying to fight "the enemy out there," rather than being proactive toward our own faults.
- *Fixation on events.* We are conditioned to see life as a series of events and to think that for every event, there is one cause; when in reality, the primary threats to our survival come not from events, but from slow, gradual processes, as illustrated in the next myth.
- *The parable of the boiled frog.* Like the frog that will sit in a pot of slowly heating water until the water boils and the frog dies, we are, while good at reacting to sudden threats, poor at recognizing gradual threats.
- *The delusion of learning from experience.* Most of the critical decisions made in organizations have systemwide consequences that stretch out over years and decades, and we never get to experience the results in a timely fashion.
- *The myth of the management team.* Most teams operate in a zone of skilled incompetence, proficient at keeping themselves from learning; the group IQ matches that of the lowest of the individuals.

Senge refers to learning organizations but points out that there is no such thing as a learning organization. However, if you use the five learning disciplines, even though you will not create a learning organization, you will foster a new wave of experimentation and advancement. Thus, the organization is dynamic and continually learning, creating, and advancing. The Plant 16 organization is guilty, in varying degrees, of any and all of the seven myths and learning disabilities mentioned above. Getting more than 600 people to rise above all of the myths, to the same level and at the same time, appears to be impossible. Based on this author's experience, when consultants and internal practitioners had faith in the employees of Plant 16, ongoing progress occurred. While Plant 16 will probably never become a learning organization, as Senge points out, we have begun to foster a new wave of experimentation and advancement never seen before in this setting, or, for that matter, any similar setting in our experience.

3.4 Chronological Events Supplement

1994

May

- The Quality Council continues to be concerned with a seeming loss of focus. The need for an off-site council meeting to address issues is apparent.

June

- Rumors abound that Anderson manufacturing plants will be sold or divested.
- The Quality Council participates in an off-site meeting, with the following results:
  - The Steering Focus Council is formed. Membership will be the plant manager and the two district committeepersons. Meetings will be conducted weekly to monitor adherence to the beliefs and values, as well as the vision and mission, throughout the plant.
  - Three other focus councils, People, Product, and Performance, are empowered to conduct the business of the plant via the mission and action plans related to them.
  - The Quality Council will begin to meet monthly, rather than weekly, for information-sharing purposes and major decision making.
  - The decision to pursue ISO 9000 registration for the plant is delayed until more data relating to the QS 9000 initiative from Chrysler, Ford, and GM are available.

- A process is developed to address employee performance issues, good and bad, so that employees receive feedback on their individual performance.

July

- It is announced that three Delco Remy plants, one in Meridian, Mississippi, and two in Anderson (all major customers of Plant 16), will be sold. The sale will be effective August 1, 1994, with employee transfer rights to be negotiated later.
- It is announced that effective July 1, 1994, the balance of the Delco Remy organization, worldwide, has merged with AC Rochester Division of General Motors. The newly formed GM division is named AC Delco Systems, and the worldwide headquarters will be located in Flint, Michigan. Anderson no longer houses a GM divisional headquarters.
- 1995 budget reviews begin, with an effort being made to establish Plant 16 as a profit center. This effort is successful.

August

- It is announced that the plant manager is being transferred effective September 1, 1994, and that the superintendent, this author, will assume the manager's responsibilities.
- A single "town meeting" with all employees is held to help alleviate employees' concerns about the loss of the manager and its potential statement about the future of the plant.
- Plant 16 hosts the NAO (General Motors North American Operations) Facilities Engineering "Maintenance Strategy" meeting. All visitors are impressed with Plant 16, and the plant is recognized by them as a potential supplier to other GM facilities.
- Plant 16 is recognized by Bosch Industries as a "basic integrator," which has the potential to lead to more non-GM business for the plant.
- The leadership, including most Quality Council members, union and management, begin developing a management restructuring to accommodate the loss of the plant manager.
- Several activities, including a plantwide recognition ceremony, are held to honor the departing plant manager and to mark the change in leadership.
- Several skilled trades departments in the AC Delco Systems—Anderson site are made a part of the Plant 16 operations, even

though they are not physically located in Plant 16. These include the following departments:

Carbide Die—50 employees
Heat Treat & Urethane—10 employees
Garage Repair—13 employees
Patternmaking—10 employees

This brings the total employment level of the plant to over 600 employees.

September

- Key executives from the new divisional headquarters in Flint, Michigan, visit Plant 16 and hear the "Plant 16 story." Employees begin to understand that entertaining visitors will become a way of life.
- The local union and management begin to meet and understand that there will be a method for movement of employees from the recently sold plants back to AC Delco Systems, Plant 16's parent company. This method will be decided by the General Motors Corporation Labor Relations representatives, the respective management representatives, and the UAW International union representatives. Plant 16 union and management representatives begin to plan for potential employee turnover as a result of the impending settlement.
- The AC Delco Systems plants in Anderson, Indiana, including Plant 16, conduct an open house in celebration of the merger of Delco Remy and AC Rochester Divisions. A New Employee Orientation Group Action Council conducts the extremely successful Plant 16 open house activities.
- Orientation and education activities are begun to bring new Plant 16 employees into the Plant 16 family.

October

- Initial discussions are held with the divisional purchasing department to allow Plant 16 to have a dedicated purchasing agent. This would allow shortening of the plant's tool and equipment lead times.
- Local labor-management meetings begin to develop the skilled trades applications referred to in the recent memorandum of understanding between AC Delco Systems, Delco Remy America, and the UAW.

November

- The plant has its first implementation workshop, a facilitated gathering of interested employees directed toward improving operations. The impending arrival of two new "wire" machines provides the opportunity for several employees to participate in forming utilization and location plans for the equipment. The results of the workshop are very encouraging, as the employees elect to "manage" the equipment by team effort rather than the usual approach of specific machine assignments. This team management approach will allow for much longer run time of the equipment. The employees benchmark their competitors and determine their goal for becoming more competitive.
- Plant 16 has its first performance review with the Anderson-site operations manager and begins identifying performance measures for future reviews. This creates some anxiety, since Plant 16 was not accustomed to reporting plant measurements. This is yet another example of adding structure to the culture of Plant 16.
- The Quality Council and other union and management staff spend two days off-site to share perceived job assignments and discuss organizational issues. The newly named sales and engineering manager and the newly named quality assurance general supervisor attend and share new insights with the group. Concerns for the plant's future are addressed. The concerns have an air of validity given the shrinking workload and increasing headcount facing the organization.

December

- The Steering Focus Council takes the Plant 16 first-line supervisors off-site to reinforce the importance of their jobs for the future success of the plant. Also stressed is the need for more structure in their expectations of employees. Employee feedback had indicated that supervisors had to step up if the urgency of the plant's situation were to be believed by employees.
- The recognition sinks in that the plant's future could be in doubt as a result of not having enough work in 1995. Over 50 percent of the 1995 business must come from new customers, and the fact that the plant will have to accept skilled trades employees from the manufacturing plants in Anderson as they endeavor to become more competitive by reducing their skilled trades headcount begins to be understood by most of the plant leadership. The Steering Council begins plans to roll out the dilemma to all plant employees.

- The first application of the memorandum of understanding between AC Delco Systems, Delco Remy America, and the UAW is promulgated, and Plant 16's headcount is increased by 39 skilled tradespeople, bringing the plant population to over 620 employees.
- The plant leadership makes the decision to intensify marketing efforts within General Motors. This allows the plant to market what it does best, designing and building integrated assembly systems. The marketing plan for the plant becomes more targeted toward the type of equipment that General Motors needs and the plant manufactures well. This decision does not preclude the utilization of plant employees on other lines of business, such as CNC machining, mold making, die making, heat treat, etc. However, it does allow for the movement of employees into the build floor on an as-needed basis. This concept allows the plant to get more competitive by increasing its more productive work and decreasing its less productive work, all the while utilizing employees to their maximum.

1995

January

- Plant 16's first year of being a stand-alone financial entity begins. Profit and loss structure begins to become a part of the vocabulary in the plant.
- Some or all of the members of the Quality Council meet with all major customers and their representatives to discuss the Plant 16 story relative to marketing plans outside of the old customer base. The intention is to create awareness among old customers that Plant 16 will be pursuing a new marketing approach but still wants to continue to have a solid relationship with them. The meetings present a good opportunity to listen to the voice of the customer. While the old customers appreciate the knowledge of Plant 16's future plans, they leave little doubt that they expect to be treated as good customers and that cost is important to them, quality is simply expected and can't be compromised, and, most of all, untimely delivery will not be tolerated. In fact, Plant 16 learns that on-time delivery is perhaps the single most important customer need in today's world, where it is necessary to get to market as quickly as possible. In essence, less cost is important, good quality is a given, but delivery can win or lose customers immediately.
- Implementation workshops continue in the plant. Each workshop involves eight to twelve employees who strive to find improvements

in their operations. This continuous improvement effort works toward identifying systemic barriers and the solutions for removing them. Periodic follow-ups maintain the integrity of the method. The plant leadership attends wrap-up sessions at the end of each workshop.
- The plant manager and the two UAW district committeepersons meet with all plant employees in groups of 25 to 40 and explain the Plant 16 story and its impact on the employees. The concern for future business, the marketing plan to move toward integrated systems work, the "voice of the customer" results, and the overwhelming need to make good on delivery dates are shared with all employees. The response appears to be positive.

February

- More effort is made to capture pertinent measurements and report on them. The Performance Focus Council takes on this task. The structure of measurements and the accountability it breeds begin to take shape.
- The plant manager starts a weekly production meeting where all jobs in the plant that are approaching being past due, or nearly so, are discussed. The accountable employee or employees report on action plans and customer contacts. The purpose is to promote on-time delivery and appropriate customer contact.
- The General Motors Automotive Components Group (ACGW) changes its name to Delphi Automotive Systems. This creates a name change for Plant 16's parent division from AC Delco Systems to Delphi Energy and Engine Management Systems.

March

- As a method for improving delivery times for jobs in the plant, the leadership elects to pursue project management concepts as a method of tracking major jobs from the original order to the time of delivery to the customer. This prompts a minor reorganization of the operations leadership. The change appears to have a positive effect on delivery and employee morale.
- The local newspaper, the *Anderson Herald-Bulletin,* does a feature story on Plant 16's activities. The Sunday feature becomes a source of great pride for the plant's employees.
- The plant manager and the sales and engineering manager are invited to present the Plant 16 story to the divisional operations

staff at corporate headquarters. The presentation is well accepted and also becomes a source of pride for the plant.
- Plant leadership attends project management training to facilitate determination of needs in the evolving manufacturing environment.

April

- Several divisional leaders visit the plant and express interest in assigning work to Plant 16 on a competitive basis.
- The editor of the UAW-GM Quality Network quarterly publication visits the plant and decides to write an article to be published GM-wide.
- The bugs associated with the financial system that allows Plant 16 to become a financial stand-alone entity begin to smooth out, and the financial data indicate that when the workload is high, the plant performs well. However, much more time needs to pass before a true assessment can be made.

3.5 Learnings and Relearnings

The past year has been very beneficial for those wanting to have learning experiences. The following reflects some of the learnings and relearnings this author, as superintendent and plant manager, experienced during the past year:

- Communicate, communicate, communicate.
- Time is a precious resource; use it wisely.
- Behavior of employees is based on behavior of leaders.
- Systemic processes and structure reduce employee anxiety by reducing ambiguity.
- Leadership is much more than just charisma.
- Not everyone fits in; be willing to make personnel changes.
- When you have no comparison to compete with, measure trends and compete with yourself.
- Systems and procedures reinforce the perception that the leadership cares.
- Employees rise to the level of the leadership's expectations.
- Expecting accountability shows that the leadership cares.
- Customers want, and expect, to be heard.

3.6 Recommendations

While these might not apply to everyone's particular situation, the following are recommendations for your consideration:

- Be prepared to spend a significant amount of time explaining cultural change activities and their relationship to the implementation of work processes and structures.
- Develop and implement measurement systems that allow you to compare your organization to itself.
- Develop and implement measurement systems that provide accountability for your employees.
- Consider problems as opportunities in disguise that allow you to demonstrate proper behavior for the organization.
- Empower as many employees as possible to be involved in the business.
- Let the employees that do not fit in move on.
- Listen to your customers, seek their input, and keep them informed.
- Prior to attempting to institutionalize structure and processes, spend time on cultural change activities.

As indicated in the *Handbook* chapter, this process is dynamic and ongoing. The Plant 16 situation changes almost daily. If you have gained some understanding of your own organization by having read this, my mission will have been accomplished. If you are in the Plant 16 neighborhood, please stop in and see us. Good luck in your endeavors. If we can be of further assistance, please let us know.

3.7 References

Collins, J. C., and J. I. Porras, *Built to Last: Successful Habits of Visionary Companies,* New York: Harper-Collins Publishers, 1994.
Darnell, G., and A. Hamood, *Highlights of Total Quality Management: Philosophies and Applications,* Detroit: General Motors Corporation, 1991.
Duff, J. L., *The Jerry Duff Group,* Dayton, Ohio, 1995.
Jablonski, J. R., *Implementing TQM: Competing in the Nineties through Total Quality Management,* San Diego: Pfeiffer & Company, 1992.
Kelly, Leslie, ed., *The ASTD Technical and Skills Training Handbook,* New York: McGraw-Hill, 1995.
Schein, E. H., *Organizational Culture and Leadership,* 2d ed., San Francisco: Jossey-Bass, 1992.
Senge, P. M., *The Fifth Discipline: The Art and Practice of the Learning Organization,* New York: Bantam Doubleday Dell Publishing Group, 1990.

Chapter 4

The University of Chicago Hospitals Move toward a Managed Care Environment

Nancy Merriam and Victoria A. Gundrum

Nancy Merriam is the Lead Educator/Trainer for the University of Chicago Hospitals Academy. Her main responsibilities are sponsorship of the Service Orientation Certificate (mandated training for all hospital employees) and supporting training needs for Sector II, which includes the ambulatory care clinics. Since September 1994, Nancy has been a member of the Managed Care Systems and Operations Committee (McSOC), serving as its liaison with the UCH Academy. Her tasks include developing training materials and assessment tools. Before coming to the UCH Academy, she spent four years as a consultant with Employee Development Systems, including time as an adjunct faculty member of the UCH Academy. The six previous years she served as internal consultant and national trainer for Joseph T. Ryerson and Sons, Inc., leading office employees through job redesign and retraining implemented as part of major technology changes. Nancy is a graduate of Smith College in Northampton, Massachusetts.

Victoria A. Gundrum is the Director of Ambulatory Services for surgery at the University of Chicago Hospitals. In addition to managing these ambulatory practices, she serves as the chairperson of McSOC at the hospitals. This committee has developed and implemented new institutional policies and procedures for the provision of care to managed care patients in the ambulatory care setting and assisted in the development of the related training program. She received her M.S. in Health Systems Management from Rush University and her B.S. in Health & Safety Studies (Healthcare Administration) from the University of Illinois in Champaign.

4.1 Introduction

The University of Chicago Hospitals (UCH) are preparing for the future in ambulatory (outpatient) clinic care. This chapter focuses on not only the short-term solutions to immediate challenges in providing ambulatory patient care, but also solutions to the enormous challenges resulting from changes in the way patient care is reimbursed. In addition to an overview of the institution and the changing marketplace, you will learn about two different kinds of technical skill training: First, managed care training responding to market-driven changes, and second, training occurring as new systems and hardware are introduced to the ambulatory clinic staff.

You will learn how challenges were identified and defined, solutions were formulated and planned for, and strategies were developed to verify that training resulted in employee behavior modifications. The chapter also examines how these initiatives are linked to strategic plans.

Because of the complexity of this chapter's terminology, a short glossary of terms is provided at the end of the chapter.

4.2 An Introduction to the University of Chicago Hospitals

The UCH, an 865-operating-bed academic medical center, made up of three separate hospitals based in Hyde Park on the campus of the University of Chicago and one hospital located on Chicago's North Side, is a not-for-profit corporation. The hospitals include Bernard Mitchell Hospital, the primary adult patient care facility; Wyler Children's Hospital, a 149-bed hospital devoted to the medical needs of children; Chicago Lying-in Hospital, a maternity and women's hospital; Weiss Memorial Hospital, a 225-bed hospital on Chicago's North Side; and more than 125 specialty ambulatory care clinics.

A specially equipped and staffed medical helicopter, UCAN (The University of Chicago Hospitals Aeromedical Network), is based at a helipad atop the Bernard Mitchell Hospital. This serves the emergency care center's Level I pediatric trauma unit as well as a number of special areawide treatment centers based at the hospitals, including regional burn, electrical trauma, and perinatal units.

The University of Chicago Hospitals are the clinical arm of the University of Chicago's Division of the Biological Sciences (BSD), which includes the Pritzker School of Medicine. Most of the 560 attending physicians who provide care in the hospital and clinic setting are full-time faculty of the BSD. Unlike the 620 residents and fellows and nearly 950 nurses, the physicians are not employed by the hospitals, but rather by the university. This relationship presents a special series of opportunities as a result of different billing, data collection, and recording systems and compatible but different reporting structures.

Physicians and researchers at the UCH are among the best and brightest in their fields. Since the first hospital unit opened in the fall of 1927, the UCH has had a proud history of breakthroughs in research and pioneering new treatments. Included in this history are 11 Nobel Prize winners in surgery, medicine, and physiology. Some breakthroughs include establishment of the first civilian blood bank, the discovery of REM sleep, and the first non-living related donor liver transplant.

The University of Chicago is home to a number of special programs, including a National Clinical Cancer Center, a National Diabetes Research and Training Center, a National Clinical Research Center, the MacLean Center for Clinical Medical Ethics (considered the leading ethics training program in the United States), a Special Center for Research in Ischemic Heart Disease, the Howard Hughes Medical Institute for research in molecular biology and molecular genetics, and the Joseph P. Kennedy Jr. Mental Retardation Research Center. The University of Chicago has one of only seven National Clinical Nutrition Research Centers in the country.

The ambulatory (outpatient) clinics at the University of Chicago Hospitals are organized as Physician-Directed Practices (PDPs). Each clinic operates as an independent practice under the direction of physician groups. This design is intended to hold physicians and hospitals management accountable for both revenues and expenses generated in each clinic. The PDP places management and fiscal responsibility for outpatient practices with clinical departments and thus attempts to control excess expenses. This approach allows the practices to create an environment which best meets the needs of their patient populations.

At the current time, ambulatory scheduling, registration, and billing systems are separate systems which run on separate computer terminals or manual devices.

4.3 Providing Care to the Surrounding Community

In addition to being a leader in research and medical education, the University of Chicago Hospitals have a long-term commitment to providing care to the community. Hyde Park is within 5 miles of 9 of the 10 poorest neighborhoods in the United States. The hospitals are the largest employer on the South Side of Chicago, with approximately 7,000 employees in the medical center, many of whom live in the area.

The hospitals provide more inpatient care to Medicaid patients than any other private hospital in the state. The patient population of the hospitals is 37 percent covered by private insurance, 35 percent covered by Medicaid, and 28 percent covered by Medicare. The lower percentage of patients covered by private insurance makes it more imperative that the hospitals provide care in a cost-effective manner.

4.4 Organizational Structure of the University of Chicago Hospitals

In 1991 the Senior Management Group of the University of Chicago Hospitals met to identify strategies for the future. The outcome of their sessions was the initiation of an ongoing process called the Transformation which describes how the UCH will achieve the following goals:

- Deliver patient-centered care to all patients
- Improve the quality of services at the hospitals
- Remain financially strong
- Strengthen strategic programs through the development of more cost-effective care

The Transformation is being achieved through a rededication to the UCH's mission of patient care in the context of structural reorganization, work redesign, and quality improvement. In addition to a new organizational structure (see Fig. 4.1), the strategic changes include substantial investments in technology and physical resources for both inpatient and ambulatory care.

Sectors I and II, Patient Services and Physician Services, are the two sectors dedicated to providing direct patient care. Some other services support both Sector I and Sector II (e.g., environmental services) and report to senior managers in both sectors.

In Sector I (providing direct care to inpatients), the investments are occurring under the umbrella of an inclusive process called Innovations in Patient Care, and are scheduled to be completed by the end of 1995. The first pilot units went live on November 1, 1994. In addition, major renovations are scheduled for many of the inpatient units to help facilitate better patient-centered care. Some of the technological innovations include a sophisticated monitoring and tracking system for communicating patient needs to the care center staff, EPIB (Electronic Patient Information Base) to provide on-line reporting of laboratory/radiology/test results, and a cook/chill system for preparing and delivering patient meals.

Sector Organization

I. **Patient Services**
(Provide direct care to inpatients)
Inpatient nursing units, pharmacy, physical therapy, respiratory therapy, environmental services, social services, patient social services

II. **Physician Services**
(Services to physicians & their patients)
Ambulatory care clinics, emergency rooms, operating rooms, radiology, laboratories, environmental services, house staff, clinical departments, and strategic programs

III. **Support Services**
(Support UCH staff, public responsibilities, physical facilities, materials handling, the President's and Executive VP offices
HR, payroll, security, UCH Academy, medical legal services, financial, regulatory compliance, plant and maintenance, clinical engineering, purchasing, receiving, supply processing, accounts payable, and laundry

IV. **Information Services**
(Monitor maintenance and use of information)
IS, admitting, billing, collection, medical records, utilization review, quality assurance, program evaluation, financial analysis, and budget

V. **Strategic Services**
(Promote a positive image of the institution, solicit and secure external funding, and develop and maintain a patient base)
Public affairs, development, planning and corporate development, advertising, and mass marketing

Figure 4.1 Sector organization.

In Sector II (providing services to physicians and their patients), the investments include the new Duchossois Center for Advanced Medicine, scheduled to open in 1996, which is a freestanding facility adjacent to the hospital where most ambulatory care will be provided. Job redesign and investment in new technologies will support physicians, employees, and patients who will use the new facility. The managed care training initiatives are part of these planned changes.

4.5 Technology in Use Today in the Ambulatory Care Clinics

Today, patients who want to schedule appointments in an ambulatory care clinic need to call each clinic individually. Clinic coordinators schedule appointments using a paper appointment book. Each clinic has its own book, and each book is shared by all employees who schedule clinic appointments for that location. Coordinating visits to more than one clinic is often time-consuming and not seamless to the patient.

Employees use a dumb terminal which has access to BHIS (Burroughs Hospital Information Systems). Scheduled patient visits are preloaded from the paper book into the hospital's computer to generate a list of appointments for the next day and to prompt the delivery of medical records and X-ray films. Once the patient arrives at the clinic, he or she is registered on BHIS. All tracking of managed care referrals is currently a manual process. Some PDPs are currently experimenting with the use of bar code scanners to scan and upload data to the billing system. This system will become more functional when patient ID numbers are incorporated into the system. Some PDPs have an automated scheduling system (IDX system); however, staff must still double-enter appointment information, once for the patient's arrival and again for billing purposes.

4.6 Anticipated Technology in the Ambulatory Care Clinics

Scheduling and registration of clinic appointments will change significantly at the University of Chicago Hospitals as changes are phased in over the next 12 months. The new policies and procedures associated with the outpatient managed care initiative are temporary operational solutions until the technical solution is installed and implemented. Patients will be able to schedule appointments at their convenience, and staff will spend less time on paperwork as a result of improved information gathering through UCH's new automated scheduling and registration system, Cadence, designed by Epic Systems Corporation. Designed primarily to serve the ambulatory clinics and ancillary areas, the new system will be phased in over the next 12 months.

Specifically, Cadence will be installed in the clinics at clinic coordinator work stations. The work stations will be Intel-based PCs with a trackball mouse keyboard and an ultra scan 17" monitor, and they will run in a Windows environment. BHIS, EPIB, Time & Attendance (the on-line employee attendance system), radiology data, and other diagnostic test information will also be accessible via a single logon. While the message and BHIS printers will continue to be used because of interface issues, network laser printers will also be installed for Cadence reporting purposes. Because of the efficiency increases anticipated with the new system, UCH will bear all hardware, software, and installation costs—costs to the PDPs will be zero.

The first phase of this automated system will replace the paper scheduling books. Physician-specific templates, created in the Cadence system, are being developed around the physicians' practice styles (e.g., clinic days, number of appointments by visit type in incremental time units, ancillaries required before the visit, directions to the clinic, etc.). Physician templates will also include the physician's other practice locations so that patients can be given location options. In addition, if a patient needs to see more than one doctor, the computer will search and find times that are convenient to both the patient and the physicians. The new system will also help patient, staff, and physicians track the necessary authorizations required with managed care contracts.

In preparation for the installation of the automated system, formal educational training is scheduled for all staff. UCH operational managers and UCH Academy staff will train and certify all staff who are involved in the scheduling and registration of patients. For example, clinic coordinators will receive 12 hours of Cadence training prior to the system's installation. Clinic managers and others designated to create physician templates received an additional 16 hours of training to learn to customize templates to reflect physician preferences. Additionally there are three practice areas where staff can try out Cadence before work, after work, or during lunch to help increase their comfort level before installation.

With the second phase, Cadence will allow for an enterprisewide registration and computerized referral tracking system. When this phase is installed, the need for duplication registration on BHIS will be eliminated.

4.7 The Impact of New Kinds of Insurance Coverage

As insurance companies move away from commercial indemnity coverage (a type of insurance that offers the enrollee/patient freedom to choose a health care provider and reimburses the provider on a fee-for-service basis) to more restrictive managed care plans (an approach to health care that closely links the delivery and financing of health care to manage patient care in a coordinated fashion), there are more rules and regulations covering the delivery of care (see Fig. 4.2).

If care providers such as the University of Chicago Hospitals and PDPs do not strictly adhere to the requirements of these new insurance plans, reimbursement for patient care may be jeopardized. Current technology allows employees to determine if a patient's

The Growth of Private Pay Patients Covered by Managed Care at UCH
It is expected that most private pay patients will convert to managed care by the year 2000.

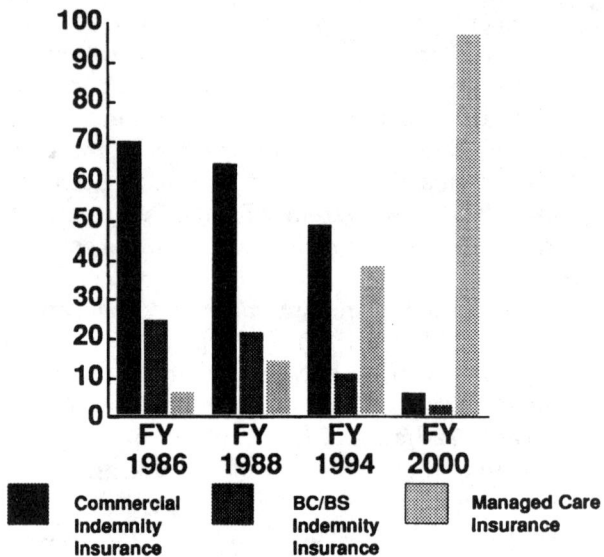

Commercial Indemnity Insurance = Fee for service insurance provided by a for profit insurance company
BC/BS Indemnity Insurance = Fee for service insurance provided by Blue Cross/Blue Shield - a not for profit insurance company
Managed Care Insurance = See glossary for definitions of HMO, PPO, POS, EPO, and IPA Insurance plan. Managed Care Insurance can be provided by any carrier

Figure 4.2 The growth in the percentage of private pay patients covered by managed care at UCH. It is expected that most private patients will convert to managed care by the year 2000.

insurance carrier has a financial contract and plan number with the hospitals by using an on-line computer screen called RINS (Request Insurance).

4.8 The Managed Care Working Group

In the summer of 1992, the Managed Care Working Group was established. As the managed care market continues to grow and becomes a larger part of the University of Chicago Hospitals' payer mix, there is a corresponding increase in delayed payments and denied claims because of the hospitals' lack of compliance with payer requirements.

In order to devise a consistent and effective response to the changing market, the working group met to examine operational issues and identify short- and long-term solutions. The goals for the working group were outlined as follows:

1. Improve compliance with payer requirements, including
   - Billing the appropriate party in the appropriate format
   - Monitoring the hospitals' performance under those requirements and responding to problems
   - Anticipating future needs and requirements of managed care organizations as the market matures
2. Improve the service the hospitals provide to referring physicians.
3. Develop a successful educational program for attending physicians, house staff, nurses, and administrative staff which is designed to provide introductory managed care information and information specially tailored to their health care roles.
4. Excel in clinical performance within the managed care paradigm by efficiently providing only authorized care with outcomes that reflect high-quality care.

4.9 The Managed Care Working Group's Recommendations

Recommendations from the Managed Care Working Group's report focused on four major issues: Referral and Clinical Management, Registration Aids, Education and Training, and Contract Management. The Managed Care Systems and Operations Committee (McSOC) was charged with developing policies and procedures and a training program for the first three goals. The fourth goal was later assigned to the Clinical Care Committee.

4.9.1 Referral and clinical management

Clinic staff must comply with authorized referrals in the ambulatory care setting. They must correctly identify those patients for whom preauthorization for services is necessary, and, once patients arrive for the appointment, the terms of the referral dictate the level of service provided. Additional services must be preapproved by the patients' PCP (primary care physician). Recommendations in this area were specific:

- During the appointment process, utilize a script developed to educate patients and remind them of their insurance restrictions and requirements.
- Modify the outpatient registration form to include insurance classification and referral information.
- Collect referral information at the point of appointment scheduling and verify this information when the patient arrives for the visit. Modify computer-generated daily clinic schedules to indicate managed care patients.
- Create computer reports to track the number of denied and delayed payments as a result of specialty areas' inability to comply with the terms of the referral and to sort information by physician and specialty.
- Develop stickers for charts and registration sheets to serve as a reminder of the patients' insurance requirements.
- Establish policies and procedures to contact the HMO or primary care physician to obtain and/or verify referrals.

4.9.2 Registration aids

To assist employees serving managed care patients, it is important to offer the employees job aids to support their information needs. The audience for these particular aids was employees who register patients for clinic visits. Unique situations exist in the emergency room (because of the necessity to provide urgent or emergency care) that require modification of the developed policies and procedures.

- Commit to continuously updating staff on the status of specific managed care contracts and their requirements.
- Generate reports that identify claims that are delayed or denied because of incorrect insurance information or data and provide feedback to registration staff. Use the reports as information and education tools to aid the support staff's understanding and use of plan codes.
- Adapt procedures for the emergency room, acknowledging that current practices in the emergency room create a unique set of challenges for dealing with managed care patients and receiving timely payment of their bills.

4.9.3 Education and training

The program must involve attending physicians, house staff, nurses, clinic coordinators, secretaries, and Patient Business Representatives (PBRs). The clinic coordinators, secretaries, and PBRs are involved with scheduling outpatient visits and registering the patients when they arrive for their appointments and the actual provision of services.

- Develop and implement a successful educational program as a critical factor for the hospitals' managed care efforts.
- Implement requirements for all relevant hospitals staff, including clinical staff, with respect to initial and continuing education on managed care.
- Develop a managed care primer for all relevant employees at UCH.
- Develop a multifaceted approach to present the primer and other pertinent information to identified target staff.
- Develop means to provide follow-up and continuation of the educational skills training program.

4.9.4 Contract management

Because many implications of managed care go beyond direct patient care to affect finances and negotiated arrangements, the final section makes recommendations for changes in these organizational and administrative areas.

- Improve coordination of hospital and physician contracts under managed care arrangements.
- Establish the Managed Care Working Group as a managed care forum that will meet regularly to identify and address issues or problems related to managed care. The group's focus is on identifying managed care issues, but it also serves as a resource for other groups affected by managed care.
- Establish a standing group to meet on billing and collection issues. The group would have representatives from the hospitals' and physicians' billing offices and would meet periodically to discuss policies and procedures and provide an opportunity for the exchange of ideas and mutual edification.

1. Develop the ability to manage "package price" and capitated patients through their course of care.
   - Identify the intake staff involved with package price patients and educate them about package price arrangements.
   - With our current registration and billing systems, the key to complying with the package price billing requirements is accu-

rate preregistration of the patient at the time of appointment scheduling and during each clinical encounter.

2. Capture and disseminate anecdotal information regarding managed care arrangements and patients on an ongoing basis. Use computer E-mail as a vehicle for sharing information throughout the system.
3. Develop the ability to identify discrepancies between expected and actual reimbursement.
   - Develop reports to identify inpatient revenue at risk or lost for lack of authorization, exhaustion of benefits, etc.
   - Relying on rejection codes and payment codes, the IDX system can distinguish and track by invoice reasons for denial or reduction in reimbursement in addition to low reimbursement under a fee schedule.
4. Centralize the collection and storage of referral forms. Implement standardized procedures for collecting, centrally filing, and storing all referral forms for one (1) year so that they can be accessed by billing staffs. After one year this information will be scanned into microfiche.

This procedure will also allow monitoring of the volume of HMO (health maintenance organizations) and POS (point of service) patients as well as provide documentation of services authorized for billing purposes.

4.10 Breaking the Task Down into Short- and Long-Term Goals

As the Managed Care Working Group (later Committee) met, it became clear to the members that major modifications to UCH policies and procedures and information systems (computers) would be necessary to meet the health care market's expectations for providers in a rapidly changing managed care environment. It also became obvious that the hospitals could not wait for these strategic processes to be implemented, but that interim solutions needed to be identified and quickly implemented.

Initial identification of issues occurred as a result of information gained from data collection efforts. Interviews were conducted in each clinic to identify current work flows and obstacles to providing consistent care in the areas of ambulatory care and ancillary services.

A number of subgroups were created to focus on specific managed care issues.

4.11 Creation and Charge of the Managed Care Systems and Operations Committee

It was understood that McSOC would address problems or obstacles that could best be addressed in the short term, but that would be ultimately affected by major long-range strategies. The specific need was to develop and implement short-term solutions to problems. Other working groups and committees were created to support the development and implementation of strategic solutions.

The Managed Care Systems and Operations Committee was charged with

- Identifying effective and efficient health care network operations requirements for meeting customer needs and functioning successfully in a mixed fee-for-service/managed care insurer and patient environment.
- Recommending systems and operations changes required if the UC network was to meet the above.
- Developing a managed care training program for all staff who interact with patients.

The Managed Care Systems and Operations Committee is a multidisciplinary team composed of individuals who have reporting structures across all sectors (see Fig. 4.1).

4.12 Where to Start: Focus on the Ambulatory Care Training Initiative

One of the short-term needs identified by the Managed Care Working Group was the development of short-term solutions for an Ambulatory Care Managed Care Initiative. This initiative included operationalizing recommendations from the Referral and Clinical Management, Registration Aids, and Education and Training sections of the patient committee's report.

As the managed care market continued to evolve, the actual terms, types, and number of products offered by carriers had become more cumbersome. (See a list of terms and plan types at the end of this chapter.) These changes had become so complicated that often the patient/enrollees of the managed care plans did not understand all of the constraints and controls of their HMOs, PPOs (Preferred Provider Organizations), or other types of managed care plans.

The staff of the UCH needed to educate patients about their responsibilities as consumers of these new insurance plans. This change meant that hospital staff working with patients needed to be able to speak knowledgeably about the basics of managed care. This knowledge base allows them to educate patients about the new "rules of the game." At this time, only the data about insurance plan codes were available on computer screens. With the new Cadence system, more automated on-line support will be available to the staff.

4.13 Gathering Data: Work Flows and Baseline Measurements

Information-gathering interviews were conducted to identify the work flows in clinic areas. Flows were generated for appointment scheduling, registration and check-in, patient care experience, and end of the day processing. New flows and procedures were created by McSOC to reflect more efficient and effective practices and to aid with more restrictive managed care plans. An example is shown in Fig. 4.3.

Baseline measurements regarding financial implications of incorrect handling of managed care patient claims were gathered from the finance department. Private pay patients covered by managed care were 10 percent of the total private pay billings at the beginning of the training in the spring of 1994. By the end of the training cycle, this percentage had grown to over 30 percent of private pay billings. These percentages will continue to increase as Medicare and Medicaid beneficiaries join managed care plans when additional managed care structures are introduced on the national and state level.

4.14 Securing Sponsorship

In order to free the time and dollar resources needed to train more than 300 individuals, it was necessary to secure sponsorship for the project. Time was right for sponsorship, as the Managed Care Committee had already alerted the management team to the need to examine long-term solutions. Communicating specifics about the effect of incomplete employee knowledge and resulting action or inaction on the bottom line of clinic operations made the need for training to demonstrate new, more proactive behaviors clear. Monies for training were approved.

Aggregate baseline data were collected in report form to communicate outcomes in terms of specific measurables. As clinics completed their training, results were monitored against baselines. Goals for each of the measurables were set and linked to a time line. Updates on attainment were presented at monthly meetings by the committee chair.

Revised Flow Managed Care - Appointment Scheduling

```
                    Patient calls
        ┌──────────▶ for appointment
        │                  │
        │                  ▼
┌───────────────┐    ╱ HMO  ╲      ┌──────────────────┐
│Follow existing│NO ╱Insurance╲    │Patient will seek │
│  procedures   │◀──╲    ?    ╱    │ PCP referral     │
└───────────────┘    ╲       ╱     │ •Staff begin     │
                      ╲─────╱      │  processing      │
                       YES         └──────────────────┘
                        │                   │
                        ▼            NO,    ▼
┌──────────────┐     ╱ PCP ╲        But  ┌──────────────┐
│Refer Back to │ NO ╱Referral╲───────────│Patient willing│
│PCP if Patient│◀──╲    ?    ╱           │to pay at Point│
│expects       │    ╲       ╱            │ of Service    │
│insurance     │     ╲─────╱             └──────────────┘
│coverage      │       │                        │
└──────────────┘      YES ◀──────────────────────┘
                       ▼
              ┌──────────────────┐
              │  Clinic Coord.   │
              │ • Schedules      │
              │   appointment    │
              │(current - manual log)│
              │Future - use Cadence │
              └──────────────────┘
                       ▼
              ┌──────────────────┐
              │  Clinic Coord.   │
              │ • Enters info into BHIS │
              │ • Notes PCP info │
              └──────────────────┘
                       ▼
              ┌──────────────────┐
              │New Patient Welcome│
              │     Office        │
              │ •Verify enrollment│
              └──────────────────┘
                       ▼
              ┌──────────────────┐
              │Confirmation Call:│
              │•Remind to bring  │
              │   referral       │
              │•Collect missing info│
              └──────────────────┘
```

Figure 4.3 Revised flowchart for managed care appointment scheduling.

4.15 Developing a Training Plan

In March 1994, the University of Chicago Hospitals Academy director became a member of the Managed Care Systems and Operations Committee. The UCH Academy is the hospitals' corporate education resource. The academy supported managed care training needs with systems and soft skills training offerings.

The first step was to design an assessment of technical skills needed by employees who schedule and register patients for clinic visits. Based on the results of the assessment, the training content group identified three training classes, supported by resource checklists and job aids (see Fig. 4.4):

- Overview of Managed Care—New Roles and Responsibilities; Appointment Scheduling and Check-In. (After the pilot, this information was adapted and presented as a series of checklists.)
- BHIS Training (using the hospitals' information systems to correctly apply plan codes when reading insurance cards and referral forms).
- Managing Patient Relations. Soft skills training for individuals scheduling appointments and identifying patient insurance coverage. (During the pilot there was a separate class outlining the patient business representatives' role. Content from both courses was included in a single course.)

Courses: Content and Developers

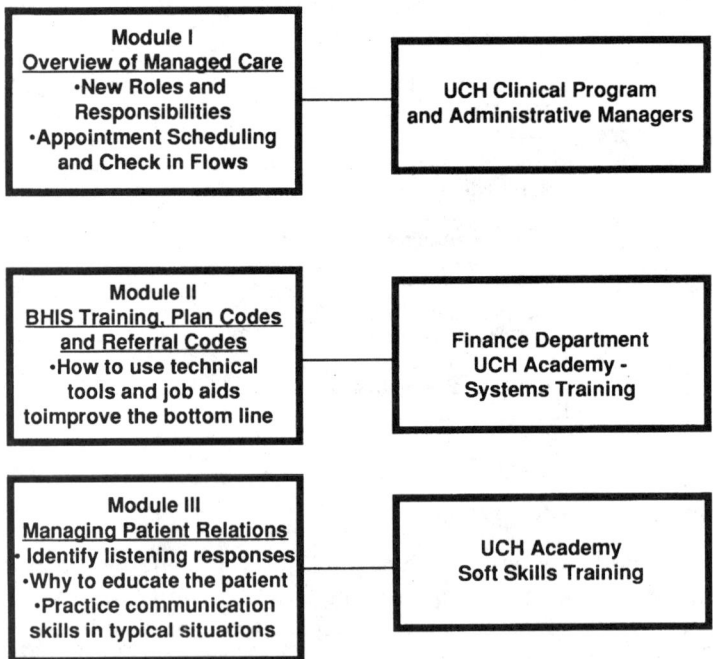

Figure 4.4 Courses: content and developers.

In each area, content experts were identified who created and conducted the training.

4.16 Selecting Pilot Sites

The UCH's main clinical departments include Medicine, Surgery, Pediatrics, and OB/GYN. The committee recommended a pilot in each of these areas. Initial training was planned for Clinic Managers, Outpatient Welcome and Registration Staff, Patient Business Representatives, Clinic Coordinators, Academic Secretaries, and other clinical staff (Nurses, Nursing Assistants, Nurse Specialists, and Technicians) prior to the implementation of new policies and procedures.

Each pilot clinic was chosen for a different reason. In Pediatrics, the Hematology Oncology clinic was selected because of a high number of HMO patients; in Surgery, the Vascular and Thoracic Surgery clinics because the physicians in the PDP felt that this was important to their practices; in Medicine, the Cardiology clinic because it has the largest HMO patient population; and finally, in OB/GYN, the Gynecology Oncology clinic because it had in place existing package pricing programs and used an automated scheduling system (IDX system).

4.17 Administering the Pretraining Assessment

Following the course design, a precourse assessment was administered to PBRs, one of the populations who would be scheduling and registering patients using the new work flows.

Prior to training, the PBRs and clinic coordinators had an average score of 57 percent in the knowledge assessment. After completing their training, the posttest assessment showed average employee knowledge at 86 percent. Based on this information and the maturing managed care market, executive sponsorship was obtained and the training became mandatory.

4.18 Developing Additional Tools to Measure Skill Transfer

At the beginning of the project, there were no easy ways to measure program success. Recall that insurance payments are denied or delayed in managed care plans because of inaccurate identification and processing of patient information and forms.

A critical success measurement is whether staff correctly identify patient insurance status and secure primary care physician referrals or other required approvals prior to delivering treatment in nonemergency situations.

Although it was possible to gather and measure data, data collection was laborious. Data were collected and reported in the following manner: PBRs submitted individual reports to their manager, who calculated the number and percent of patients in each of the following measured categories:

- HMO patients on the schedule
- HMO patients seen in the clinic
- HMO patients with referrals
- HMO patients seen by PBR to obtain referral
- Referrals obtained by PBR
- Patients rescheduled
- Patients reclassified to self-pay
- Patients seen without a referral
- Total referrals obtained

With the installation of Cadence, on-line data collection will become automated. Until that time, manual collection and tally remains a burden on an already busy staff. Interim changes were made to the computerized batch processing mode to generate clinic-specific data files summarizing HMO patient schedule activity and patient registration activity. Planned changes to existing programs call for loading the data files from the production system into a spreadsheet to facilitate report generation. This change will result in less manual calculation by clinic managers. E-mail is used to communicate report results.

4.19 Pilot Sessions

In June and July 1994, 55 employees in the pilot clinics were trained. Attending physicians and house staff (residents, fellows, and interns) received written communications and process flowcharts prior to pilot implementation. In addition, meetings with section chiefs were held to describe the changes in patient processing in order to obtain their input and physician buy-in to the new ways of working.

The following modifications to the training and process implementation were identified and adapted:

- A process for on-line update and communication using SNTE (Show Notes screen) on the hospitals' internal information systems for recording financial and referral information prior to contacting the admitting and finance offices of the Hospitals was developed.
- Multiple copies of the authorization referral are given to the patient to give to clinic staff as needed.
- Cross coverage for PBR assignment is provided to assure that each clinic has support even during sick days, vacations, and scheduled lunch times.
- Clinic coordinators enter the correct financial plan code and PCP information during preregistration.

The following support systems and tools were developed to ease the transition:

- Pilot newsletters were developed to ease communication during the changes. Each pilot clinic had a designated liaison to answer questions and communicate issues and suggestions to McSOC.
- Laminated financial plan code cards were created to provide easy access to plan code information. (Because of market maturation, these cards are in their fifth revision in 9 months in an attempt to keep current with changes.) On-line information is available through the RINS (Report Insurance) screen.

A schedule was developed for four tracks of training and implementation of new policies and procedures (see Fig. 4.5). All specialty clinics on the UCH Hyde Park campus were included in the program, which had a completion deadline of November 11, 1994.

4.20 Measuring Pilot Results

Reports showed positive changes from the pilots and from the total clinic population. Baseline data collected from June 1994 to December 1994 showed an improvement in outcomes. Pilot clinics not only began with strong numbers, but continued to show improvement in each report.

4.21 Reporting to the Sponsor Committee and Setting New Goals

When the results were examined in January 1995, different levels of success indicated varying commitments to the new processes. As in any health care provider organization, there are many conflicting

Training Schedule - All Onsite Clinics	
9/26 Greater General Surgery Pain Management Dermatology Endocrinology Endocrinology / Infertility Pediatric Speciality - Neurology - Neurosurgery - Nephrology - Child Development - Sleep - Urology	10/10 Urology Ophthalmology Neurology Neurosurgery Gynecology Generalist Gastroenterology Pediatric Speciality - Gastroenterology - Liver Transplant
10/24 Otolaryngology-Head & Neck Surgery Oral/Dental Renal Pulmonary Obstretical Specialty Pediatric Speciality -Pediatric Surgery - OrthopaedicSurgery - Plastic Surgery	11/11 Ortopaedic Surgery Chest Oncology Hematology Oncology Rheumatology Psychiatry Pediatric Speciality - Infectious Disease - Allergy / Immunology - Cystic Fibrosis - Endocrinology

Figure 4.5 Training schedule—all on-site clinics.

demands on staff time and attention. Because the initial reporting process was cumbersome, key indicator goals had not been established previously.

In order to reemphasize the importance of the initiative, the management group examined data and determined that setting specific, progressive goals would be the best way to improve compliance outcomes.

To help determine if each clinic is on track for the new goals, data are shared weekly via E-mail with McSOC members, clinic managers, and senior managers. The data are shared monthly at the Committee on Ambulatory Care Systems and Procedures meeting, and with members of the Managed Care Committee.

4.22 Certifying Employee Competency

The senior management group has also charged McSOC with creating a competency assessment certification for all clinic employees who are participating in training sessions and/or are responsible for patient scheduling and registration.

A commitment was made to have all employees demonstrate competency by passing an annual competency assessment. Passing is defined as a score of at least 84 percent for employees who schedule appointments and a score of at least 80 percent for employees who have patient contact but who do not schedule appointments.

Employee competency is publicly celebrated at staff meetings. Clinic managers receive report of participant scores and are given UCH Managed Care mugs to acknowledge employee success and certification. Clinic managers distribute the awards to employees as recognition of their achievement.

To prepare employees for the assessments, the following supports are offered:

- Refresher training sessions are offered in each of the three training classes.
- A Managed Care Study Guide is provided which can be used to prepare for taking the competency assessment and as a tool while participating in the "open book" assessment session. (The staff use the book as a job aid during daily work with managed care patients.)

By the middle of May 1995, 78 employees had demonstrated managed care competency.

4.23 Where Are We Now and Where Are We Going?

As you can see from the section on anticipated technology, the technical skills training challenge has just begun. Two internal consultants have been identified and are beginning to design training and prepare employees to use new hardware and software. Universal workstations are being installed, practice areas are being designated, and a second systems training room is being completed. Employees are continuing to learn about Windows, trackballs, logons, and using multiple applications from a single workstation.

In the spring of 1996 the ambulatory clinics are scheduled to move into the new Duchossois Center for Advanced Medicine. In addition to new systems (Cadence will be up and running, providing improved support for patient scheduling, registration, and on-line data recovery of important patient care and insurance information), the physical space has been designed to create a patient-centered outpatient experience. Training plans are taking shape to prepare employees to optimize patients' experience of the improved physical and technical systems incorporated in this state-of-the-art building.

4.24 Glossary of Terms and Titles

4.24.1 University of Chicago Hospitals titles and terms

Attending Physician The physician who is responsible for the patient's care while the patient is in the hospitals or clinic. The attending physician is often a specialist and not the PCP, and is affiliated with the UCH.

Clinic Coordinator The person at each clinic who registers patients and records charges resulting from the clinic visit. Some coordinators also schedule appointments.

Gatekeeper or Primary Care Physician (PCP) A physician who manages patient care and controls utilization of a managed care organization's resources. Often this is a referring physician, not affiliated directly with the UCH. The physician requires updates on patient treatment, diagnosis, and prognosis. Nonemergency care from providers other than the PCP must be authorized by the PCP in advance for treatment to be eligible for reimbursement for patients in managed care plans.

Housestaff Resident physicians and fellows. These are young physicians who are graduates of some of the world's best medical schools. They already have, at a minimum, eight years of education in science and medicine. They provide care under the guidance of the UCH attending physicians.

Medical Students Working under direct supervision of attending physicians and residents, they help give tests and observe patient care as part of their education.

Outpatient Welcome and Registration A newly created department which contacts new patients (patients new to the UCH clinics, or who have not been seen in the last 24 months) prior to their initial clinic visit. Staff answer patient questions and verify insurance information, informing managed care patients about the importance of PCP referrals.

Patient Business Representatives (PBRs) Staff members who help patients understand the financial implications of their insurance coverage. They assist patients in contacting their PCP for a referral if needed. If no referral is given, they inform patients of their options, e.g., contact the PCP and request a referral or elect to visit the clinic as a self-pay patient. If self-pay is elected, PBRs collect the average fee for a clinic visit before the patient is seen by a physician and facilitate the completion of forms for the provision of services.

Referring Physician The physician of a non-managed care patient who has made a patient's appointment with a UCH physician or instructed the patient to make the appointment.

UCH The University of Chicago Hospitals.

4.24.2 Managed care terminology list

Authorization The requirement for preapproval of services and a care plan by the referring primary care physician prior to the scheduling or delivery of services (tests, X-rays, surgical procedures). The document which indicates authorization is also known as the referral.

Capitation A method of reimbursing providers or provider groups in which a managed care organization (MCO) pays a flat fee per member per month for a defined set of services. The amount is fixed regardless of how many services the health care provider provides. Capitated payments are usually expressed as a certain rate per member per month (PMPM).

Carrier Another term for a company that provides insurance plans.

Carve-Outs Health care services that are not included within the scope of a capitated rate. These are typically specialty services, e.g., mental health services and transplants.

Coinsurance A certain percentage of an individual's total medical expenses, over and above any deductible, which insurers require a covered individual to pay. Also known as patient portion or co-payment.

Commercial Insurance Insurance plans supplied by for-profit insurance carriers and organizations.

Diagnosis-Related Groups (DRGs) A method of reimbursing providers that prescribes a flat fee based on a patient's diagnosis. They were first instituted by Medicare in 1983 to reimburse hospitals.

Exclusive Provider Organization (EPO) A type of managed care organization that is a hybrid of an HMO and a PPO. Like an HMO, an EPO does not reimburse members for services provided by nonnetwork providers. EPOs are similar to PPOs in structure and organization; i.e., they assemble a panel of preferred providers and are regulated by state insurance laws.

Gated PPO A type of managed care organization which assembles a panel of independent medical providers (preferred providers) to provide care to its members. An authorized referral from the primary care physician (PCP) is required in order to obtain the services of another physician or a specialist.

Group Practice Three or more physicians formally organized to provide medical care, consultation, diagnosis, and/or treatment through the joint use of equipment, records, and personnel, with income from the medical practice distributed according to some prearranged plan.

Health Maintenance Organization (HMO) An organization that provides comprehensive health care benefits to enrolled members for a fixed monthly fee. A member selects a PCP and hospital provider within the network. If services are not authorized by a PCP, the member pays out of pocket and the health care provider must bill and collect from the patient.

Indemnity Insurance A type of insurance that offers the enrollee/patient freedom to choose a health care provider and reimburses the provider on a fee-for-service basis. May be offered by commercial carriers such as Blue Cross and Blue Shield (BC/BS).

Independent Physician Association (IPA) A type of HMO managed care construct which contracts for the services of many unrelated caregivers from which the members can choose to receive health care services. An authorized referral from the PCP is required to obtain services from a specialist. The medical group, not the HMO, pays the claims.

Managed Care An approach to health care that closely links the delivery and financing of health care in order to manage patient care in a coordinated fashion. Effective managed care organizations are designed to reduce costs associated with health care and improve patient outcomes.

Managed Care Organization (MCO) An organization or insurance plan that emphasizes bringing providers and payers into a close relationship in order to manage patient care more effectively.

Package Price A single payment that covers hospital and physician services for a particular service, e.g., cardiac catherization. In some instances, the package may include preoperative care and follow-up care after patient discharge. Also referred to as global or flat fees.

Point of Service (POS) A type of managed care plan that is a hybrid of HMO and indemnity insurance plans. Members are provided full coverage for services delivered by network providers, but reduced coverage when using out-of-network providers.

Preferred Provider Organization (PPO) A network of preferred providers who will provide care at a discounted rate for patients in the network. Patients may go out of the network for health care services, but the out-of-pocket expenses are greater. No PCP or referrals are required.

Referral A form required of all HMO or gated managed care patients. The form is provided by the PCP. It authorizes the hospitals and physicians to perform specific care and/or procedures. No other procedures or treatments can be provided without prior authorization by the PCP.

Subscriber An employer, union, or association that contracts with an HMO for its prepaid health care plan. The plan is offered to eligible enrollees.

Utilization Management or Utilization Review Organized programs instituted by insurers, managed care organizations, and other entities to ensure that their contracted providers and resources are used in the most efficient, appropriate, and cost-effective manner possible.

Chapter 5

Competency-Based Technical Training on an International Scale

Rick Sullivan

Dr. Rick Sullivan is Director of Training for the JHPIEGO Corporation (a nonprofit training organization affiliated with Johns Hopkins University). Rick completed his Ph.D. at The Ohio State University, after which he served as a professor at the University of Central Oklahoma for twelve years, where he was responsible for the Training and Development degree program.

5.1 Introduction

Uttar Pradesh state in India has a population of approximately 140 million people. There is an immediate need to train thousands of auxiliary nurse-midwives and medical officers to provide family planning services to this growing population. Similar challenges confront ministries of health in Indonesia, Nepal, Brazil, Kenya, and many other countries around the globe. The challenge facing the JHPIEGO Corporation, a nonprofit training organization affiliated with Johns Hopkins University, is how to design and deliver competency-based technical training programs simultaneously in many different countries.

Designing a technical training program to be conducted in another country is not an easy task, and it becomes even more difficult when training is to be delivered in several countries. In 1995 JHPIEGO is involved in family planning training activities and programs in more than 40 countries. Conducting effective technical training on an international scale is not achieved without overcoming several challenges. The primary challenge facing JHPIEGO was to develop and maintain an appropriate approach for conducting what is often highly technical clinical training. What methods would work? Which of the numerous approaches currently in use would best fit the needs of the doctors and nurses trained by JHPIEGO? Should our training approach be similar to those used in traditional colleges and universities to prepare medical professionals?

Throughout the world, millions of students go to universities and schools every day. These schools are part of educational systems that have existed for centuries. Students in traditional public schools still study subjects such as science, language, and mathematics in classes and courses that are usually scheduled to last the duration of the school year. Progression through the various subjects in school is *time-based,* and so at any given time during the year the teacher is expected to be at a specific point in the textbook or course content. Although students may not all progress at the same rate, the schedule typically requires everyone to move at the same rate as the teacher. Tests are periodically administered to ensure that students understand the concepts and practical aspects being taught. Test scores are often compared to determine the grades of the students. Unfortunately, when a student does not do well on a test, there is often little time for individual assistance, as the teacher must move on in order to adhere to the established time schedule.

While traditional, time-based approaches to education have met with varying levels of success over the years, they can be ineffective when the goal is to train individuals to perform specific job-related technical skills. For example, a doctor requiring training in order to perform a specific clinical procedure used in family planning attends a two-week course. If the doctor attends each day of the course, will this ensure that he or she is qualified to perform the procedure? Of course not; attendance and qualification are two very different things. Obviously, the time-based educational system used in schools and universities is not appropriate when conducting skill-based technical training.

After considerable research, JHPIEGO personnel found that an effective approach to conducting international technical training is one that is *competency-based.* However, before implementing competency-based training (CBT) programs around the world, we felt it was important that we define this training approach, examine the characteristics of CBT, consider the advantages and limitations of CBT, and determine how we would evaluate the effectiveness of our training. Before we describe one of our CBT courses, it will be helpful if we share the information we used to form the foundation of this approach to training. This information will also be of assistance to those readers considering the use of CBT.

5.2 What Is Competency-Based Training?

The unit of progression in a traditional educational system is time, and the system is teacher-centered. In a competency-based training system, the unit of progression is mastery of specific knowledge and skills, and the system is learner- or participant-centered. Two key terms used in competency-based training are

- *Skill:* A task or group of tasks which often use motor functions and typically require the manipulation of instruments and equipment (e.g., IUD insertion, Norplant implants removal). Some skills, such as counseling, are knowledge- and attitude-based.
- *Competency:* A skill performed to a specific norm or standard under specific conditions.

There appears to be substantial support for competency-based training. Norton (1987) believes that competency-based training should be used instead of the "medieval concept of time-based learning." Foyster (1990) argues that using the traditional "school" model for training is inefficient. After in-depth examinations of three competency-based programs, Anthony Watson (1990) concluded that competency-based instruction has tremendous potential for training in industry. Moreover, in a 1990 study of basic skills education programs in business and industry, Paul Delker found that successful training programs were competency-based.

A competent clinician (e.g., physician, nurse, midwife, medical assistant) is one who is able to perform a clinical skill to a satisfactory standard. CBT for reproductive health professionals, then, is training based upon the participant's ability to demonstrate attainment or mastery of clinical skills performed under certain conditions to specific standards (the skills then become competencies). Norton (1987) defines competency-based training by describing five essential elements of a CBT system. These elements apply not only to JHPIEGO technical training courses, but also to any competency-based technical training course. In a CBT training approach:

- Competencies to be achieved are carefully identified, verified, and made public in advance.
- Criteria to be used in assessing achievement and the conditions under which achievement will be assessed are explicitly stated and made public in advance.
- The instructional program provides for the individual development and evaluation of each of the competencies specified.
- Assessment of competency takes the participant's knowledge and attitudes into account but requires actual performance of the competency as the primary source of evidence.
- Participants progress through the instructional program at their own rate by demonstrating the attainment of the specified competencies.

5.2.1 Characteristics of CBT

How does one identify a competency-based training program? What does CBT look like? Other than a set of competencies, what characteristics are associated with CBT? JHPIEGO staff needed to answer these questions before designing and delivering competency-based technical training programs simultaneously in many different countries. According to Foyster (1990), Delker (1990), and Norton (1987), there are a number of characteristics of competency-based programs. These characteristics are summarized in Table 5.1.

5.2.2 Advantages and limitations of CBT

One of the primary advantages of CBT is that the focus is on the success of each participant. If all participants master the skills and knowledge presented during the course, that's great! Imagine the concern and questions if all students in a university course were to score 100 percent on a final examination.

Watson (1990) feels that the competency-based approach "appears especially useful in training situations where trainees have to attain a small number of specific and job-related competencies" (p. 18). Benefits of CBT identified by Norton (1987) include the following:

- Participants will achieve competencies required in the performance of their jobs.
- Participants build confidence as they succeed in mastering specific competencies.
- Participants receive a transcript or list of the competencies they have achieved.

TABLE 5.1 Characteristics of Competency-Based Training Programs

Competencies are carefully selected.

Supporting knowledge is integrated with the practice of technical skills, as opposed to being taught separately.

Training packages and materials are keyed to the competencies to be achieved and are designed to support the acquisition of knowledge and skills.

Training methods involve mastery learning and include immediate feedback to participants.

Participants' knowledge and skills are assessed as they enter the program. These assessments involve the use of both knowledge and skill criterion-referenced tests.

Learning should be self-paced.

Individuals conducting training function less as traditional teachers and more as coaches or facilitators.

A training environment which simulates the workplace is used.

A variety of methods and approaches are used to deliver training.

Participants with appropriate prerequisite skills and knowledge may bypass training on competencies they have already attained.

Satisfactory completion of training is based on achievement of all specified competencies.

Flexible training approaches including large-group methods, small-group activities, and individual study are essential components.

A variety of support materials including print, audiovisual, and simulations keyed to the skills being mastered are used.

- Training time is used more efficiently and effectively, as the trainer is a facilitator of learning rather than a provider of information.
- More training time is devoted to working with participants individually or in small groups than to presenting traditional lectures.
- More training time is devoted to evaluating each participant's ability to perform essential job skills.

While there are a number of advantages of competency-based training, JHPIEGO staff also considered the potential limitations. Prior to implementing CBT, it is important to consider these limitations:

- Unless initial training and follow-up assistance are provided for the trainers, there is a tendency to "teach as we were taught," and CBT trainers quickly slip back into the role of the traditional teacher.
- A CBT course is only as effective as the process used to identify the competencies. When little or no attention is given to identification of the essential job skills, then the resulting training course is likely to be ineffective.

- A course may be classified as competency-based, but unless specific CBT materials and training approaches are designed to be used as part of a CBT approach, it is unlikely that the resulting course will truly be competency-based.

5.2.3 Models and simulations in CBT

Models and simulations are used extensively in competency-based technical training courses. Airplane pilots first learn to fly in a simulator. Supervisors first learn to provide feedback to employees using role plays during training. Individuals learning to administer cardiopulmonary resuscitation (CPR) practice this procedure on a model of a human.

Norton (1987) believes that participants in a competency-based training course should learn in an environment that duplicates or simulates the workplace. Richards (1985), in writing about performance testing, indicates that assessment of skills requires tests using simulations (e.g., models and role plays) or work samples (i.e., performing actual tasks under controlled conditions in either a laboratory or a job setting). Delker (1990), in a study of business and industry, found that the best-case scenario for training involved learner-centered instruction using print, instructional technology, and simulations.

5.2.4 Evaluation and assessment in CBT

In traditional courses, evaluation typically involves administering knowledge-based tests. While knowledge-based assessments can certainly be used in CBT to measure mastery of information, the primary focus is on measuring mastery of skills. In keeping with this, Thomson (1991) reports that the decision to recognize a performance as satisfactory and to determine competence should be the basis for success in a competency-based program. Moreover, Foyster (1990) argues that assessment in competency-based programs must be criterion-referenced, with the criterion being the competencies upon which the program is based. Finally, Richards (1985) indicates that simulation and work sample performance tests should include a checklist or some type of rating scale. He also indicates that performance tests can include paper-and-pencil tests.

5.3 International Technical Training

As organizations and companies conduct more and more business in other countries, individuals within these companies find themselves designing and delivering training in international settings. There are often differences between delivering training in one's own country and doing so in another country. When designing an international training course, it is important to become familiar with the local culture, learn about the potential trainees, and prepare for the delivery of training. Before describing JHPIEGO's approach to CBT, let's consider some important aspects of conducting training internationally.

5.3.1 Cultural differences

The first mistake trainers traveling to another country make is that they do not learn enough about the local culture. It is critical that you do not approach this audience the way you approach an audience within your own organization. Take the time to understand the people and their society. Anyone traveling to another country may appear to be different—not wrong or right, just different.

Becoming familiar with the culture of another country is a critical first step in planning an effective international training course. Avoid mistakes by reading books and learning about the local customs, religious practices, geography, environment, goods and services, history, and politics. You can also talk with someone who is familiar with the country. Do whatever it takes, but learn as much as you can about the country and its people.

5.3.2 Understanding your audience

Conducting training internationally requires gathering some information about those you will be training. In some situations you may know only the general background of those likely to attend. Other times you will have a list of specific individuals. In either case, gather as much information as possible. Consider these questions as you collect details about your audience:

- What are the backgrounds of the individuals attending?
- Can you acquire a list of the potential participants? What are their titles?
- Do you have the correct spellings and pronunciations of the names?
- What are the participants' reasons for attending training? What are their expectations? Are they attending because they want to, or are they required to attend?
- Are the participants aware of the need for training, the course content and schedule, and the language you will use to deliver your training? This information should be available to your participants in advance.

5.3.3 Preparing for conducting training

Preparing for any training course is important. Preparing for an international training course is crucial. Assuming that the needs assessments have been completed and that the materials have been developed (in the participants' language, if appropriate), there are several other considerations.

Begin by identifying a local contact person. Having a liaison in the other country can be of great importance. Your contact can help you to learn about your audience, develop a schedule, distribute information to participants, and arrange for facilities, and can answer questions about local culture and customs.

Forward information regarding your course and schedule to your contact person. Ensure that the schedule reflects the local culture. Are there typical start and stop times? Are there times of the day when it would be inappropriate to ask people to attend training? For example, in some countries morning and afternoon tea breaks are expected. You may also need to take religious services and events into account. Once details are finalized, ask that this information be forwarded to participants.

Review your plans with someone who is familiar with the country and the people attending training. In some countries you may be making your presentations through an interpreter. If so, practice with the interpreter in advance. Review your presentation notes and ensure that they will be clear to the members of your audience. Carry originals of your notes and media (transparencies, slides, and videos) with you on the plane. Despite what you are told in advance, you never really know what media equipment will be available and working. It's a good idea to have your presentation ready both on slides and transparencies.

Develop participant notes or materials. It is important that participants have a set of materials in a text or outline format so that they will not be required to take notes. You may consider providing copies of your transparencies and slides. Also, in some situations it may be helpful to have participant notes translated into the participants' language.

Look into all aspects of the training facility. Here are some things you should do:

- Ensure that the size of the room is appropriate.
- Check that the tables and chairs are comfortable.
- Make sure that there are power outlets in the room and that you will have the correct adapters and extension cords for media equipment.

- Find out if there could be power outages during your training course. If so, what is your backup plan?
- Check on the availability of refreshments and meals, if applicable.
- Determine the availability of breakout rooms if participants will be involved in small-group work during training.

Find out what types of instructional media equipment will be available. Here are some things you should do:

- Ensure that your videotapes are in the correct format and that the appropriate player is available.
- If you are taking slides, check on the type of slide tray and machine you will be using.
- Check that you will have access to a flipchart. Determine whether it is an actual flipchart or sheets of newsprint. Also, make sure there is an easel available.
- Carry your own flipchart pens or markers. The pens that are available are often markers that were not designed for flipcharts. They are usually one color and bleed through the pages.
- Take masking tape if you plan on posting flipchart pages around the room.
- Carry a supply of blank transparency film and pens, as in some countries these items are difficult to locate and may be very expensive.

Allow sufficient time to ship your handouts and other materials in advance. If possible, verify that the materials have been received by your contact before you leave the country. Materials have been known to be lost, misplaced, or stuck in customs. Check that your laptop or notebook computer power supply or battery charger will run on voltages ranging from 110 V ac to 240 V ac. Make sure that you have the correct electrical adapter so that you can plug in your computer or charger.

Verify your housing and transportation logistics. Do you have hotel reservations? Will you need to travel to the training site? If so, will transportation be provided, or will you need to make your own arrangements? Check that you have the names, addresses, and business and home telephone and fax numbers of your local contact and any other individuals connected with your training course.

Determine what the dress requirements will be. Appropriate dress will depend on the type of training, your audience, and the time of the year that you will be visiting the country. It would be inappropriate to either over- or underdress.

Check on the protocols or customs regarding introductions and opening remarks. Who will bring a welcome? How formal are the opening remarks, if any? Determine if you will be expected to present gifts to your hosts. In many situations, you will be presented with a gift. You will feel awkward if you do not have a gift in return. By the way, make sure that your gifts are made in your own country.

Communicate closely with any in-country copresenters with whom you may be working. Conducting training can be difficult enough, but coordinating details with someone in another country is a challenge.

Plan to arrive early to allow time to recover from any jet lag. This will also give you an opportunity to meet with your local contact, visit the training site, check on room setup, look over your materials, verify arrangements for media equipment, and finalize all details related to training. Be sure to check the media equipment and ensure that you are familiar with the operation of each piece of equipment.

5.3.4 Delivering training internationally

Prior to delivering training, you should check your plans, ensure that your materials arrived, and set up the facilities. Here are a number of tips you can follow to ensure the success of an international training course:

- Begin with an initial welcome and introduction of all appropriate people. You should learn to say "welcome" in the participants' language.
- Deliver an overview of the course. This lets your audience know the scope and sequence of training.
- Speak slowly, clearly, and distinctly.
- Summarize periodically. This affords the participants an opportunity to digest your key points.
- Check for understanding by asking questions without embarrassing anyone. Be sure to provide positive feedback once they respond.
- Encourage questions and repeat participant questions and responses.
- Repeat key points.
- Connect key points to your media. When you are making an important point, show a transparency or slide of that point.
- Avoid acronyms and phrases that are unfamiliar to your audience.
- Use humor carefully. Humor is still an important presentation technique, but what is funny in one country may not be so in another. Look for humor in your travel arrangements, hotel accommodations, food, or local weather.

- Avoid saying, "In our country, we…" This can come across as a "better than thou" attitude, which can create a negative climate.
- Be patient and flexible. The schedule may not go the way you planned. There may be discussions in the participants' language. Or the participants may want to discuss topics you did not plan to cover. While you want to accomplish the training objectives, be flexible and try to meet the needs of your audience.

Planning and delivering training in another country offers some unique challenges and equally unique rewards. Meeting these challenges begins with learning as much as possible about the local culture and acquiring information about your audience.

Now that we have examined the principles of competency-based training and considered some suggestions for conducting training internationally, let's look at how JHPIEGO approaches training.

5.4 JHPIEGO's Approach to CBT

Based on our research and experience, JHPIEGO Corporation has adopted a competency-based approach to conducting training. Using the principles summarized in this chapter as a foundation, JHPIEGO staff have developed an approach to CBT that involves key design, delivery, and evaluation activities. These activities are summarized here and explained in detail in JHPIEGO's *Clinical Training Skills for Reproductive Health Professionals* and *Advanced Training Skills for Reproductive Health Professionals* reference manuals.

The key events around which JHPIEGO's competency-based training is built include design, delivery, and evaluation activities. The best way to describe these is to briefly define each and give examples from one of our training courses. As JHPIEGO's training courses are clinical in nature (i.e., they prepare doctors and nurses to perform specific family planning procedures), the content may not be familiar to the reader. Therefore, examples will be taken from a training skills course. This course is designed to prepare individuals to be trainers.

5.4.1 Design activities

The first step in the design process is the *identification of the specific family planning clinical skills* that will form the basis of a competency-based training course. These skills could be clinical, counseling, or, in our example, training skills. Figure 5.1 is a list of JHPIEGO's essential training skills. We feel that clinical trainers must master these skills or competencies in order to be effective. A similar list of skills is developed for every CBT training course.

JHPIEGO Training Skills
- Conduct a needs assessment
- Design a training course
- Develop course materials
- Prepare and use audio-visuals
- Create a positive training climate
- Use interactive training techniques
- Use coaching in a clinical setting
- Develop and administer knowledge-based assessments
- Develop and administer performance-based assessments
- Evaluate training
- Conduct a clinical training course

Figure 5.1 JHPIEGO essential training skills.

Identification of the conditions under which the skills must be demonstrated is the next step in the design process. Examples of conditions include working with anatomic models, demonstrating skills during role plays, and working with actual clients. In our training skills courses, the participants demonstrate acquisition of their new skills by developing training materials, making presentations, and delivering a training course.

The third step in the design process is the *development of the criteria or standards* to which the skills must be performed. These standards are very clear when training is focused on specific medical procedures. These standards appear in learning guides (used for skill acquisition) and checklists (used for skill assessment) which list each of the steps required to perform each skill. In terms of training skills, we have learning guides which describe the standards for making effective classroom presentations, presenting clinical demonstrations, and using coaching in a clinical setting.

Development of training objectives which outline what the participant must do in order to master the family planning clinical skills is our next step. Figure 5.2 presents a training skills course terminal objective and the supporting enabling objectives.

Once we have a clear picture of the specific competencies and objectives those attending training are expected to master, the next step is the *development of reference manuals* which contain the essential, need-to-know information related to the competencies. The reference manuals for our training skills courses include *Clinical Training Skills for Reproductive Health Professionals* and *Advanced Training*

> **Objective:** After completing this training session, the participant will be able to use interactive training techniques when introducing new knowledge and clinical skills.
>
> **Enabling Objective:** To attain the chapter objective, the participant will:
>
> - Introduce a training session
> - Summarize a training session
> - Use effective questioning techniques
> - Plan and present an illustrated presentation
> - Conduct a brainstorming session
> - Facilitate a discussion
> - Facilitate the use of a role play
> - Facilitate the use of a case study

Figure 5.2 Training skills course terminal objective and supporting enabling objectives.

Skills for Reproductive Health Professionals. These manuals serve as texts for the participants and as reference manuals for the trainers.

For our clinical courses, the next step is the *development of anatomic models and supporting audiovisuals* to be used during training. Use of anatomic models allows participants to develop their initial skills in a classroom setting prior to working with clients in a clinical setting.

The next step in the design process is the *development of pre- and midcourse questionnaires* which will be used to measure participants' acquisition of knowledge. These questionnaires are based on the training objectives and the information contained in the reference manual.

The final step in the design process is the *development of course outlines, syllabi, and schedules* which describe how training courses are to be delivered. The course syllabus and schedule contain information about the course and can be sent to participants in advance so that they are aware of details concerning the course. The course outline is a plan or map that outlines the flow of the course. Figure 5.3 is a portion of a course outline for a JHPIEGO train-the-trainer course. The outline is divided into four columns:

- *Time.* This column indicates the approximate amount of time to be devoted to each training objective and activity. This helps the trainer to budget time so that all objectives are addressed in the allotted amount of time.
- *Objectives/Activities.* This column lists the objectives and training activities. The objectives (taken from the reference manual

TRAINING OF TRAINERS (TOT) COURSE OUTLINE: STANDARD COURSE (10 days, 20 sessions)

TIME	OBJECTIVES/ACTIVITIES	TEACHING/LEARNING METHODS	RESOURCES/MATERIALS
Session One: Day 1, AM (continued)			
15 minutes	**Module 1:** Developing a Participatory and Humanistic Approach to Training **Objective:** Identify the purposes of training	Ask participants to describe the differences between training and education. Ask for examples of training and education. Review the information in the module.	Clinical Training Skills Manual (Module 1) Transparencies 10-11
30 minutes	**Objective:** Define competency-based training (CBT)	Ask participants to describe the difference between competency-based training and traditional time-based training. Discuss the information in the module.	Transparencies 12-17 Flip chart and markers
30 minutes	**Objective:** Interpret the model for JHPIEGO's philosophy or training	Ask participants to form groups of 3-4. Each group is to examine the model shown in Figure 1-1 in the module. Each group is to prepare a brief description of the philosophy of training communicated by the model. Each group will share their comments during a brief group discussion.	Transparencies 18-21 Flip chart and makers for each group
10 minutes	**Activity:** Session summary	Review the key points and concepts presented in the morning session	

Figure 5.3 Training of trainers course outline, standard course (10 days, 20 sessions)

chapters) outline the sequence of training and are presented here in the order in which they will be addressed. The combination of the objectives and activities (introductions, small-group exercises, practice sessions, breaks, etc.) outlines the flow of training.
- *Teaching/Learning Methods.* This column lists the various methods, activities, and strategies to be used to deliver the training for each objective. Sufficient detail is provided so that different trainers will follow essentially the same plan for delivering the same course in different locations, either in one country or in several.
- *Resources/Materials.* The fourth column in the outline lists the reference materials and audiovisual resources needed to deliver training for each objective.

The course outline, syllabus, and schedule appear in the trainer's notebook and participant's handbook. These documents, along with the reference manual, anatomic models, and audiovisuals, form the basic training package (see Fig. 5.4) that JHPIEGO staff develop for each CBT training course.

5.4.2 Delivery and evaluation activities

A precourse questionnaire to assess the participants' knowledge about course content is administered at the beginning of each of our training courses. In those courses with a clinical component, the *administration of precourse skill assessments using models* is used to either standardize participants' skills or ensure that participants possess the entry-level clinical skills required to successfully complete the course. Based on the results of the precourse knowledge and skills

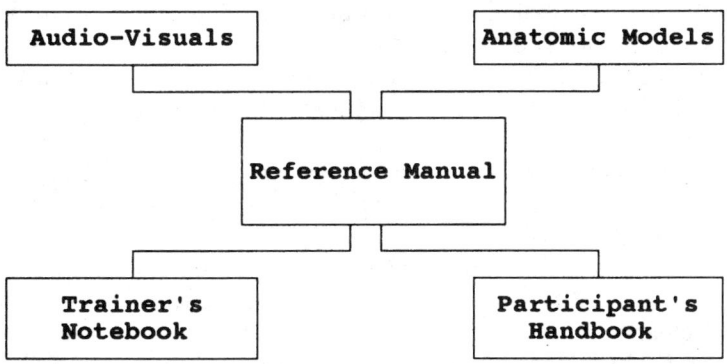

Figure 5.4 A basic training package for a CBT course.

assessments, the trainer may modify the course schedule to meet the needs of the participants.

Critical to the success of our training courses is the *delivery of the course by a trainer/facilitator using an interactive and participatory approach.* Every effort is made to design and deliver the course in such a way that those attending the training are highly involved. Medical training is notorious for "talking heads" that lecture for long periods of time. One of the identifying features of JHPIEGO's approach to training is participation.

During courses with a clinical component, *development of the participants' skills using a humanistic approach* is used. This means that participants acquire the skill and then practice until competent, using a model. Only when participants are assessed and determined to be competent on a model do they work with clients. Once participants have observed a skill being demonstrated, they *practice the skill following the steps in the learning guide* until they become competent at performing the skill. During this practice time, the trainer functions as a *coach,* providing constant feedback and reinforcement to participants.

When the information in the reference manual has been transferred to the participants, the trainer will *administer a midcourse questionnaire* to determine if the participants have mastered the knowledge. Those participants who have not mastered the knowledge (i.e., achieved a minimum score of 85 percent correct on the questionnaire) are afforded opportunities to study and work with the trainer until they have mastered the knowledge.

Essential to JHPIEGO's CBT approach is the *assessment of each participant's skills.* In a clinical course, these skills are demonstrated on an anatomic model, with the assessment by the trainer being conducted using competency-based checklists. In a training skills course, participants deliver a series of presentations and receive feedback from other participants and the trainer.

In clinical courses involving clients, the next step is the transfer of skills from the trainer to the participants through *clinical skill demonstrations using clients.* Participants observe the demonstrations and then practice under the direct supervision of the trainer. Assessment of each participant's skills on a client are made by the trainer using competency-based checklists.

The participant is either qualified or not qualified *as a result of both knowledge and skills assessments.* During the course closing ceremony, participants receive a statement of qualification which identifies the specific knowledge the participant has mastered and the skills the individual is qualified to perform.

5.5 Transfer of Training

JHPIEGO staff and consultants provide assistance to countries that want to strengthen the training system that supports their family planning efforts. To ensure that the training system is sustainable and will function after our work in a country is complete, we help develop a national training system that will continue to produce qualified service providers. We use a four-step process to help create a national training system:

1. Standardize clinical skills and modify or adapt standard JHPIEGO training materials (if necessary) to meet the needs of the country.
2. Train service providers to perform standardized clinical skills.
3. Prepare proficient service providers to function as clinical trainers so that they are able to train other service providers.
4. Prepare clinical skill trainers to function as master trainers so that they are able to train other clinical trainers.

The first step is to standardize the clinical skill(s) to be used in the delivery of family planning services (e.g., IUD and Norplant implants). In a country, for example, there may be a need to train clinicians to perform IUD insertions and removals. The first activity conducted is to identify and observe a group of clinicians who are performing these procedures. The steps the clinicians perform are observed and compared to the standard approach outlined in JHPIEGO's competency-based IUD learning guides and checklists. This observation process gives JHPIEGO trainers an idea of the skill levels of those who are to be trained to be service providers. As necessary, JHPIEGO's learning guides and checklists are modified to meet the specific needs of service delivery standards or norms. The standardized procedure then forms the basis for the service provider training courses conducted within the country.

The second step is to train a specific group of service providers to perform the standardized clinical skills. The clinical skills course is based on the training package, consisting of a reference manual, supporting audiovisuals, anatomic models, and trainer and participant handbooks. Following the clinical skills course, these competent service providers provide family planning services to clients. After providing services for a period of time, a group of the most proficient service providers who have demonstrated an interest and willingness to become clinical trainers attend a train-the-trainer course.

The third step in the transfer process is to prepare a group of proficient service providers to be clinical trainers. These service providers attend a clinical training skills course. During this course, participants learn how to demonstrate clinical skills, how to transfer knowledge and skills during training, how to function as a clinical coach, and how to use competency-based learning guides and checklists to assess participant performance. Following the training skills course, these clinical trainers conduct service provider training courses. During their first service provider course, they cotrain with a master trainer. After they have delivered service provider training courses for a period of time, a small group of proficient clinical trainers are ready to become master trainers.

The final step in the process of creating a national training system is to prepare a small group of proficient clinical trainers to become master trainers. These clinical trainers attend an advanced training skills course. During this course, participants learn how to conduct needs assessments, design training courses, develop training packages, facilitate the group dynamics occurring during a course, and evaluate training. Following the advanced training skills course, these advanced trainers conduct training skills courses. During their first several training courses, they cotrain with a master trainer. After successfully delivering several training skills courses, these individuals can be qualified to function as master trainers. Figure 5.5 summarizes JHPIEGO's approach to ensuring that a country has a sustainable system for preparing service providers and trainers.

5.6 Summary

Delivering competency-based technical training in multicountry settings requires a great deal of planning and organization. JHPIEGO's vision is to design a CBT system for a country or region that will allow local trainers and master trainers to eventually assume full responsibility for the design, delivery, and evaluation of family planning training. Through comprehensive needs assessments, the design of training packages, delivery of competency-based courses, and providing support for in-country trainers, we feel we can help improve the quality of family planning programs around the world.

5.7 References

Delker, Paul V., *Basic Skills Education in Business and Industry: Factors for Success or Failure*. Contractor Report, Office of Technology Assessment, United States Congress, 1990.

Foyster, John, *Getting to Grips with Competency-Based Training and Assessment*, TAFE National Centre for Research and Development, Leabrook, Australia, ERIC: ED 317849, 1990.

Norton, Robert E., *Competency-Based Education and Training: A Humanistic and Realistic Approach to Technical and Vocational Instruction*, Paper presented at the Regional Workshop on Technical/Vocational Teacher Training in Chiba City, Japan, ERIC: ED 279910, 1987.

Richards, Beverly, "Performance Objectives as the Basis for Criterion-Referenced Performance Testing," *Journal of Industrial Teacher Education,* 22(4): 28–37, 1985.

Thomson, Peter, *Competency-Based Training: Some Development and Assessment Issues for Policy Makers,* TAFE National Centre for Research and Development, Leabrook, Australia, ERIC: ED 333231, 1991.

Watson, Anthony, *Competency-Based Vocational Education and Self-Paced Learning,* Monograph Series, Technology University, Sydney, Australia, ERIC: ED 324443, 1990.

JHPIEGO Training Path

	The person completing this . .	Training course is then . .	Qualified as a
Level 1	**Clinician** (doctor, nurse, midwife)	**Clinical Skill Course** focusing on the knowledge and skills necessary to provide one or more family planning services	Competent **service provider** able to provide one or more family planning services
Level 2	**Proficient service provider** (several months of practice following clinical skills course)	**Clinical Training Skills Course** focusing on the knowledge and skills necessary to train clinicians to be service providers	Competent **clinical trainer** able to conduct a clinical skills course
Level 3	**Proficient clinical trainer** (successfully conducted several clinical skills courses)	**Advanced Training Skills Course** focusing on the knowledge and skills necessary to train service providers to be clinical trainers	Competent **master trainer** able to conduct a clinical training skills course

Figure 5.5 JHPIEGO training path.

Chapter 6

Vocational Education and Technical Training in the Netherlands

Jan Waldus

Jan Waldus, B.Sc., is director of Waldus Consultancy for Training Projects in Apeldoorn, the Netherlands. He has over 25 years' experience as a trainer, 15 of which were in the paper and corrugated industry, and he has served as an adviser to the Dutch government in an entrepreneurial project for five years. After being a part-time lecturer for entrepreneurial education for more than 15 years, he was appointed Director of Entrepreneurial Education in the Agriculture Maintenance Area. Since 1990 he has had his own Consultancy in Training and Development Projects, working in the Netherlands and several other European countries. Mr. Waldus is a Lead Auditor for CEDEO and was a member of the Dutch Visitation Committee for Higher Technical Vocational Education. He was one of the founders of the Dutch Trainers' Institute and served this Institute for many years as International Secretary. During his 10 years of service to the International Federation of Training and Development Organizations (IFTDO), he was a board member and chair of the Conference Coordinating Committee.

6.1 Introduction

This chapter contains some examples of the technical education and training systems available to young people in the Netherlands. While it would difficult to describe these systems in detail, it is possible to outline their essential components.

The Dutch system has a regular education track, a vocational education track, and, by law, an entrepreneurial training track for students in all sectors of business. Some of the terminology varies from that of the United States, and as the chapter progresses, terms will be further defined.

6.2 The Netherlands

Understanding the country will help the reader to somewhat better understand the Dutch system of education and training. Unlike the American system, the Dutch system includes all phases of technical training leading to the highest level of training available. The U.S. educational system does not provide such job skill training. Typically, what is commonplace in the Dutch system is attained outside the traditional American educational system. For example, in the Netherlands, skilled trade apprenticeships are part of the regular school curriculum—a young person can graduate as a certified electrician. The Netherlands' system is much closer in structure to the Singapore educational system (see *The ASTD Technical and Skills Training Handbook,* McGraw-Hill, 1995, for a complete discussion), which has been developed to meet the high-tech needs of Singapore's business and industry. Both the Netherlands and Singapore are small nations that are dependent on international companies for their livelihood, and so they have developed their education and technical training systems to support workforce readiness and technical competence. The Dutch have historically been dependent on their ability to be the tradespeople of the world. The Dutch education system has evolved so that it guarantees that well-trained trade and technical people are available to business and industry. Since many people are not familiar with the Dutch system, some detail is included.

At this moment there are about 15.5 million inhabitants of the Netherlands (see Fig. 6.1). In 1900 there were 5.1 million inhabitants. The country has a total of 41,800 square kilometers of land, of which 4,300 square kilometers is under water! In the last 100 years the Dutch have reclaimed approximately 2,500 square kilometers of land from the sea to provide more space for people to live. For example, a traveler to Amsterdam who lands at the main airport, Schipol, is on reclaimed land. More than 20 percent of the Netherlands consists of reclaimed land.

CHINA 1050 million inhabitants		BRAZIL 143 million inhabitants	UNITED STATES 241 million inhabitants
■■■■■ ■■■■■ ■■■		■	■■
JAPAN 121 million inhabitants	FRANCE 55 million inhabitants	HUNGARY 11 million inhabitants	NIGERIA 105 million inhabitants	THE NETHERLANDS 15 million inhabitants
■■■■■ ■■■■■ ■■■■■ ■■■■■ ■■■■■ ■■■■■ ■	■■■■ ■■■■	■■■ ■■	■■■ ■■■	■■■■■ ■■■■■ ■■■■■ ■■■■■ ■

■ 10 persons per km²

Figure 6.1 Population density in a number of countries. The Netherlands has 438 people per square kilometer.

Of the approximately 15 million people, 12 percent are older than 65. It is forecasted that this will rise to 14 percent by the year 2000. Also, 40 percent are under the age of 25 years. The working population is around 7 million. More than 630,000 inhabitants are legal aliens. Almost 140,000 are Moroccans, 210,000 come from the former Dutch colony of Surinam, 175,000 are Turkish, and the rest are of other origins.

6.2.1 Government profile

The Dutch government is a constitutional monarchy with a parliamentary system. The States General, or Parliament, consists of two houses: the Upper House, which has 75 members indirectly elected by the Provincial Councils, and the Lower House, with 150 members elected by universal suffrage of all electors over the age of 18. Parliament forms the legislature, and the sovereign and ministers form the executive branch. The Dutch government has been faced with the need to educate a dense population to ensure that unemployment stays low. This is a very tough job, since the country does not have the industrial base that some other European countries have.

6.3 The Educational System in the Netherlands

The Dutch educational system's origins can be traced to the Batavian Republic, a unitary state that came into being after the French Revolution. Education has occupied a central place in the Civil and Constitutional Regulations of the Netherlands. The system is made up of the following:

- Primary schools
- Special schools
- Secondary schools
- Institutes of higher education

Of the 15.5 million people who live in the Netherlands, about 4 million are in full-time education (see Fig. 6.2). Education is free during the compulsory period up to the age of 16. The Netherlands annually spends more than 30 billion guilders (U.S. $20 billion) on education, or roughly 17 percent of the national budget.

Primary education is for children of ages 4 through 12. There are no schools for children below the age of 4, only playgroups and crèches for young children. Primary education is not final, nor do pupils receive a graduation certificate when they are finished. They go on to

Vocational Education and Technical Training in the Netherlands 115

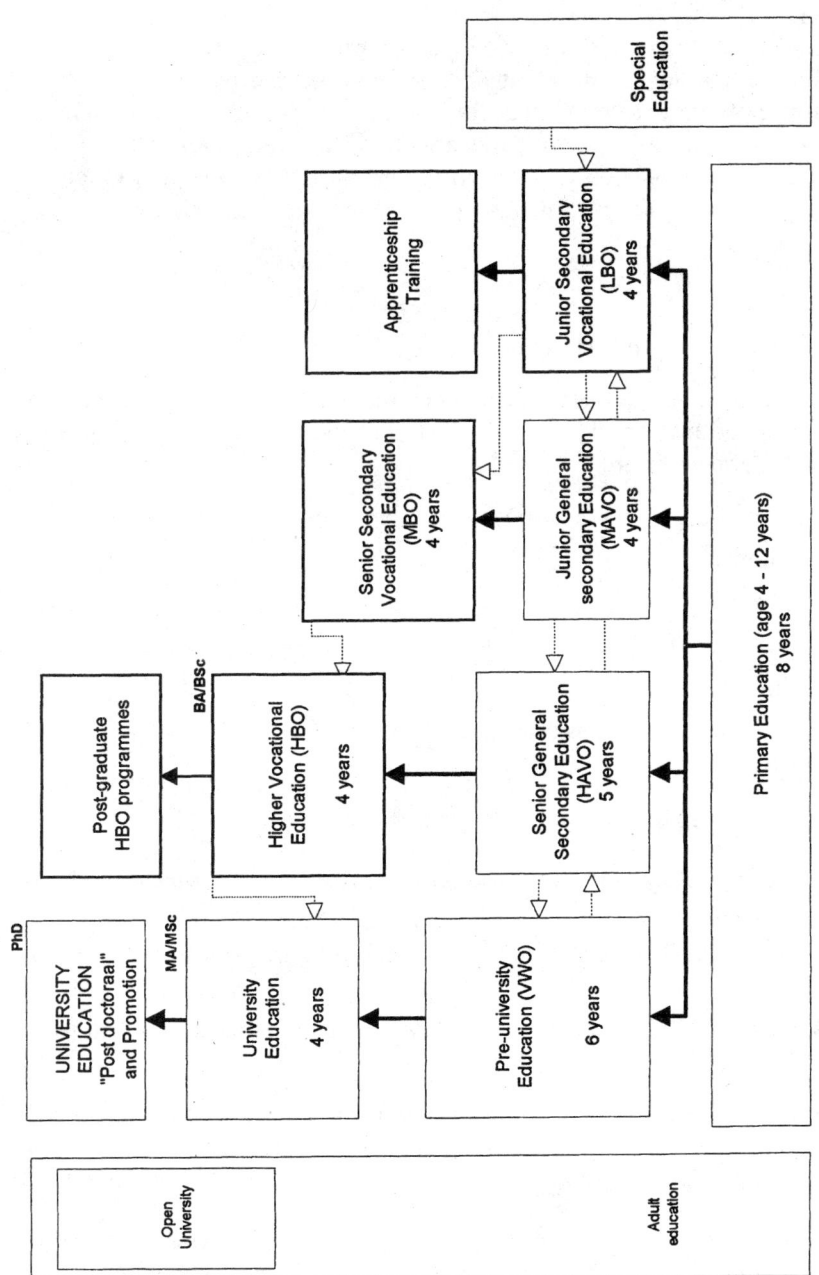

Figure 6.2 The Dutch educational system.

secondary school, the type of which depends on their test results, intelligence testing, attitude (motivation), and assessment by the teachers.

As noted, full-time education is compulsory up to the age of 16. Children who leave school at age 16 are required by law to continue training or education courses for one or two days a week, depending on the type of educational program that they select and their career direction. For the remainder of the week they may have a paid job.

Secondary education consists of the following:

- General secondary schools
- Preuniversity schools
- Vocational secondary schools

Like those in the United States, Dutch vocational schools focus on technical education. Typically a Dutch student has several courses of study to choose from:

- Agriculture
- Commercial
- Technical
- Social services and health care
- Home economics
- A trade (e.g., mechanics)
- Nautical

Most of these areas provide three levels of mastery:

- Junior (LBO)—Junior Vocational Education, *Lager Beroeps Onderwijs*
- Senior (MBO)—Senior Vocational Education, *Middelbaar Beroeps Onderwijs*
- Higher (HBO)—Higher Vocational Education, *Hoger Beroeps Onderwijs*

Students with an LBO or a junior general secondary education certificate may take short senior secondary vocational courses, enroll in an apprenticeship program, or follow a senior secondary vocational course.

Higher education includes higher vocational education and university education. The latter is provided at 10 universities and 21 *hogescholen* (equivalent to universities). Higher vocational education courses are available in the following areas:

- Higher agriculture education
- Higher commercial education
- Higher technical education
- Higher health care education
- Higher home economics education
- Higher trade education
- Education in the arts
- Teacher training

Students with certificates from senior general secondary schools, pre-university secondary schools, and senior vocational education schools can be admitted to a higher vocational education course which takes four years to complete. It is important to understand that in the Netherlands vocational education can be selected very early in a child's education; this is done through the testing systems mentioned earlier in the chapter.

6.3.1 Adult continuing education

In addition to the regular educational system, adults are increasingly interested in courses which were not previously available to them. Special facilities for adult education have been or will be created in a large number of municipalities. The Dutch have called them open schools and open universities. Further technical education will be available through these schools. Technical training involves industry-related training on machines and technology-related equipment. Vocational training can be technical or nontechnical. It refers to training in a person's career area, such as home economics or accounting.

6.3.2 Technical training in Dutch companies

Technical training in Dutch companies has grown considerably, as indicated in a recent national survey. Every two years there is an extensive national survey to determine Dutch business and industry trends in training. The 1993 survey showed that big companies are increasing their spending on training relatively less rapidly than companies with less than 500 employees. Growth in spending on training in larger companies averaged 1 percent. Smaller companies showed a much larger growth, 13 percent, in the amount spent on training.

The survey did not include vocational education, but did include technical training. Big companies are spending the most on training [1750 guilders ($1147) per employee. Companies with 100 to 500 employees spend 870 guilders ($580) per employee, and small companies spend only 380 guilders ($274) per employee on training] (see Fig. 6.3).

Some other results of the 1993 survey included the following:

- Of the employees, 25 percent attended courses.
- Of the companies with less than five employees, 35 percent spent time and money on training.
- Of all training activities, 58 percent are in-company training courses.
- External courses are attended by the following portion of employees:
  Small companies, 67 percent
  Midsized companies, 46 percent
  Large companies, 34 percent
- Types of training institutions used by companies include the following:
  A course in a regular education institution, 11 percent
  The branch training institutes (e.g., metal, baker's), 31 percent
  A private training institute, 58 percent
- Types of courses attended include the following:
  Technical (e.g., welding), 18 percent
  Automation (e.g., CAD/CAM), 17 percent
  Management, 9 percent
  Marketing, 8 percent
  Communication and teamwork, 9 percent
- Length of the courses varied:
  Two to five days, 55 percent
  Six or more days, 25 percent
  One day, 19 percent
- Four times more men than women attend courses (a normal proportion for the Netherlands).
- Training offices or departments exist in companies in the the following proportion:
  Companies with 100 to 500 employees, 31 percent
  Companies with more than 1000 employees, 71 percent
- Of the corporate trainers, 62 percent are full-time trainers.

Cost of Training in Companies	Total	% of labor costs	per employee
	million Dfl. ($)	%	Dfl. ($)
1990 (excl. social work-facilities)	2996 (1997)	1,7	910 (407)
1993	3515 (1757)	1,7	990 (607)
Per branch of industry			
Agriculture and fishing	9 (6)	0,4	150 (100)
Industry and mineral mining	1084 (723)	1,7	1160 (773)
Energy- and water authorities	75 (50)	2,2	1690 (1127)
Building industry	151 (101)	0,8	480 (320)
Commerce	390 (260)	1,1	510 (340)
Hotel and catering industry	22 (15)	0,6	200 (133)
Transport and communication	707 (471)	3,1	1940 (1293)
Financial institutes	549 (346)	3,6	2870 (1913)
Business services and other services	528 (352)	1,4	700 (467)
Per size of company			
5 - 100 employees	573 (382)	0,7	380 (253)
100 - 500 employees	615 (410)	1,3	870 (580)
500 and more employees	2327 (1551)	3,0	1750 (1167)

Figure 6.3 Training costs.

6.3.3 Outside educational opportunities

In addition to entrepreneurial education (described in the next section), there are other options available after four years of junior secondary vocational education. Most of these pupils, age 16 and older, begin intermediate vocational training. This means that they work in a company for four days and attend school for one day each week (similar to the United States' cooperative education program). The company in which they work makes an agreement with the young employee. The employer pays for the work and allows the trainee to go to school. At school the trainee is educated in the particular fields in which he or she is working. Most of the time the company also helps the trainee prepare special reports about the work he or she has done during the working time.

Intermediate vocational education is for two years. After two years the person is called a *skilled worker*. The trainee can receive another two years of intermediate vocational education and become an *advanced skilled worker*. For example, a person who wants to be a metal worker will begin an apprenticeship which after an average of four years of work will result in the person's becoming a qualified metal worker.

Once these types of courses are completed, there are additional courses and certification options available. All additional education is available through Dutch government programs and sanctioned institutions. For a Dutch person, the interconnectedness of all the programs allows him or her to be on one continuous track from early childhood to adulthood.

6.3.4 Entrepreneurial education: starting a business

People who want to start their own small business will have to complete all the requirements for an advanced skilled worker before they are allowed to take the two courses on starting their own business.

Unlike the United States, the Netherlands has developed a very sophisticated set of regulations for starting a business. The Dutch feel that helping each person succeed is very important. As a result, only 25 percent of the businesses fail. Two-thirds of all businesses started in Europe survive. (In the United States, less than 50 percent survive the first five years, and over 80 percent fail or are closed by the tenth year.) To start a business, a rigorous set of courses and tests are required over a two-year period. For example, a person who wishes to become a metal worker in the agricultural maintenance field and run his or her own business must take all the courses necessary to become a certified metal worker in agriculture maintenance (an advanced skilled worker). Then the worker must take the two courses required to start a business: a management course and a bookkeeping and economics course. Each course concludes with a test.

The content of the management course includes the following:

Enterprise and society

- Developing goals for the company and society
- Understanding how a successful company functions
- Understanding how to manage a company
- Learning Dutch rules and regulations for small business owners
- Learning all the social security laws and tax law regulations

Company organization

- Learning how to plan

- Understanding work preparation
- Calculating how long each job takes
- Understanding quality and logistics

Cost price and calculations

- Learning cost concepts
- Learning how to do cost price calculation
- Learning how to evaluate company results, such as profits

Personnel organization

- Learning to manage people
- Learning how to communicate effectively
- Learning how to evaluate performance
- Learning how to train employees

The management course is a prerequisite for the bookkeeping and accounting course. Consequently, trainees must spread their studies over a two-year period.

6.3.5 Higher vocational education and universities

Because of its key role in technical training and workforce competence, higher vocational education is monitored and evaluated, to ensure that all curricula are up-to-date and that job skill development will enable Dutch employees to be competitive in the world market. To oversee higher vocational education and universities, the Dutch Ministry of Education has established visitation committees. These committees visit the schools after they read the self-evaluation reports done by the schools. This evaluation is not based on ISO 9000; however, some schools use the design of ISO 9000 for the self-evaluation report. The visitation committee does a lot of questioning which further reveals the level of quality assurance in that particular school. After visiting all the schools of one type (e.g., for technical education), the committee produces one report that summarizes all its experiences and outcomes. This report is made available to all the administrators and teachers in these schools. There is no award system like a Baldrige Award. The idea is to learn from each other and improve the quality of education.

6.4 Certification Programs through Training Institutes

Three types of certification exist:

System certification through ISO 9000

Institute certification by CEDEO

Individual certification by SKO

6.4.1 System certification

In addition to all the Dutch certifications, several other types of certifications are now required by the European Community, to which the Netherlands belongs. Quality concerns worldwide have increased the need for technical education. ISO 9000 is being used worldwide. Many companies doing business with the European Community are being required to be certified. In the Netherlands, training institutes are active in implementing and assessing quality systems. They are doing this to improve the competitive situation and to satisfy increasingly demanding customers.

Institutes use one of two systems: ISO 9000 or EFQM. ISO 9000 is well known. EFQM stands for European Foundation for Quality Management. It is similar to the Malcolm Baldrige National Quality Award. The quality assessment system an institute chooses depends on the type of business it is assessing.

EFQM is used for service businesses—those not producing a product. Those businesses are *knowledge-intensive service organizations* (KIS). Professionals in this type of organization produce nontangible products, such as giving advice on how to invest money. The ISO 9000 standard is a method to assure the quality of core processes in the organization. The EFQM model is more a diagnostic and growth and development model. In practice, both systems can be used together. The quality audit by external auditors is crucial to the EFQM process, just as it is to the ISO 9000 process. Auditors who often audit training and education organizations have the right skills to audit KIS organizations. These auditors work closely with organizations to identify concerns and recommend improvements. Continuing improvement is important to the process.

6.4.2 Institute certification

CEDEO, an independent information system of business education in the Netherlands, is an example of the type of organization that conducts certification audits. CEDEO is an institute that is in charge of doing audits for training and educational institutes. The method used by CEDEO is called "the way to continuing quality improvement" and is explained graphically in Fig. 6.4.

CEDEO's activities focus on business courses and training. Figure 6.5 shows the scope of CEDEO's activities. CEDEO tries to be as clear as possible about the kind of information available in its publications or databases.

Included are

- Business courses and training
- Oral and written instruction
- Services for national and regional markets

Excluded are

- Government-sponsored primary, secondary, technical, and academic education
- Education activities aimed at the unemployed
- Day-school activities (6 months on end)

Gray areas included in CEDEO sources are

- Business education given in foundations attached to government-sponsored schools
- Open universities and schools and distance learning
- BBA/MBA program at universities

The products of CEDEO are in listed in a book published each year that describes the services of all controlled institutes. Mentioned in the book are training databases, an on-line help desk for trainers, contract evaluations of training institutes with companies, and established networks in training and education. CEDEO enjoys a close connection with the Dutch Trainers' Institute.

6.4.3 Individual certification

SKO (*Stichting voor de Certificatie van Keurings en Inspectiepersoneel en niet-destructief Onderzoekers*) is an example of a system of individual certification. SKO stands for the Dutch Foundation of Certification of Professional Competence of Inspection Personnel and Nondestructive Inspectors (*nondestructive* refers to using technology like ultrasound to evaluate the soundness of a structure; *destructive* requires tearing a structure apart to see what has happened). This is a certification of technical work, and in particular that of welders. For welding, the specialist technical worker is dependent on the judgment

124　Chapter Six

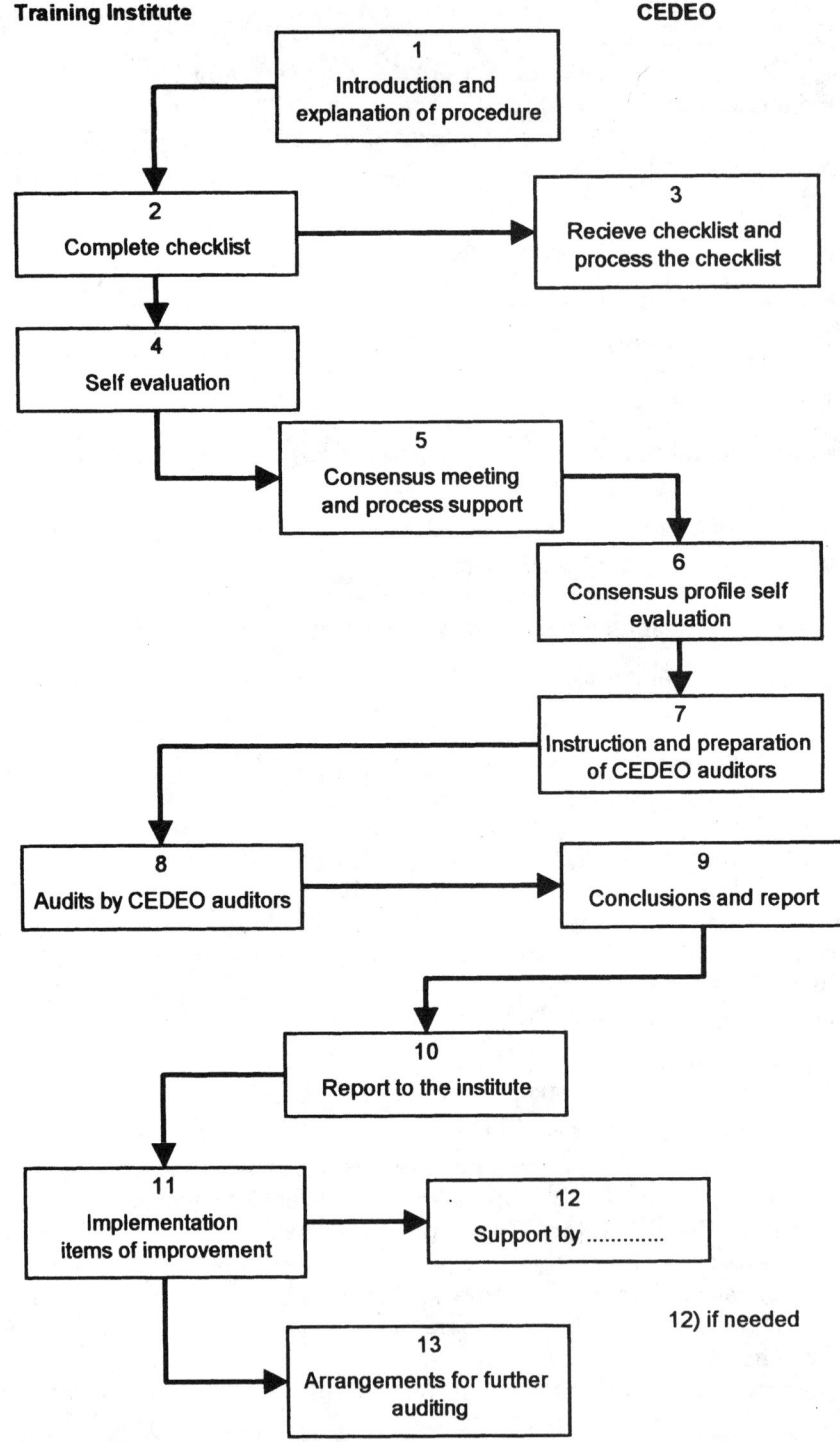

Figure 6.4　Procedure for quality improvement.

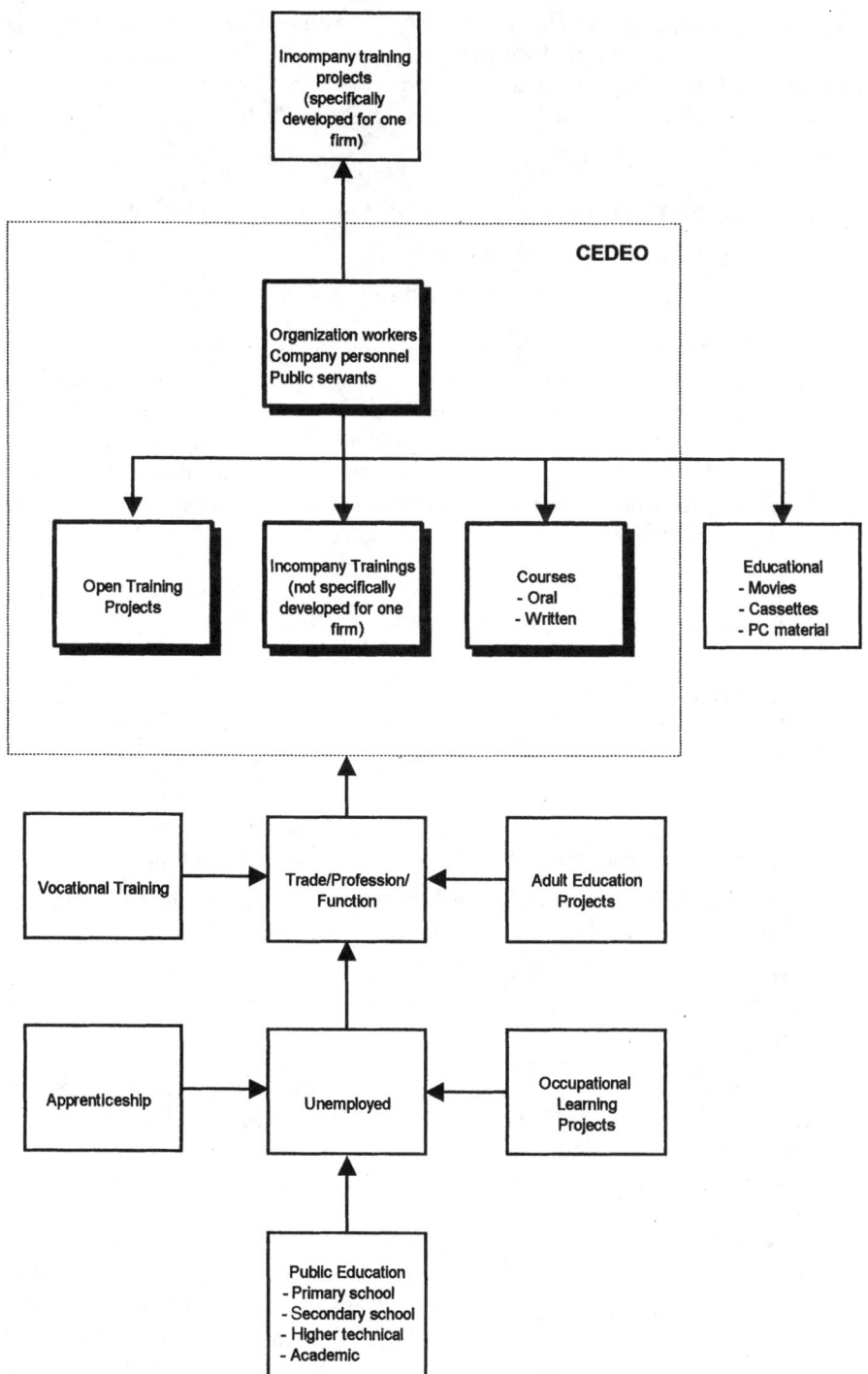

Figure 6.5 CEDEO's scope.

of other people about the quality of his or her work. This judgment is based on the outcome of an inspection process, which can vary from a simple visual inspection to an extensive inspection. Over time, criteria have evolved for the inspections. These include

1. A project-specific inspection procedure
2. A standard that defines how the inspection should be conducted
3. Criteria for judging exceptions
4. A skilled use of the criteria to complete a final report

The supervision of the inspection is critical to the process. Those doing the inspecting must pass an examination of competence. In addition, the welders to be inspected and the inspectors must demonstrate professional competence. Figure 6.6 shows the certification procedure for a welding specialist. The certification process shows how the Dutch approach technical education and training for welding specialists and welding inspectors.

Preparatory education: The skilled worker should have enough general education to be successful in the profession. Most of the time the students come from the LBO and MBO education levels (see Fig. 6.2).

Professional education: Standards are set for various levels of education, and each subject requires that a certain number of hours of training be completed.

Examination: During the tests, not only the theoretical knowledge but also the practical skills of the individual will be tested.

Certification: The SKO is accredited by the Dutch Council of Accreditation and has the official status of a certification body.

Authorization: The SKO certificate gives the employer the guarantee that the holder of the certificate is a professional welder or inspector.

The employer bears the responsibility for the competence of the worker and has to take the responsibility for seeing that any additional training needed occurs in a timely manner. Recertification has to be carried out from time to time to keep the level of competence up to date.

SKO certification from the Netherlands is recognized by Belgium and France; in addition, certified individuals have no problem passing certification tests in other European Community countries. Within a short time it is expected that SKO certificates will be accepted in all European Community countries.

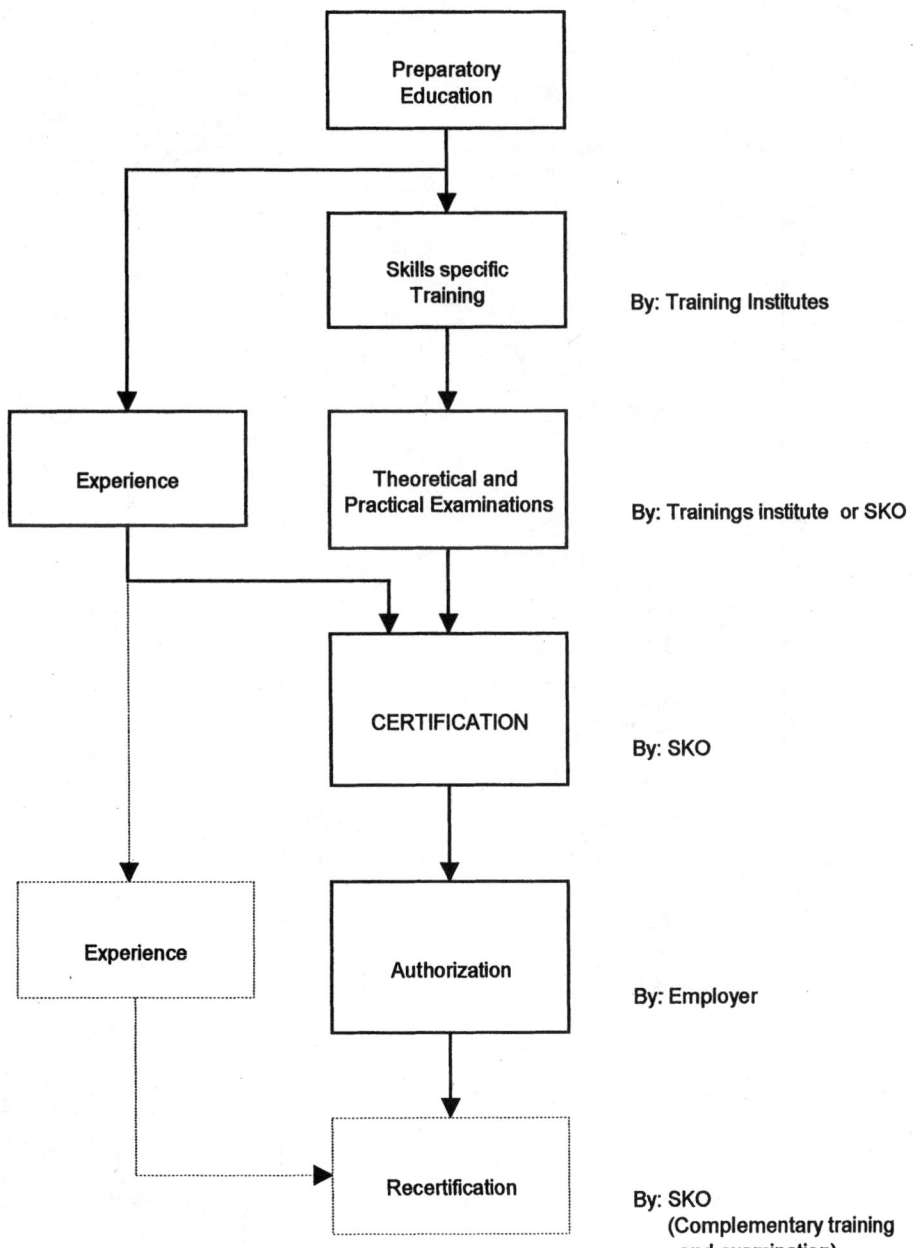

Figure 6.6 The SKO certification procedure.

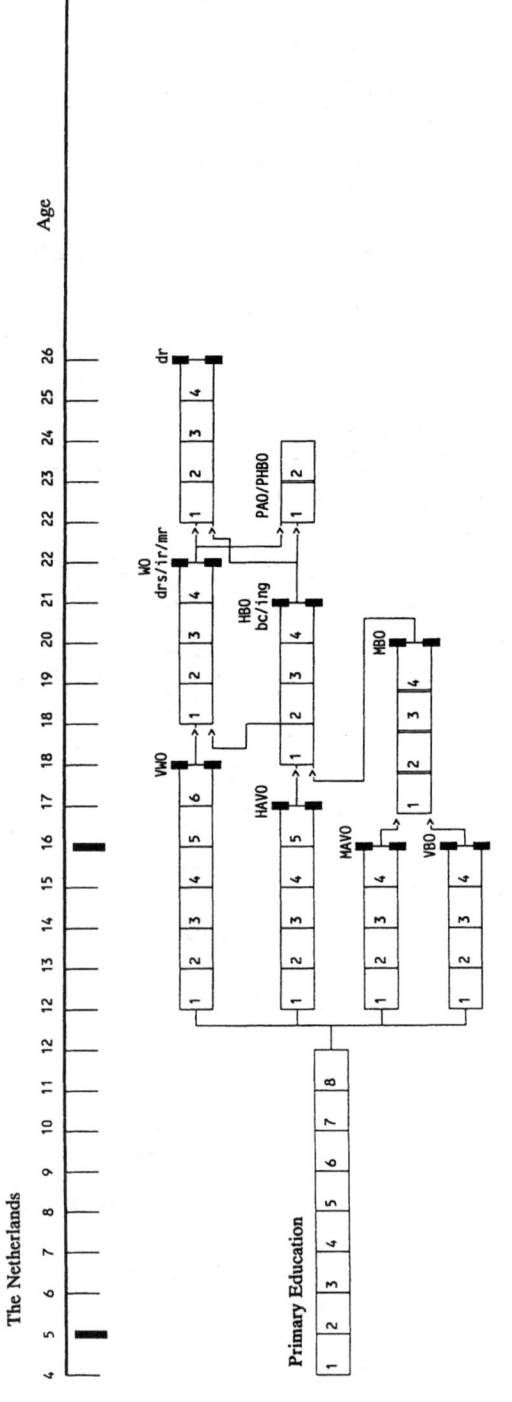

Figure 6.7 The educational system in the Netherlands.

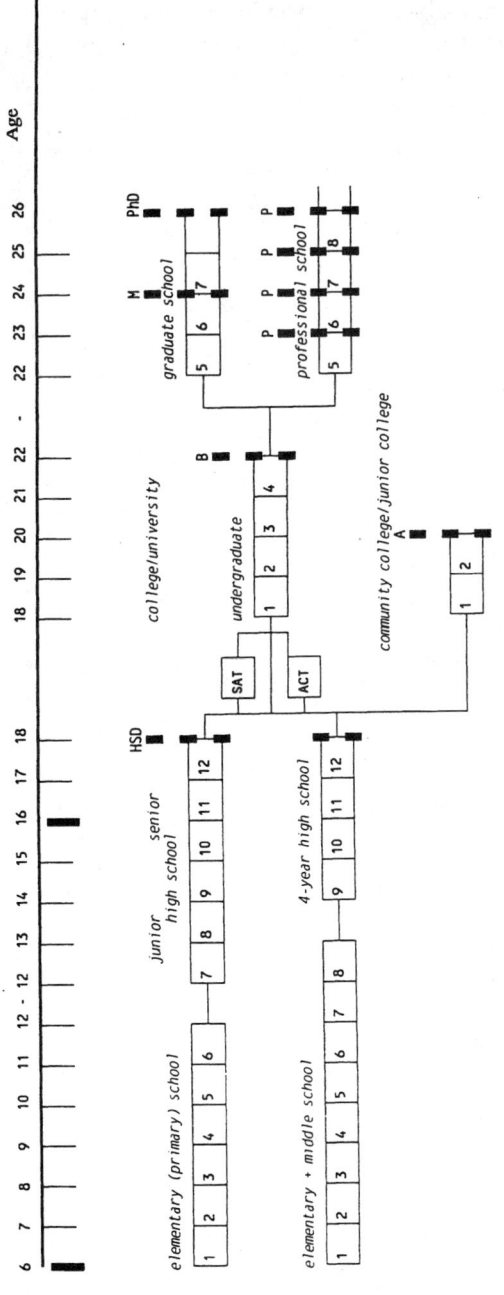

Figure 6.8 The educational system in the United States.

6.5 Conclusion

The Dutch, like all Europeans, have struggled with double-digit unemployment and the need for new markets. They have been inventive and resourceful as a nation. By tying together their educational and technical training systems, they have provided their employees with an extra edge. They are thereby better prepared to tackle the challenges that new market configurations and rapid introduction of technology are posing for economies worldwide.

6.6 Resources

CEDEO
Postbus 85510
2508 CE DEN HAAG
The Netherlands
TEL. +.31.70.346 37 39
FAX. +.31.70.362 50 94

SKO
POSTBUS 190
2700 AD ZOETERMEER
The Netherlands
TEL. +.31.79.53 13 43
FAX. +.31.79.53 13 65

For the Dutch Education System
Dutch Ministry of Education and Science
ZOETERMEER
The Netherlands

Chapter 7

Liability and the Technical Trainer: Recent Cases and Comments

John Sample, Ph.D.

John Sample, Ph.D., is the Director of Professional Development and Public Service at the Florida State University Center for Professional Development (Tallahassee, Florida). He has over 20 years' experience as a consultant, developer, facilitator, and evaluator of performance improvement programs for the private and public sectors. One of his areas of research and practice involves the impact of regulation and our legal system on technical training and human resource development.

> It has been the intention of the author to provide summary reviews of recent court cases affecting the work of technical trainers and their managers. Managerial and instructional solutions to several problems have been offered. Questions regarding legal issues must be sought from competent legal counsel. There has been no intent by the author to offer legal advice in this chapter.

7.1 Introduction

This chapter is an extension of the author's earlier work found in *The ASTD Technical and Skills Training Handbook* (Sample, 1995). Topics covered in that chapter included OSHA and work safety training, employer negligence in the workplace, human resource management issues (EEO and ADA), experiential and adventure-based training, intellectual property (copyright and trade secrets), and liability and the independent consultant.

Based upon the cases discussed, one will deduce rather quickly that liability for failure to train to standard is no longer a peripheral issue for corporate America. In this context, potential liability runs the gamut from "soft skills" training and development to human resource management. Technical trainers and their managers are already broadening the scope of their responsibilities to include this broader array of instruction that will be necessary if technical environments are to survive and succeed (Carnavale, 1993).

The focus of this chapter is on several instances of liability in which technical training may have had a specific role. Three cases are reviewed and summarized. A fourth section of the chapter focuses on a method for analyzing data and using subject matter experts in the identification of high-liability tasks.

7.2 Sex Discrimination, Technical Training, and Human Resources Management

The recently approved settlement of a massive sex discrimination class-action suit against Lucky Stores in California for more than $90 million clearly demonstrates the importance of strategic cooperation between training programs and human resource management. The 1994 settlement was based upon a 1992 decision rendered in the U.S. District Court for the Northern District of California (*Stender v. Lucky Stores Inc.*).

7.2.1 Case summary

In August 1988, Nancy Stender and five other women filed a complaint on behalf of themselves and of a class of female, black, and Hispanic past, present, and future employees of Lucky Stores. They alleged discrimination based upon sex, race, and national origin. The lawsuit was brought under Title VII of the 1964 Civil Rights Act and the California Fair Employment and Housing Act. A subsequent 1991 separate class action against Alpha Beta stores for the period when those stores became Lucky Stores (*Anders v. American Stores Company*) was joined with the Stender suit.

The Lucky Stores lawsuit is best described as a three-stage process. The first stage consisted of extensive discovery and pretrial practice and more than ten weeks of fact and expert testimony during the trial. The second stage was a series of hearings regarding the liability for back pay and the consideration of alternative methods for calculating such damages. No formal findings were made by the district court during the second stage. The third stage consisted of arguments and negotiations by opposing counsel and the agreement to a settlement by the district court.

The key finding by the court was that Lucky Stores' decisions on hiring, initial placement, training, and promotion were based on no objective standards and that training and promotion were founded on nonexistent criteria and were left to the sole discretion of store managers. The following circumstances are also noteworthy:

- The store managers and assistant store managers were not instructed about standards applicable to hiring or making promotional decisions. There was no documentation of decisions about whom to hire, train, or promote, or about why certain people were selected and not others.
- There was no paperwork showing which employees received training or requested additional hours of training.
- There were no job descriptions to provide guidance in evaluating whom to hire, promote, and train.
- Management consistently failed to follow its own established posting policies.

The district court found that the absence of personnel policies requiring decision makers to collect accurate information about applicants and employees, apply written selection criteria, and be accountable for their decisions increased the likelihood that gender stereotypes would influence their decisions. (*Stender v. Lucky Stores*, 803 F. Supp. At 331). The court also found that a lack of clear and objective guidelines on placement, promotion, and training elevated the potential for abuse by discrimination to a level sufficient to deduce the intent necessary for a finding of direct and intentional discrimination (legally termed *disparate treatment*).

Further intent of disparate treatment was concluded from two previous class action settlements by Lucky Stores for sex discrimination in the early 1980s. An affirmative action policy established in 1983 required the human resources manager to make recommendations concerning the lawful recruitment and selection of employees, the preparation of formal job descriptions, and the need for more equal representation of women in departments that offered employees better opportunities for advancement. Information from the corporate office determined that there was an awareness of the low percentage of women in management, and that based upon the affirmative action policy, the company needed to reemphasize the importance of compliance.

In addition to evidence of discriminatory intent, the plaintiffs' attorneys established, through expert testimony, statistical evidence sufficient to establish *an inference of intentional discrimination,* also known as *disparate treatment.* Expert testimony established gross statistical disparities in the initial placement of men and women, and statistically significant shortfalls in the promotion of women, the movement of women from part-time to full-time positions, and the allocation of additional hours to women.

The plaintiffs also established *disparate impact,* which is different from disparate treatment. In disparate impact, proof of intent is not required because personnel practices may be neutral or appear fair on their face, but be discriminatory in practice. In the Lucky Stores lawsuit, the district court cited court precedent that leaving decision-making power to the sole discretion of lower-level supervisors whose conscious and unconscious prejudices are unchecked by objective, published criteria can satisfy the causal requirement of a disparate impact claim. The plaintiffs established conclusively that management at Lucky Stores did not consistently follow the policies.

One of the most important facets of this case involves punitive damages. The district court ruled that the plaintiffs had sufficiently established their claim for punitive damages, as provided for in the Civil Rights Act of 1991. The court based its conclusion on Lucky Stores' prior knowledge of the sufficient problems with the underrepresentation of women in managerial positions and its repeated failure to implement appropriate recommendations. The court also relied on evidence of the discriminatory attitudes of some of the store managers and the company's abandonment of two affirmative action programs despite continued evidence of gross gender imbalance. This finding of reckless indifference by the court allowed the plaintiffs to pursue punitive damages pursuant to the Civil Rights Act of 1991.

7.2.2 Details of the settlement

The financial settlement was the third stage of the Lucky Stores lawsuit. The settlement agreement, which was approved in January 1994, provided monetary relief and attorneys' fees to the plaintiffs and to the class, and established detailed guidelines and procedures to correct prior violations of the antidiscrimination laws and to ensure equal employment opportunities for women in the future. See Table 7.1 for a detailed summary.

7.2.3 Implications for technical trainers

The critical lessons to be learned from Lucky Stores' experience are that senior management in all organizational contexts, including

TABLE 7.1 Summary of Settlement in the Lucky Stores Lawsuit

- Payment of $1,205,000 damages to the six individual plaintiffs.
- The establishment of three separate funds totaling $59,145,000 for allocation among three separately defined groups of class members by Lucky Stores.
- The establishment of a $20,000,000 pool to implement the terms for injunctive relief and the affirmative action program.
- Assessment of $13,750,000 in attorneys' fees and litigation costs against Lucky Stores.
- Lucky Stores will contribute up to an additional $13,000,000 if specific goals and targets for hiring and promotion are not met.

---

technical, must be accountable for compliance with the antidiscrimination laws and that this responsibility involves a series of distinct responsibilities and obligations. The special case for training supervisors and managers in EEO and other regulatory requirements must not be ignored (Sample, 1995, pp. 198–200).

Given the context of the Lucky Stores lawsuit, the following obligations of management are minimally required:

- Formulating and disseminating clear, concrete, and comprehensive personnel policies and procedures
- Ensuring through appropriate training and instruction that managers and supervisors understand their responsibilities with respect to EEO laws
- Monitoring these personnel policies and procedures to guarantee that they are being consistently and properly followed

Lucky Stores' problems appeared to derive precisely from management's failure to articulate and circulate distinct standards and guidelines, and from the freedom of local store managers and assistant managers to make discretionary and subjective decisions—often with disastrous consequences. In the Lucky Stores context, there were indications of potentially deep-seated employment problems. It is insufficient for a company to deal with personnel issues on a superficial basis. Grievances and complaints can appear to be dealt with, and yet the infrastructure of the human resource system may in fact conceal broader improprieties. Goldstein and Gilliam (1990) contend that training and fair employment practices will continue to be a training system issue into and beyond the year 2000. Senior management, corporate counsel, human resource managers, risk management specialists, and technical trainers must continue to forge strong internal strategic partnerships as a preventive tool against the threat of employment law litigation (Sample, 1995).

7.3 Adventure-Based Training: An Example from a Corporate Utility

Imagine that you are contract trainer for one of the largest telecommunications corporations in the country, and that one evening about 8:00 P.M. a civil process server rings your doorbell at home. When you open the door, you are face to face with a man wearing a badge who says, "Is this the residence of..., and what is your name, sir?" The officer of the court hands you a legal document, and states that you have 20 days to respond to the allegations stated in the complaint.

As you are reading over the document, you become aware of 14 allegations of negligence against you and your employer, the telecommunications corporation. You tell your wife the devastating news and talk for some time about the ominous implications (Sample & Hylton, 1995).

7.3.1 Case summary

The employer, a telecommunications company, contracted with a local consultant to provide a series of management development experiences for higher-level employees. Each offering of the program had between 9 and 15 participants, and the contract trainer had conducted more than 12 of these programs. Although formally titled "Team Work," the program was often referred to as "the Rambo course" by its many participants and by others who had heard about the program. The contract trainer was certified in the development and facilitation of the teamwork program by a business specializing in adventure-based programs.

The program in question was attended by employees from two work groups within the corporation. On the morning of the first day of this particular program, the contract trainer explained the parameters for participation by the employees. He explained that teamwork in the program was directly linked to working together on the job, and that the members of both work groups could improve their working relations by successfully completing the program.

The contract trainer explained that any participant could "challenge out" of any exercise if personal safety or injury was a concern. However, it was important that everyone participate in the team planning portion of each exercise. The exercise that is the subject of this analysis is called the "swinging log" exercise.

In the swinging log exercise, a 20-foot pole is suspended on two cables at each end. The highest point of the log is 19 inches above the ground. The cables are tethered to upright poles, with the swinging log suspended between them. The planning for the exercise requires the team to strategize how to get all participating team members standing on the log with all of their body parts above the horizontal halfway mark of the log for a count of 10. Spotters are arranged around the log, and other safety checks are routinely observed.

Three members of the team "challenged out" of the exercise. Eleven members of the team attempted the swinging log exercise. The team attempted the exercise several times. Two of the women who had attempted the exercise had twice attempted to remain on the log for the required count of 10. On the third attempt, one of the women fell over sideways and broke her leg as she was climbing down off the log. She later sued. During the trial, she alleged that the swinging log had hit her leg, causing the fracture. It was not clear whether another woman had stepped on her foot as she was dismounting the log. The plaintiff was a 59-year-old employee of the defendant corporation, and she had over 25 years of employment to her credit. She was designated a craft union employee. Her attendance in the teamwork program was mandatory.

On the same day as the accident, the contract trainer wrote a three- to four-page report of the events prior to and shortly after the accident. A copy was given to the corporation, and a copy was retained for the trainer's file. Several days later, the contract trainer did a walk-through of the events leading up to the accident with a safety inspector from the corporation.

The contract trainer became the key witness for the corporation. Fortunately for the trainer, he had kept meticulous notes and records on the current and previous teamwork programs. He also maintained the posters used during each program. As the corporation began to develop a defense to the multiple allegations of negligence, it was the contract trainer who provided the most detailed and vivid recollection of what had occurred. Additionally, the trainer had nearly memorized the manual from the certification program he had attended on how to facilitate the teamwork program. He knew in detail the purpose of each exercise, the conditions under which it could be used safely, and how to modify it to meet varying conditions.

Prior to the trial, there were discovery proceedings designed to bring to the surface important information for the plaintiff and defense. Depositions were taken of witnesses and the contract trainer. During the eight-day trial, the contract trainer testified for approximately 6½ hours. The plaintiff's attorney went through the certification manual page by page with the trainer. Attempts were made to portray the trainer as a "Rambo trainer" who bullied little old ladies into performing physically dangerous stunts. The defense attorney had the contract trainer explain the program in a factual and unemotional manner. Flipcharts and easels were brought into the courtroom, and the contract trainer, as witness for the defense, explained to the jury the content and process of the teamwork program. Ironically, the skills the contract trainer ordinarily needed to train participants were now being used to educate the jury about the facts of the case before the court.

The responsibility of the jury when multiple defendants are involved is to determine the amount of negligence of each defendant. In this case, the jury determined that the contract trainer was not negligent, and that the corporation was negligent (*Colatacari v. Bell South & Hylton*). A judgment of $875,000 was initially awarded against the defendant corporation by the jury. The judgment was appealed by the defendant corporation as excessive, and a subsequent settlement in excess of $300,000 was agreed upon by the parties.

7.3.2 Implications for technical trainers

Technical trainers can expect to be more involved in nontechnical, or "soft skills," training. They may be expected to design, develop, and perform the training themselves, or, as in this case, they may purchase training from a contract provider. In either circumstance, technical trainers are well advised to follow a systematic and defensible approach in developing or providing training that has legal implications. The following admonitions may be useful in this regard (Sample, 1995):

- When using adventure-based or experiential training, ensure that participants have legitimate alternatives for accomplishing their required management development through other acceptable means.
- Do not punish personnel during employee appraisals or at opportunities for promotion for failure to participate in adventure-based programs.
- If contract trainers are used, assess their competence and certification requirements. Send corporate personnel to attend a program before committing to an agreement for services. Inquire into the insurance coverage of the business that certifies a trainer. Determine previous litigation against the contract trainer and the business that certified him or her.
- For contract trainers, have your contract reviewed by a competent attorney. Discuss with him or her the need for insurance or bond as a safety net.
- Consider including language in the contract that requires the corporation to provide legal assistance under the corporate umbrella as long as the trainer operated within the scope of the contract.

- For both contract and internal corporate trainers, keep copious notes of activities during the training program. Do not stray significantly from program manuals and materials, since that would invalidate your certification. Inspect equipment used in adventure-based programs prior to each use, make notes of equipment problems, and require immediate attention to defective equipment. If possible, cotrain with another certified trainer, and use each other to make informed decisions affecting safety and potential injury.

7.4 Negligent Technical Training in a Retail Store

A retail store environment is not the usual context for discussing technical training. One might expect sales training to be the predominant focus in a retail store. Not so, according to a Maryland civil court case in which the plaintiff alleged negligence when she fell on a display treadmill.

7.4.1 Case summary

This is a negligence action brought by a female plaintiff, age 55 at the time of the injury, against the defendant, a large retail store, alleging negligence in failing to properly train its employees in the safe operation of exercise equipment on display (*Martha Hood v. Sears, Roebuck & Company*). The plaintiff additionally alleged that the defendant retail store was vicariously liable for the negligence of the employee who activated the treadmill while the plaintiff was standing on it.

The testimony established that the plaintiff, who was totally deaf, entered the retail store to look at exercise equipment. She stepped up onto a treadmill machine which at the time was unplugged. Unbeknownst to the store employee on duty in the exercise equipment department, the treadmill machine had been left on the highest setting. The evidence indicated that the store employee asked the plaintiff if she needed help, not knowing that the plaintiff was deaf. The plaintiff made a gesture with her hand which the employee interpreted as meaning that she wished the employee to plug in the machine.

The employee proceeded to plug in the machine while the plaintiff was standing on it, and the plaintiff lost her balance and fell. The plaintiff contended that the defendant's employee was negligent in activating the machine while it was set in the highest-speed mode and while the plaintiff was standing on the machine. The plaintiff further contended that the defendant was negligent in failing to properly train the employee with regard to safe operation and demonstration of the treadmill machine.

The medical evidence indicated that the plaintiff sustained soft tissue injuries, carpal tunnel syndrome, and an aggravation of a preexisting arthritic condition. The plaintiff, who was employed as a seamstress at the time of the fall, claimed total disability as a result of the injuries sustained in the accident. She presented medical claims approximating $35,000 and claimed lost income, past and future, of $186,000.

The defendant retail store denied negligence and contended that the plaintiff was comparatively negligent in failing to heed the large warning signs in close proximity to the treadmill and other exercise display equipment. The defendant's evidence indicated that the signs posted instructed customers to ask for assistance before attempting use of the machine. The defendant also called two orthopedic experts, who testified that the plaintiff had suffered a minimal soft tissue injury which resolved shortly after the accident and that her present complaints were solely attributable to her preexisting arthritic changes.

The jury found in favor of the defendant retail store.

7.4.2 Implications for technical trainers

Senior management must constantly be aware of potential liability for failure to train to standard and to invoke appropriate learning technologies to ensure competent performance, regardless of the setting. Technical training occurs in a variety of business, industrial, and governmental settings. In this instance, technical training combined with sales training was called for in a retail store setting.

Task analysis is a useful first step in identifying performance outcomes and the knowledge, skills, and attitudes necessary for competent task performance (Swanson, 1994; Ward, 1988). The required use of job aids in the demonstration of exercise equipment in the display area would reinforce classroom instruction and on-the-job training of sales personnel (Rossett & Gautier-Downes, 1991).

7.5 Framework for Identifying High-Liability Tasks

There are several approaches to predicting the likelihood of organizational liability for failure to train to standard. The most traditional approach is to monitor civil (and sometimes criminal) case law for precedent cases that guide the legal system in its deliberations and findings. Such an approach is largely reactive, since the manager of technical training must rely upon advice from legal counsel to keep him or her informed about cases that have already been decided.

A second approach uses existing statutes and regulations to guide strategies and instructional programs for compliance. Examples of such statutes and regulations include EEO, OSHA, Nuclear Regulatory Commission rulings, and most recently the Americans With Disabilities Act. This approach has the advantage of technical assistance from the regulating agency (Ledvinka & Scarpello, 1991). Although too much assistance can become unwelcome, at least there is a source of legal and technical information for designers of training programs!

A third approach is more proactive in nature; when combined with the first two approaches, it will ensure the identification of potential high-liability tasks. This approach uses a validated task inventory, routinely maintained risk-management and personnel records, and subject matter experts (SMEs) to identify high-liability tasks.

7.5.1 Identifying high-liability tasks

Most business enterprises are aware of the areas in their operations that engender the most liability. Unfortunately, there is usually no systematic method, or requirement, for generating and analyzing the various sources of such information within the organization.

Sources of information regarding potential liability for business and industry include the following:

- *Professional and trade associations.* Some associations will provide research on specific topics, and may even employ attorneys who will provide advice.
- *Corporate attorneys.* They can provide legal documents on sustained and dismissed complaints alleging negligence and other forms of liability.
- *Risk management programs.* These provide analysis of types of accidents, statistics on paid claims on workers' compensation cases, and fines by regulators such as OSHA.
- *Safety programs.* These can be used for analysis of types of accidents resulting from improper use of equipment, driving-related accidents, and failure to follow a procedure resulting in an accident.
- *Personnel files.* These can be used for statistical analysis of progressive discipline records; training records; job descriptions stating knowledge, skill, and attitude requisites; applications for employment indicating previous experience; and sick leave.

Law enforcement and corrections is an area of the public sector that depends substantially on technical training for improving performance and reducing the potential for liability for failure to train to standard (Gallagher, 1990). The conventional wisdom in law enforcement and corrections is to group potential high-liability tasks into several general areas: driving, first responder/first aid, use of force, firearms, and sometimes civil rights issues (Berringer, 1987). Identification of these broad areas has served to put administrators, supervisors, and training personnel on general notice about potential liability in law enforcement. What has been lacking is a specific process for identifying potential high-liability tasks within those broad areas.

The following example from a medium-sized law enforcement agency describes a process for identifying potential high-liability tasks from divergent sources of information within the agency (Boone, Sample, & Koenig, 1992). The heart of the process lies in the use of a valid task inventory, routinely kept records, and the use of subject matter experts (SMEs).

Given this framework, the following steps are employed:

1. Develop an inventory of tasks performed by sworn personnel in the law enforcement agency.
2. Analyze routinely kept risk-management and personnel records for tasks associated with the following: auto accidents, workers' compensation claims, professional liability, and internal affairs complaints.
3. Utilize SMEs to review summary reports to determine which tasks have the most potential for high liability.

Step 1, development of task inventory. Most efforts involving task analysis result in a list of tasks and the identification of the knowledge, skills, and attitudes (KSAs) necessary for selecting, training, and supervising personnel to standard (Swanson, 1994).

The task inventory used in this example was generated from the *Job and Task Analysis of Florida Law Enforcement Officers*. The original task list of 528 items was updated by 18 representatives of the law enforcement agency. This group identified an additional 22 tasks performed by sworn personnel in the department.

An inventory consisting of 550 tasks and 11 demographic variables (sex, assignment, etc.) was distributed to all sworn officers and their sergeants. Each "Law Enforcement Task Inventory" included a mark-sensitive optical scanning scoring form. Instructions for completing the task survey were also included, and the respondents were given two weeks to complete the assignment. Each booklet and scoring form was assigned a number that corresponded to the officer's identification number.

Each officer was to determine if he or she had performed each task during the past year, and if so, to use a 5-point scale to estimate "relative time spent" on the task (1 = very much below average; 5 = very much above average). One hundred fifty-four task surveys (92 percent) were returned to the personnel unit for processing. The optical scanning forms were scored by the testing and evaluation center at a major state university, and statistical analysis was provided by the computing center at the university.

Step 2, data analysis. The author and a representative of the staff services unit of the law enforcement agency reviewed incident reports from existing records to determine what specific tasks were being performed at the time the incident occurred. In this context, "incident" means any single occurrence of an automobile accident, professional liability claim, internal affairs/citizen complaint, or workers' compensation claim. Incidents were gathered for an 18-month period, and a summary report was written for each of these topics.

Step 3, use of subject matter experts. Subject matter experts are individuals who have specialized expertise in a specific area of a job, and whose judgment and professional opinion will withstand rigorous scrutiny. In a law enforcement context, SMEs must have the experience and ability to provide credible testimony and to withstand cross-examination if they are ever required to testify in their area of expertise. SMEs must be chosen carefully, for a department's future liability may turn on their expertise. It was recommended that the sheriff's department use external and internal SMEs to provide the required expertise. In this regard, the use of SMEs is similar to using external observers for assessment center activities.

In this instance, the sheriff requested the assistance of seven internal and external SMEs. The SMEs for this project represented driving, firearms, first responder/first aid, defensive tactics, and general law enforcement administration. Included as SMEs were a representative of the state sheriff's association and an attorney from the insurance company that represented the department. They did not receive any compensation for their assistance.

The SMEs met for a half-day to assist the department in identifying tasks with high-liability potential. As a group, the SMEs reviewed the summaries of the automobile accidents, internal affairs complaints, professional liability, and workers' compensation claims.

The next objective for the SMEs was to determine a practical definition of high-liability tasks. After lengthy discussion, the SMEs agreed upon the following working definition: A high-liability task

- Results in claims involving death or significant injury to members of the public or deputies, or
- Results in a loss (settlement or judgment) of $50,000 or more, or
- Results in multiple incidents involving the same task or person, each incident causing $5,000 or more loss, or

- A combination of the above.

Having reviewed the report summaries and given the above definition, the seven SMEs were instructed to review the task inventory to determine potential high-liability tasks for the department. Working independently, each SME used his or her experienced judgment to determine tasks with potential high liability. For tasks of their choice, the SMEs assigned an "H" (for high) or an "M" (for moderate) liability.

The SMEs were also instructed to determine potentially high-liability tasks using an alternative method, a nominal group technique (Martinko & Gepson, 1983; Moore, 1987). This approach to group decision making requires that SMEs identify high-liability tasks and silently vote to determine a priority ranking. In this instance, each of the seven SMEs was instructed to assign votes to the ten tasks having the potential for the highest liability. The task with the highest liability received ten votes, the next highest liability task received nine votes, and so on.

7.5.2 Triangulation: task list, needs analysis, subject matter experts

Table 7.2 gives the consensus of subject matter experts arising from the above-described procedures for determining high-liability tasks for the sheriff's department. The rank order in the left-hand column is the result of the SMEs' assessing each task in terms of liability potential. The second list of rankings represents the rank order from the nominal group technique (NGT).

Note that the NGT method resulted in two additional tasks that were not identified by the first method:

1. Conduct active patrolling of assigned areas.
2. Set up roadblocks. These were ranked fifth and ninth, respectively.

It is of some significance that the two methods essentially resulted in similar rankings. Multiple methodologies are always preferable in applied research of this nature, and in this instance, confidence in the validity of the final task list is increased, since both methods yielded very similar results (Cascio, 1991).

There is no particular magic to be attributed to the final consensus list of high-liability tasks reported in this article. A different group of equally competent subject matter experts could have identified a different mix of high-liability tasks. What is defensible is the process by which the tasks were systematically and rigorously identified. In this instance, the sheriff's department can have confidence that a grand

TABLE 7.2 Ranking of High-Liability Tasks by Subject Matter Experts

Rank	NGT	Task description
1	4	Pursue vehicles or vessels
2	2	Apprehend suspects
3	3	Control disorderly or irate persons
4	1	Make arrest
5		Confront or monitor groups
6	6	Conduct felony stop
7	7	Administer first aid
8		Rescue trapped persons
9		Act or respond to extortionist or kidnapper
10		Use animals to control crowds
11		Conduct traffic stop
12		Detain suspect vehicle or vessel
13		Participate in the execution of arrest warrants or make return of them to proper authority
14		Protect victim or other threatened person
15		Seize or confiscate illegal apparatus (such as distillery, traps, drug equipment, or gambling devices)
16		Guard prisoners outside of jail
17	8	Search for explosives related to bomb threats
18		Use animals to detect or apprehend intruders
19		Transport ill or injured persons from remote area to meet emergency medical team
20		Investigate hazardous materials violations
—	5	Conduct active patrolling of assigned areas
—	9	Set up roadblocks

jury or civil trial jury would conclude that reasonable steps were taken to identify high-liability tasks.

7.5.3 Strategies for preventing liability

The results of this applied research project cast the identified high-liability tasks into what the courts refer to as foreseeable field incidents that officers could be reasonably expected to experience (*Canton v. Harris,* 1989). Having identified high-liability tasks, the sheriff's department is now on notice to adequately prepare sworn deputy sheriffs and their supervisors to respond competently to situations in which these tasks are required (Sample, 1995). Failure to do so could result in civil liability against the department's insurer and the county. It is important that chief executive officers require extensive written policies, training, supervision, and discipline for such foreseeable tasks.

Further research using the above-indicated procedures is in progress (Sample, 1994). A statistical procedure for assessing the level of interrater agreement of subject matter experts known as Kendall's coefficient of concordance (Siegel & Castellan, 1988) has been utilized with SMEs in a correctional setting.

7.6 Conclusion

The potential for and actual liability in corporate America continues to pose a serious and continuing threat to CEOs, senior management, and managers of technical training programs (Fenton, Ruud, & Kimbell, 1991). Corporate personnel must continually balance appropriate risk taking in the spirit of sustainable competition with a high regard for the rights of employees and their safety in the workplace. Risk management programs, including various types of insurance, provide reasonable protection for employers. Such coverage is costly, and may be subject to abuse.

Reducing costs associated with a company's risk management program must be a continuing aim of line managers. Technical trainers may assist in this endeavor through effective analysis, design, development, implementation, and evaluation of performance-based learning (Ward, 1988, Sample, 1989).

7.7 Glossary

Disparate treatment Direct and intentional discrimination.

Disparate impact Employment practices that appear to be neutral, but that have a discriminatory impact or effect in practice.

Plaintiff One who wishes to file a lawsuit against a defendant in court.

Punitive damages Monetary damages designed to punish the defendant.

Vicarious liability The liability of one person for the actions of another.

End Note

The author appreciates permission from the National Society for Performance and Instruction to use a revised version of "Using Subject Matter Experts to Identify High Liability Tasks" from the June 1995 volume of *Performance and Instruction*.

7.8 References

Berringer, H. G., *Civil Liability and the Police,* Evanston, Ill.: The Traffic Institute, Northwestern University, 1987.

Boone, E., J. Sample, and R. Koenig, "Florida Sheriff Uses Experts to Identify High Liability Tasks," *Sheriff,* 1992, pp. 10–12.

Carnavale, A., "Outlook: Job Skills and Technical Training," *Training & Development,* 47(2):24–30, 1993.

Cascio, W. F., *Applied Psychology in Personnel Management.* Englewood Cliffs, N.J.: Prentice-Hall, 1991.

Fenton, J. W., W. N. Ruud, and J. A. Kimbell, " Negligent Training Suits: A Recent Entry into the Corporate Employment Negligence Arena," *Labor Law Journal,* 1991, pp. 351–356.

Gallagher, G. P., "Risk Management for Police Administrators," *The Police Chief,* 1990, pp. 18–28.
Goldstein, I. L., and P. Gilliam, "Training Issues in the Year 2000," *American Psychologist,* 45 (2):134–143, 1990.
Ledvinka, J., and V. Scarpello, *Federal Regulation of Personnel and Human Resources Management,* 2d ed., Boston: Kent Publishing Company, 1991.
Martinko, M., and Gepson, J., "Nominal Grouping and Needs Analysis," in F. Ulschak (Ed.), *Human Resource Development,* Reston, Va.: Reston Publishing Co., 1983.
Moore, C. M., *Group Techniques for Idea Building,* Newbury Park, Calif.: SAGE Publications, 1987.
Rossett, A., and J. Gautier-Downes, *A Handbook of Job Aids.* San Diego: Pfeiffer & Company, 1991, pp. 189–205.
Sample, J., "Using Subject Matter Experts to Identify High-Liability Tasks," *Performance and Instruction,* 34(5): 34–37, 1995.
Sample, J., and R. Hylton, "The Anatomy of a Lawsuit against a Contract Trainer: A Case Study," work in progress, 1995.
Sample, J., " Liability and the Technical Trainer: An Overview of Issues and Prevention Strategies," in L. Kelly (Ed.), *The ASTD Technical and Skills Training Handbook,* New York: McGraw-Hill, 1995, pp. 175–210.
Sample, J., "A Pilot Test for Determining Inter-rater Agreement of Subject Matter Experts and High Liability Tasks," work in progress, 1994.
Sample, J., *INFO-LINE Series—Legal Liability and HRD: Implications for Trainers and Their Managers,* Washington, D.C: American Society for Training and Development, 1993.
Sample, J., "Civil Liability for Failure to Train to Standard," *Educational Technology,* 29 (6):32–26, 1989.
Siegel, S., and N. J. Castellan, *Nonparametric Statistics for the Behavioral Sciences,* New York: McGraw-Hill, 1988.
Swanson, R. A., *Analysis for Improving Performance,* San Francisco: Berrett-Koehler Publishers, 1994.
Ward, G., *High-risk Training,* New York: Nichols Publishing, 1988.

7.8.1 Court cases

Anders v. American Stores, Civ. No. C91 1763 MHP—sex discrimination, training, and human resource management.
Canton v. Harris, 109 S Ct 1197 (1989)—failure to train to standard in the public sector.
Colatarci v. Bell South Corporation, Bell South Human Resources, and R. L. Hylton, Case Number 91-10260(1), 17th. Judicial Circuit, Circuit Court of Florida—negligent adventure-based training.
Martha Hood v. Sears, Roebuck & Company, Judge Duckett, Ann Arundel County, Md., (Feb. 9, 1993)—negligent store training.
Stenger v. Lucky Stores, 803 F. Supp. 259 (N. D. Cal. 1992)—sex discrimination, training, and human resource management.

Chapter 8

Developing Legally Defensible Tests

Robert Bass, Ph.D.

Robert I. Bass, Ph.D., is a human resources consultant. He provides consulting services to large and small companies, primarily in the areas of organizational analysis, attitude surveys, developing and validating selection instruments, developing training programs, and individual assessment. He is an active ASTD local member, currently serving on the board of directors of the North New Jersey chapter of ASTD. He is also the recipient of the 1993 Quality & Innovation Award from the ASTD North New Jersey chapter.

8.1 Introduction

You just developed a course to train your technical employees. The first group of trainees is about to start the course. You wonder, will the participants learn the course material? Will they perform their job better after the course? You decide that the best way to evaluate the trainees is to give them an end-of-course test to determine how much they learned.

Because you are an experienced course developer, you think developing a test should be a piece of cake. You're probably right. But, will the test evaluate how well the trainees can do their job? You probably already know that an end-of-course test will not answer that question directly. Will the test evaluate how much the trainees learned? Maybe. Will the test be defensible in a court of law? That depends on how the course was developed, how the test was developed and validated, and the quality of the documentation.

8.2 Case Studies

Let's look at two case studies. The first case study is adapted from a real legal case in which I was involved. The second is a fairly common situation; you or your colleagues have probably done the same thing. I am called regularly to discuss essentially this exact situation. A discussion of possible outcomes follows each case study.

8.2.1 Case study 1

You are a newly promoted human resources or training manager. Your predecessor, with whom you worked for several years, developed a set of training programs and end-of-course tests to evaluate the trainees' performance in the course. Because you worked with and respected your predecessor, you continue to use the courses and tests which were developed.

Is there anything wrong with this situation? What, if anything, can happen to you?

Case study 1 discussion. This case study was adapted from a real legal case. During the legal proceeding, the human resources manager was being deposed by the attorney for the plaintiff. The attorney asked why the test was used and why certain specific test procedures were used, and there were many questions about the development of the employment procedures. During over a half hour of testimony, the only responses from the human resources manager were (1) that she did not know, or (2) that the testing procedure was implemented by her predecessor and she did not know why the points in question were done in specific ways. The human resources manager explained that her predecessor had developed many tests and procedures, and that she, the new human resources manager, had not reviewed all the procedures that had previously been developed. As it turned out, the predecessor did not leave any notes or reports explaining why things were done the way they were, and so the new human resources manager could not really answer any questions.

Is this the kind of testimony that you would want to present to defend a lawsuit? Is this the kind of testimony that will endear you to your employer? We are all very busy, but assuming that everything your predecessor did was fine can get you into a very embarrassing and potentially costly situation.

As a postscript, the "new" human resources manager had been in the position for over a year, but things were very busy and she had never had time to review the previously developed tests or procedures.

8.2.2 Case study 2

You are a fairly seasoned training professional. You have just finished developing a course for computer technicians. The first group of trainees is about to be trained. It is now time, you decide, to develop a test to evaluate their performance or knowledge. You will be using the test primarily to evaluate your training course. You feel confident because you have done this many times before, but is there a reason to be concerned? You know that if the test is going to be used for an employment decision, it must be properly developed and validated. You know, though, that the test will not be used for any employment decisions, so you are okay. Later, if you find that the course is fine, the test may be used to evaluate the trainees, but you will take care of that situation when the need arises.

Everything is okay, right? Is there anything that can go wrong with this scenario?

Case study 2 discussion. The first case study has some obvious problems, but this case study might seem to be problem-free. As I mentioned, this is a common scenario; you or your colleagues may have done the same thing yourself. Most of the time everything *is* okay. Let's see some of the possible problems.

The use of a test needs to be clarified immediately. Stating that a test will not be used for an employment decision when in fact it will be is often the first mistake that trainers make. How could they make such a basic mistake? Why wouldn't they know how they will use the test? Trainers know how *they* will use the test, but they do not always know how other people in the company will use it. For example, suppose a trainee takes a test and passes with a satisfactory score. No problem. Yet, what if the trainee goes back to work, and the supervisor asks to see the test score? While it is passing, the score is lower than the score of another employee. The supervisor gives the employee with the higher score a better assignment. A year later the employee with the better assignment gets a promotion based on success in the new assignment. Did the test score lead to an employment decision? Probably, and a plaintiff's attorney will be certain to argue this line of reasoning.

Once a test—or any employment procedure, including a training course itself—is used for an employment decision, the procedure must be properly developed and validated (Sample, 1995). In addition, *the development and validation must be properly documented.* Few of us like to take the time to document why we did what we did, yet this really is a vital component of a test development effort.

About now, you may be asking why there is such concern about documenting the test development: "I won't have to give my report to anyone anyway; it is my work, and I can do what I want with it." Well, in a legal proceeding there is a process called *discovery*. Discovery is the process of determining what relevant information is available from the other side that can help the attorneys prepare their case. In most jurisdictions, discovery is very liberal. Certainly every jurisdiction would allow the discovery of all relevant reports and documents concerning the test. Well, you think, the attorney does not really understand what it takes to properly develop a test, and so almost any report will do. This is absolutely wrong if the attorney has any experience in the field.

Most attorneys who practice employment law are extremely knowledgeable in all areas of human resources. They are often more knowledgeable than many human resources and training professionals.

Whether or not the attorney is knowledgeable in the field, he or she is likely to retain an expert witness to review the case, prepare for trial, and testify at the trial. An expert witness is paid to review a case and render an opinion concerning the test development and validation effort. Any good expert will review your documentation to identify areas where your work is not consistent with the highest professional standards. If you have no documentation, that in itself is a departure from the standards expected of professionals in test development and validation. The expert will have a good time pointing out any mistakes or omissions in your documentation, and explaining how you deviated from professional standards. Your employer will realize the litigation exposure issues immediately.

Suppose that, as in case study 2 and as often occurs, you decide that if you later use the test for an employment decision, you will take care of the validation and documentation then. What if "later" is three to four years from now and you have to write a report or answer questions? Some of the questions might be the following:

What did you do?

What was your job analysis procedure?

Who did you interview during the job analysis?

How did you determine each of the content areas?

How did you determine how many questions to include for each content area?

Who did you interview to determine what questions should be included on the test?

What did you do to determine the relevance of each question?

Could you recall the details in your office three years later? Could you recall the details on a witness stand in front of a jury? And could you testify that you were absolutely certain of your recollection without having a report to refer to that was prepared at the time you developed the test?

Okay, let's test your memory about some other things. This might be a proper rebuttal question from the plaintiff's attorney to make you look like someone with poor recall. How happy do you think your company would be with your testimony?

8.3 Test Development Guidelines

Before we go into a discussion about developing tests, it is important to review the standards that will guide the development, validation, and documentation of the test. There are three sets of guidelines that you should be familiar with, two professional and one legal. The professional guidelines are the *Principles for the Validation and Use of Personnel Selection Procedures* (Principles) and *Standards for Educational and Psychological Testing* (Standards). The legal guideline is the *Uniform Guidelines on Employee Selection Procedures* (Uniform Guidelines).

The three guidelines are given different consideration in a legal case. The Uniform Guidelines are generally given precedence by the administrative agencies, such as the EEOC, that may decide to pursue a legal case against your company. The two professional guidelines will most likely be given precedence and greater authority by an expert witness. Experts are generally chosen because of professional expertise in the field and, therefore, will most likely agree with the professional standards.

The primary difference between the Uniform Guidelines and the professional guidelines is that the Uniform Guidelines specify many developmental steps as essential, whereas the professional standards describe the same steps as recommendations rather than strict requirements. If you follow the professional standards rather than the more stringent Uniform Guidelines, you should at least be aware of the differences and explain in your report why you did not do the things that the Uniform Guidelines describe as essential. A checklist of the different requirements can be found in Cascio (1987). Cascio also provides a checklist of documentation requirements for the Uniform Guidelines.

8.4 Test Development

So how would you develop a legally defensible test? Figure 8.1 gives an overview of the process. This process should look familiar to many of you because it is similar to a standard instructional systems design model. Actually, developing a test is not very different from developing a good training course.

8.4.1 Conduct job analysis

As can be seen, the first step in developing a test is performing a job analysis. There are many methods of conducting a job analysis, and none of them is considered inherently superior to the others (see, for example, the Principles and the Uniform Guidelines).

One method that I find useful is a functional job analysis. A functional job analysis identifies the tasks performed on the job and the results of the behavior. The knowledge, skills, abilities, and other characteristics (KSAOs) required to perform the tasks are usually also identified. To perform a functional job analysis, workers are typically observed, interviewed, and sometimes surveyed. The end product of a functional job analysis is a complete list of the tasks performed on the job and a list of KSAOs required to perform the tasks. The KSAOs are evaluated to determine their criticality (see the Uniform Guidelines), and the test is developed based on the results of

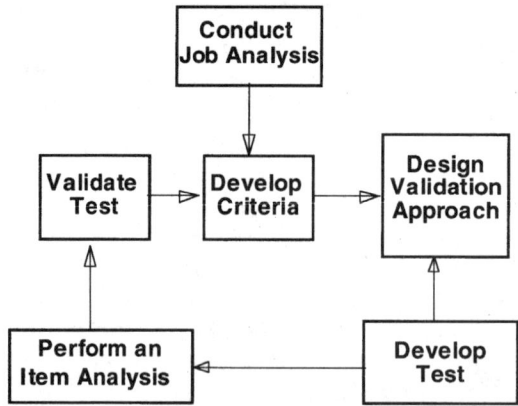

Figure 8.1 Test development model.

the job analysis. Information about the different methods of job analysis can be found in Gael (1988).

A format for writing task statements is presented in Fig. 8.2. Following this four-part format makes conducting job analysis interviews easy. If you ask the job incumbents to describe the work that they perform in this format, it will be easy to write the task statements.

Common specifications exist for writing task statements. For example, one specification is that task statements are written to describe observable and measurable actions. When the tasks are action-oriented, action verbs are used. Task statements are written in the first person singular, present tense. By keeping task statements in a consistent format, it is possible to ensure that differences in task descriptions reflect differences in tasks rather than differences in job analysts.

8.4.2 Develop criteria

The second step in test development is developing the criteria, or the evaluative standards. These are the standards that you will eventually use to evaluate the validity of the test, or how well the test does what it is supposed to do. Criteria are developed based on information obtained during the job analysis. Inexperienced test developers sometimes develop criteria at the end of the test development process, rather than at the beginning of the development phase. However, the criteria should be chosen for their relevance and importance rather than for the ease of collecting them.

Figure 8.3 provides guidelines for evaluating criteria.

Examining the issue of reliability requires some knowledge of statistics. While it is not necessary to be a statistician or psychometrician, it is useful to have a basic understanding of correlations.

8.4.3 Design the validation approach

The next step is to design the validation approach. There are several common validation strategies. These include content validation, criterion-related validation, and construct validation. Criterion-related validation has two subcategories, predictive and concurrent. The most

Format			
What is being done?	To what is it being done?	How is it being done?	Why is it being done?

Figure 8.2 Format for writing task statements.

> **Relevant:** Criteria should be related to the job. This means *to important aspects of the job*, not chosen simply for ease or convenience in collection.
>
> **Sensitive:** Criteria should be able to be measured in a way that differentiates between effective and ineffective performance.
>
> **Reliable:** Reliable in a psychometric sense. (See Nunnally, 1967, for a discussion of reliability.)
>
> **Practical:** The collection of the criterion measure(s) must be able to be accomplished in a manner that does not unduly interfere with the organization, or be so costly as to present an unreasonable expense.
>
> **Free from Contamination:** Criteria are biased when they are contaminated or when they measure things that are not relevant to job performance.

Figure 8.3   Evaluating criteria.

commonly used validation approaches are content and concurrent criterion-related. Each approach will be discussed briefly.

A *content validation* approach entails showing that the content of the test is directly linked to the job. In a content validation approach, the content of the job is identified through a job analysis. The test is then constructed based on the content of the job. Identifying the relationship between the job and the test gives an indication of the content validity of the test. Because content validation is very similar to developing a training course, it is generally the best approach for trainers to use.

The relationship between a test and a criterion measure is determined with a *criterion-related validation* approach. This involves determining the statistical relationship between the test and the criterion measures. The two criterion-related approaches, predictive and concurrent, refer to the temporal relationship between the collection of the predictor and criterion measures. In a concurrent approach, the predictor and criterion measures are collected at about the same time. An example of a concurrent approach is giving current employees a test, and at the same time collecting data about their job performance, such as the number of widgets that they produce. The test results are correlated with the job performance measure to assess the validity of the test. In a predictive approach, the predictor measure is collected first, and then at a later point in time the criterion measure is collected. An example of a predictive approach is having trainees take a postcourse test and then at a later time—for example, a year later—collecting job performance data. The test results are correlated with the job performance measure to assess the validity of the test. While there are theoretical differences between the two approaches, and many test development professionals prefer a predictive validation approach when feasible, the primary difference between the two approaches is the time between collecting test scores and the job performance measures.

In a *construct validation* approach, the relationship between the test and some psychological construct is examined. This approach is not often used in industry because it is less practical than the other approaches. For a construct approach, it is usually necessary to conduct a content validity study and several criterion-related studies. The criterion validity studies are performed to determine the relationship between the construct and variables that should be related to the construct and to determine that the construct is not related to variables that should not be related to the construct.

Let's examine how we might validate an intelligence test to illustrate construct validity. We first recognize that intelligence is a psychological construct; it is not something tangible that we can measure directly. To develop the test, we identify characteristics that appear to be related to intelligence (the job analysis). We then determine the relationship between the test and the characteristics that we determined are related to intelligence (content validation). Finally, and this is really an ongoing process, we determine the statistical relationship between our intelligence test and variables that should be related to intelligence (criterion-related validity), such as analytical ability, and between our test and variables that should not be strongly related to intelligence, such as manual dexterity. We expect that our test is strongly related to analytical ability, but not strongly related to manual dexterity. If we find the relationships that we expect, we have demonstrated evidence of the construct validity of the test.

In addition to the traditional validation approaches just discussed, there is an alternative approach that is gaining in popularity, validity generalization.

Validity generalization is based on research that indicates that test validities are not specific to an organization, or often even to a job, but rather are often transportable or generalizable across different jobs and organizations. Throughout the history of test development, the best thinking has been that test validities are specific to a particular job in a particular organization. Recent meta-analytic studies have shown that this traditional approach to situationally specific validities resulted from flawed validity studies utilizing small sample sizes (see, for example, Schmidt & Hunter, 1977). Meta-analysis is a method of calculating an average validity coefficient from many validity studies. An advantage of validity generalization for test developers is that tests validated in one company can be used in another company as long as the jobs in the two companies can be shown to be relatively similar. This showing of similarity is based on the job analyses, and is similar to a content validity study.

As mentioned above, for most trainers, the best approach to validating a test is to utilize a content validity approach. This is a fairly straightforward approach, and the one closest to the approach trainers use to develop courses. In addition, no special statistical knowledge is required for a content validity approach, unlike other approaches.

8.4.4 Develop the test

The next step is to develop the test. Before the test can be developed, however, a decision must be made about the best type of test to use. While there are many different types of tests and different taxonomies for categorizing tests, we will limit our discussion to three common formats, multiple-choice, essay, and performance, and two types of content, job knowledge tests and aptitude tests. It is preferable to first choose the type content and then choose the type of test question.

Job knowledge tests by definition test the knowledge required to perform the job. A typical example is testing technicians about a method of installing or repairing computer hardware. Job knowledge tests are generally the most appropriate type of test for trainers to develop because they are directly related to training material.

As the name implies, *aptitude tests* are designed to determine if someone has the aptitude to perform the job or, in some cases, the aptitude to learn material that is necessary to pass a course. Because they evaluate aptitude rather than course knowledge, aptitude tests are generally not appropriate for an after-course test, although they may be appropriate for screening a group of applicants prior to taking a course. There are some questions that should be asked before deciding to use an aptitude test as a screening device, including the following:

1. Are there a large number of people who *cannot* learn the course material?
2. Is the time to learn the course material to a specified proficiency level a serious concern?

If the answer to these questions is yes, an aptitude test may be appropriate to prescreen people for a course.

Be aware, however, that the use of an aptitude test for current employees may cause unanticipated problems. Because of their nature, it is often difficult to study for an aptitude test. Current employees who are not allowed to take a course, especially one that may lead to a promotion or better assignment, may be resentful if they believe that they can do the job but are not allowed to because they have not passed a prescreening aptitude test. There may be additional legal considerations if an employee in a provisional title is performing well, but cannot become permanent because he or she does not pass an aptitude test.

The type of test items is determined by the format, the types of information or knowledge that you are trying to assess, and practical issues. For example, if you are interested in assessing how well someone performs a skill, then a performance test is an obvious choice.

When we think of tests, *multiple-choice tests* immediately come to mind. Multiple-choice tests are by far the most common type of test, probably because they are relatively easy and inexpensive to develop. Multiple-choice test questions also lend themselves to objective scoring. While they will not be discussed in this chapter, *fill-in* and *matching test* questions are also relatively easy and inexpensive to develop.

Figure 8.4 presents some basics about writing multiple-choice test questions.

Several common mistakes made by inexperienced test writers when writing test questions are as follows:

- The correct response is either the longest or the shortest answer.
- Distractors do not logically or grammatically follow from the stem.
- The correct answer and the distractors are written in different jargon or technical terms.

Inexperienced test writers often introduce a "response bias." In this case, the correct answers are mostly the same choice; for example, choice "c" is the correct choice more of the time than would be expect-

---

Three parts: Stem, correct answer, and distractors.

The **stem** can be written as a question or as an incomplete sentence.

- Provide sufficient information to convey the central point of the question, but not telegraph the correct answer.
- Questions should be independent. One question should not provide the answer to another question.
- Questions should be clearly written, not mean to confuse.
- Negatives should generally be avoided. If they are used, negatives should be highlighted so they are not misunderstood.

The **correct answer** should be clear and unambiguous.

The correct answer should be indistinguishable from the distractors except for content, e.g. some length and grammar.

The **distractors** should be common misconceptions of the correct answer and indistinguishable from the correct answer except for the content of the answer.

Figure 8.4 Writing multiple-choice test questions.

ed to occur by chance. As a corollary, inexperienced test writers often avoid making the first and last choices the correct response because they think that the choice is more obvious when it is first or last. If the distractors are properly written, the correct answer can appear in any position and not be more likely to be chosen.

Another common error in writing distractors is using the same concept and wording it in two slightly different ways. If the person taking the test can determine that the concepts are the same, he or she can immediately eliminate two alternatives.

For the same reason, "all of the above" is generally not recommended. If the test taker can determine that two of the responses are correct the answer is determined, and other distractors serve no purpose. Also, if the test taker can determine that one or more of the answers is incorrect then "all of the above" can be eliminated as a possibility.

"None of the above" is also generally not recommended. If a test taker recognizes a possible correct answer he or she will tend to avoid this distractor, thereby rendering it less useful than other possible distractors. An exception to the general rule of avoiding "none of the above" is when the question requires computation, because the test taker may try each alternative. Because errors in computation can be made, leading the test taker to reject the correct response, "none of the above" can be a good distractor. For obvious reasons, "all of the above" should never be used for computational questions.

Essay tests can be very useful if you are attempting to evaluate whether the test takers have conceptual understanding of the material. They are also useful if you are trying to assess written communication skills. Be warned, though, that scoring essay questions can be a problem. What you will have to do is develop and document a large set of possible answers and also develop and document a consistent scoring method for each variation of response, and for each variable that you want to score.

Performance tests, as their name implies, are designed to assess actual performance. In some instances this is the sole interest. For example, if you want to assess whether hardware technicians can install a new hard drive, the best method is to have them install a hard drive as the test. Performance tests, though, are often more difficult to score than multiple-choice tests. For example, how do you score a technician who correctly installs a serial interface board, but forgets to select the COM port? The board is correctly installed, but it does not work. Is partial credit given? How much? What about a repair technician who fixes a problem accidentally? These issues and the scoring method need to be addressed logically and consistently, and documented accordingly. When they are properly developed, performance tests can be excellent, and well worth the time and effort spent in their development, because you can be fairly certain that you are assessing actual job performance.

8.4.5 Perform an item analysis

While performing an item analysis is an important step, a complete discussion of item analysis and reliability is beyond the scope of this chapter. Anastasi (1988) presents an excellent overview of item analysis.

Whenever possible, an item analysis should be performed. An item analysis is a systematic examination of the psychometric characteristics of the test and test items. There are several reasons to perform an item analysis. According to classical test theory, all the test questions should come from the same domain. This implies that the test questions should be related to one another and to the total test score. Calculating the internal consistency of a test tells us how the items are related.

An item analysis can quickly tell us some important information about a test: Are the test questions good? How difficult are the questions? Is there sufficient variability in responses so that the questions are useful? You might, for example, find that a test question is not answered correctly by people who do the best on the test. This test question may be miscoded, with an incorrect answer coded as the correct answer, so that people who do poorly on the test get the test question correct more often than people who score higher on the test. Test questions can be confusing; this can also lead to incorrect answers being given often because the questions are misunderstood. Test questions that are too difficult, are too easy, or have very little variance should generally be avoided. An item analysis will provide these data about the test questions.

8.4.6 Validate the test

This step involves carrying out the validation procedure determined earlier: content validation, criterion-related validation, or construct validation. As part of the content validation strategy, you should confirm that the test is related to the criteria that you developed. This is the feedback loop from the test validation to the criteria you originally developed.

8.5 Additional Issues

In addition to following the test validation model, there are several additional issues with which you should be familiar. These issues are the documentation requirements, determination of the passing score, test administration, test security, evidence of discrimination, fairness, and the search for alternatives.

8.5.1 Documentation

The test development effort must be documented so that the test administrator knows how to administer and score the test. Test development also has to be documented in case any legal proceedings arise. As discussed above, recreating the test development effort years later is an almost impossible task.

Because one of the reasons for documenting the test is possible review by the Equal Employment Opportunity Commission, documentation should be consistent with the requirements specified in the Uniform Guidelines. An outline of these reporting guidelines can be found in Cascio (1987).

8.5.2 Passing score determination

While it appears to be very simple, determining the passing score can actually be one of the more difficult things to do. Passing scores can be arbitrarily set at some level, for example, 65 percent correct, in which case it is easy to set a passing score. But this may not be a useful passing score. The test developer needs to ask, "Will many people pass or fail at an arbitrary passing score simply because the questions were written to be either hard or easy?" Passing scores can be set at a specific criterion performance level, such as minimally acceptable job performance, or they can be set at an estimated level of satisfactory performance. Two commonly used methods of setting the passing score can be found in Angoff (1971) and Ebel (1972).

8.5.3 Test administration

The individuals who are responsible for administering the test need to be trained in the proper procedure. The test procedure should be documented in the administrator's manual. Special conditions, such as time limits for test sections, and any equipment needed to take the test are to be documented in the administrator's manual.

8.5.4 Test security

Test security is an important issue for several reasons. First, it does not make any sense to go to the trouble of developing a test and then allow everyone that is interested to obtain a copy of that test. Also, if there is a differential passing rate between groups, and it can be shown that one of the groups had access to the test as a result of your negligent actions or lack of action, it may be to your detriment in court.

8.5.5 Evidence of discrimination

First, it should be made clear that it is not illegal to discriminate. In fact, all tests are developed to discriminate between acceptable and unacceptable levels of knowledge or performance. What is potentially illegal is for a test to discriminate based on subgroups, including race, color, religion, sex, and national origin. The definition of illegal discrimination used most often is the one stated in the Uniform Guidelines.

According to the Uniform Guidelines, discrimination is defined as adverse impact, as measured by the four-fifths rule. The four-fifths rule states that the passing rate of the minority group must be at least four-fifths the passing rate of the majority group. If the passing rate is less than four-fifths, it is taken as prima facie proof that the test is discriminatory. The defense to a showing of adverse impact is to demonstrate that the test is job-related and valid. Job relatedness is also referred to as bona fide occupational qualifications (BFOQs). So, while it is preferable to have a test without adverse impact, showing that the test is properly developed and valid for its intended use can be a reasonable defense. It is also important to note that many good tests that are currently in use do not pass the four-fifths rule. Simply failing the four-fifths rule is not a reason to avoid using the test, but it does raise a red flag. You had better be certain that the test is properly developed and validated, and that the documentation is complete.

8.5.6 Fairness

When a criterion-related validity approach is used, both the Uniform Guidelines and professional standards recommend that tests be investigated for evidence of unfairness. The issue of test fairness concerns whether or not different subgroups perform differently on a test. A problem exists if the difference in test performance is not associated with different levels of job performance. For example, a racial subgroup may perform worse than another subgroup on a test, but perform as well on the job. From a legal perspective, the subgroups that must be investigated are racial, ethnic, and gender. When a criterion-related approach is used, and especially when there is a large sample, the readers should refer to a source on determining test fairness (see, for example, Peterson & Novick, 1976). It should be noted that while the Uniform Guidelines require an evaluation of the fairness of tests, the professional community is in general agreement that there is very little evidence that cognitive tests are unfair to different subgroups (see, for example, the Principles).

8.5.7 Search for alternatives

The Uniform Guidelines state that when a test has been found to have adverse impact, it is necessary to search for alternative tests that may have equivalent validity and less adverse impact.

8.6 Summary

Although this may surprise you, the purpose of this chapter was not to discourage you from using after-course tests to evaluate your trainees. Rather, our purpose was to share a structured approach to developing and validating legally defensible tests. The purpose of pointing out areas where mistakes can cost you dearly was designed to make you aware that tests must be properly developed and validated, and supported by properly written documentation.

8.7 References

Anastasi, Anne, *Psychological Testing*, 6th ed., New York: Macmillan, 1988.

Angoff, W. H., "Scales, Norms and Equivalent Scores," in R. L. Thorndike (Ed.), *Educational Measurement*, 2d ed., Washington, D.C.: American Council on Education, 1971.

Cascio, Wayne F., *Applied Psychology in Personnel Management*, 3d ed., Englewood Cliffs, N.J., Prentice-Hall, 1987.

Ebel, R. L., *Essentials of Educational Measurement*, Englewood Cliffs, N.J., Prentice-Hall, 1972.

Gael, Sidney, *The Job Analysis Handbook for Business, Industry, and Government*, New York: John Wiley & Sons, 1988.

Peterson, N. S., and M. R. Novick, "An Evaluation of Some Models for Culture-Fair Selection," *Journal of Educational Measurement*, 13: 3–39, 1976.

Principles for the Validation and Use of Personnel Selection Procedures, Society for Industrial and Organizational Psychology, a division of the American Psychological Association, 1987.

Sample, John S., "Liability and the Technical Trainer: An Overview of Issues and Prevention Strategies," in Leslie Kelly (Ed.), *The ASTD Technical and Skills Training Handbook*, New York: McGraw-Hill, 1995.

Schmidt, F. L., and J. E. Hunter, "Development of a General Solution to the Problem of Validity Generalization," *Journal of Applied Psychology*, 62: 529–540, 1977.

Standards for Educational and Psychological Testing, American Educational Research Association, American Psychological Association, National Council on Measurement in Education, 1985.

Uniform Guidelines on Employee Selection Procedures, 29 C.F.R. 1607.1, et seq.

Chapter 9

On-the-Job Learning: A Look at the Papermaking Industry

P. J. Marsh

P. J. Marsh is the principal of P. J. Marsh and Associates. Before starting this service in 1982, he spent 18 years with Fortune 500 companies: He was Manager of Human Resource Development and Productivity Improvement, Northern Telecom INS Group; Director of Human Resource, Harris Corporation Semiconductor Sector; and Director of Organization Development, NL Industries.

He graduated from George Washington University with an M.A. degree in Personnel Management, and from the University of Colorado with a B.A. degree in English Literature. He completed an Internship for Specialists in Organization Development with the NTL Institute for Applied Behavioral Science, and has published articles on skills training and management and organization development.

9.1 Introduction

On-the-job learning (OJL) is an approach to on-the-job training (OJT) that emphasizes learning and performance rather than training. The approach is learner-based and learner-paced; the learner "partners" with the trainer during the learning and training process. The approach corrects the deficiencies often associated with unstructured OJT. It uses our knowledge about learning, and especially adult learning, to help the trainee more quickly attain skill mastery and desired performance levels. Because OJT usually cannot adequately convey complex cognitive materials, OJL supplements it with performance-based off-the-job training sessions. (I first compared and contrasted traditional, unplanned OJT with OJL from the perspective of learning principles in "On-the-Job Learning," *Technical and Skills Training,* August/September 1994).

This chapter first describes papermaking. It then presents three case studies in which OJL was used to modify unstructured OJT. Each case involves a manufacturing operation that had performance problems. Two of the cases take place in paper-making mills, and one takes place in an envelope manufacturing company. Each operation had depended on unstructured OJT for operator training until senior management concluded that inadequate training had become a major factor in unacceptable performance.

The cases describe the changes which were made in the way training was conducted and the results of the changes. After the changes, most training was still conducted on the job, but it was planned, uniform, and conducted by trainers who had learned how adults learn and how to use prepared OJT materials. The OJT was supplemented by off-the-job training. In each case, OJL helped improve performance to an acceptable level.

The chapter summarizes six OJT deficiencies which appeared in the cases and then describes seven characteristics of effective OJL. These "building blocks" can be used to fashion effective on-the-job learning and to improve operating results in any organization.

9.2 Papermaking

Paper mills convert wood pulp into paper. The stock preparation function in a paper mill mixes the wood pulp with water, starch, and other additives to prepare it for delivery to paper-making machines. Stock preparation operators have traditionally progressed through five jobs, bailer room operator, additive room helper, additive room operator, control room operator, and assistant head stock operator, to reach the senior classification, head stock operator.

The paper machines in these cases are huge. They are two stories high, as wide as a two-lane highway, and as long as a football field. Wood pulp is formed on these machines, dried, and rolled into a reel of paper. Another huge machine, a rewinder, unrolls the reel and rewinds it at speeds of up to 60 miles per hour into a roll that may weigh up to 27 tons. As the paper is rewound, it is cut into designated widths. Paper machine operators usually progress through five jobs, seventh hand, sixth hand, fourth hand, winder operator, and back tender, to reach the senior classification, machine tender.

Because of their size and complexity, paper machines represent huge investments. They are operated by four shift crews which keep them running 24 hours a day, 7 days a week, all year long to maintain profitability. The best machine operators keep the machines running, and producing acceptable-quality paper, without interruption.

In both the paper mills we discuss here, the senior paper machine operators had traditionally set up the machine in accordance with their own individual preferences. At shift change, the new operator changed the operating parameters from the previous setup to his or her own. When problems occurred, the operator who had set up the machine was the only operator who knew the parameters. Troubleshooting was an almost impossible task.

Operator training in most mills and "secondary industries" like envelope and container-making companies is still conducted on the job, as it traditionally has been. Each new operator learns from an experienced operator, often his or her immediate predecessor, who has already moved up to a higher classification. This means that each operator has a different instructor. Each instructor has different ideas about how the job should be performed, and often these ideas are inconsistent with desirable practices.

9.3 Paper Mill South: Developing Training Checklists

Paper Mill South makes linerboard on three paper machines. Linerboard is a heavy brown paper used for six-pack cartons, pizza boxes, and other types of packages. In February 1989, the division vice president responsible for Paper Mill South expressed concern that operating results on paper machine number one showed a twelve-month trend toward decreased machine utilization, increased scrap, and decreased productivity.

The discussion soon focused on operator errors, a perceived lack of operator know-how, and the fact that operator training had received little management attention. Mill managers agreed to assign a respected supervisor, Bruce, who had an engineering degree, and Dave, the mill's most respected foreman, to the task of designing and conducting an operator training program.

In March, Bruce began developing materials for classroom training sessions. The materials he developed reflected his engineering orientation; he focused on how the systems and machine components work. After he had developed many of the materials and shifted his attention to classroom delivery, he asked for assistance from an outside consultant.

The consultant recommended a training needs analysis before any more work was done on materials preparation. The recommendation was accepted, and the analysis began with interviews of hourly operators and supervisors. The objective was to determine their perspective on operating problems and training needs, and to build interest in and commitment to the process. The interview data showed that OJT was essential to operations but was currently seen as ineffective. They also showed that operators had concerns about the scheduled classroom training. They saw it as potentially difficult to understand, boring, and impractical. The interviews strongly suggested that OJT needed to be changed and that classroom training must be practical and interesting, and must be linked directly to the operators' jobs and OJT.

When Dave assumed his new role as training coordinator, development of OJT materials began. Dave worked with the consultant in conducting a task analysis for each of the stock preparation and paper machine jobs, starting with the lowest-level job in each line of progression.

Next, work instructions, called learning/training (L/T) checklists, were written for each job. As they were drafted, they were reviewed with as many operators as practical. A semiformal review process was followed for senior operator checklists (winder operator, back tender, and machine tender). An appointed scribe took notes of the meeting. The review meeting's objective was to hear from each operator to ensure that each had a chance to improve the checklist before its approval and adoption.

As Dave talked with machine tenders, he realized that many of them were producing excessive scrap when changing from one paper grade to another. He developed an arithmetical formula to use as a guide in adjusting machine speed to paper weight when changing grades and had it printed and laminated in plastic. This formula became a very useful job aid for senior operators, eventually contributing to a significant scrap reduction.

Learning/training checklists for the lower-level jobs were two pages long. The checklist for the machine tender was 35 pages long and referred to a six-page job aid. These checklists described the agreed-upon most desirable way of performing the job's tasks.

As materials to improve OJT were developed, Dave helped reshape classroom training materials. In the perspective adopted after the needs analysis, classroom training became a supplement to OJT rather than stand-alone training. Materials were revised to reflect an operator's orientation, not a machine and systems orientation. The new approach focused on the operator's actions and reactions and deemphasized engineering. Both OJT and classroom materials were written in a simple, operator-friendly style. When there was a choice between an engineering term or an operator term for a part or process, the operator term was used.

As materials were developed, operators discussed them, and excitement about learning grew. Bruce and Dave conceived of a practical "learning center" near the production area where operators could discuss problems and review checklists away from the noise and hazards of the production floor. They converted an 18-square-foot storage area into this learning center by installing bookshelves, tables and chairs, an overhead projector with a screen, a TV monitor and VCR, a small refrigerator and coffee urn, easels, and pads. Copies of checklists, classroom reference materials, and job aids were placed there for ready reference.

In May, Bruce and Dave began conducting two-hour classroom sessions using visual aids and handouts. Sessions started with a brief discussion of objectives and how the content could be used on the job. Both Dave and Bruce worked hard to encourage questions and solicit answers from the groups of operators. Dave reflected, "We had to show that we were just as vulnerable to making a mistake as anyone in that room so that they'd feel free to speak up." The sessions were so well received that operators from all jobs began asking to attend all sessions. After a brief period of euphoria, in which open attendance was encouraged, the instructors tightened up on attendance. They found that participants to whom sessions didn't apply lost interest quickly and became a distraction to learning.

The use of checklists to conduct OJT, however, stalled. The intention was that operators who helped write and review checklists would use them to conduct training. Operators, though, continued training the same way as always, without checklists. As one operator put it, "I just don't know what to do with it." Dave realized that operator/trainers needed to learn how to use checklists for OJT and that they also needed to learn how people learn. He and Bruce decided that a workshop for trainers was needed.

The foundation for the workshop was a visual aid called the On-the-Job Training Cycle (see Fig. 9.1). It positions the trainee as the focal point of the training process. Checking with the trainee after each step for responses that can be reinforced or corrected is essential. Closure assures that the trainee can perform the job safely and competently and can meet all of the quality standards. The train-the-trainer workshop presented "Training Dos and Don'ts," practices that trainers should follow or avoid during training. Participants critiqued a trainer exhibiting desirable and undesirable training practices.

The workshop also introduced all operators to a self-paced orientation and initial training module that the mill had developed for new

Preparation
- ▼ Review the checklist for the job.
- ▼ Prepare for each step in the cycle.

Check: What do trainees already know about the job?

Information Presentation
- ▼ Put trainees at ease.
- ▼ Involve them with the learning checklists.
- ▼ Show and tell with "digestible bites."
- ▼ Stress and repeat safety and quality points.

Check: Verbal and nonverbal clues. Do they understand?

Demonstration
- ▼ Make sure trainees can see.
- ▼ Think out loud.

Check: Verbal and nonverbal clues. Do they understand?

Practice
- ▼ Guide and prompt, but let trainees do it.
- ▼ Ask them to show and tell you now.
- ▼ Correct them before they get into trouble.
- ▼ Reinforce correct responses with feedback.

Closure
- ▼ Check performance with the checklists.
- ▼ Reinforce the learning with feedback.
- ▼ Identify areas requiring more practice.

Figure 9.1 The on-the-job training cycle.

winder crew members (seventh and sixth hands). This interactive videotape module illustrated how the five winder crew members work as a team to convert paper from reels to cut rolls of paper ready for shipment to customers. Trainees stop the tape and complete exercises asking them to describe the action they take at specific stages as the reel of paper is rewound into a shippable roll.

Despite the increased comfort that most operators felt after their train-the-trainer workshop, some continued to train in the old way, teaching their own eccentricities without the structure of L/T checklists. The mill superintendent asked supervisors to ensure that no training was conducted without checklists and issued a memorandum that specified the use of checklists. The memorandum stated that checklists were to be

- Given to trainees at the outset of OJT to focus their attention and reduce confusion.
- Reviewed by foremen with operator/trainers to assure that the trainers were ready to conduct training.
- Used by operator/trainers to show trainees how to do the job. (Training conducted with checklists would be the only approved method of OJT.)
- Used by foremen to determine if trainees were qualified or if they needed more training. (When the union president was asked how he felt about the training program, he said, "I wasn't too excited when I first heard about it, but it's been good; it has really helped.")

Dave, who had progressed through every paper machine job over a 25-year career, and who had previously trained machine tenders without checklists, used the machine tender checklist to continue conducting individual coaching for this critical job.

9.3.1 Results

In September 1991, 18 months after training began, the effects of training were evaluated for the number one paper machine. Machine utilization had improved by 8.5 percent, and productivity, as measured by tons of paper shipped to customers, had also improved. These improvements took place while the time required to qualify operators as machine tenders was halved.

The changes in operator training were made concurrently with efforts to improve other operational aspects of the paper mill under a total quality management program. The TQM effort culminated in application for ISO 9000 certification in the spring of 1992. During preparation for certification, managers and operators realized the contribution that OJL played in the new uniformity of the paper-making process and the quality of paper shipped. ISO 9000 required additional procedures specifying how training was documented and how training records were kept. Consequently, a filing system for master copies of all L/T checklists was initiated. Both supervisors and trainers were required to sign off when they considered new trainees qualified for the job.

The 24-hour-a-day, 7-day-a-week nature of the paper mill operation made it difficult to reach consensus on the changes. Differences in the ways shifts conducted training still remained in April 1992. After searching for ways of ensuring consistency between shifts, the mill manager and his staff settled on the use of foreman expectation checklists.

All foremen were interviewed to determine what they told new or recently transferred employees. Some of the questions focused on work policies, such as attendance, on-time reporting, and sick time. Others probed orientation and training practices. Significant differences were discovered in the foremen's expectations of operators. Interviews revealed that the average length of time required to reach performance standards varied more because of differences in foreman expectations than because of differences in trainee abilities. Interview results were assembled by category (e.g., attendance, reporting on time, etc.) in preparation for a rare meeting with all foremen. At that session, agreement was reached on appropriate expectations in each category and on options for discussing these expectations with operators. Agreements were summarized in foreman expectation checklists. These tools have further helped standardize job and shift orientations as well as training and work habits.

9.4 Paper Mill North: Hourly Workers Develop and Deliver Training

Paper Mill North makes high-quality printing and copying paper in 15 colors on two paper machines. The stock preparation additive room is particularly important to this operation because the chemicals that produce good printing and reprographic qualities and the dyes to produce colored paper are added here. In April 1993, paper mill management was concerned about operating results. Machine utilization and productivity were among the lowest in the corporation. Operating results were inconsistent, and the mill frequently exceeded its operating budget. Discussion centered on both equipment problems and operator errors that were being made throughout the operation.

The relationship between the union hourly group and the nonunion salaried group was strained because of a prolonged union-management contract negotiation and strike in the late 1980s. There was also resentment between groups of hourly paid workers remaining from the strike. The mill management team had changed almost yearly in the five years since the strike, intensifying the lack of trust.

About a year before the contract dispute, a classroom training program had been inaugurated. Reactions to its usefulness were mixed. Some senior operators resented it, believing that it undermined their positions as key employees. These operators believed that they should have complete responsibility for training and that the management team shouldn't interfere with training. Because of the hostility and differing views about how training should be conducted, OJT had not been conducted as effectively since the strike as it had traditionally been. The inadequacy of training made it difficult for managers to deal with errors. Managers could not be sure if operators were making mistakes deliberately, because of carelessness, or because they didn't know how to do the job. If they honestly didn't know how to perform their jobs because they hadn't had the chance to learn, disciplinary action would make the already tense situation worse.

Informal discussions between supervisors and hourly workers revealed resistance by hourly workers to outside consultant assistance with training in the mill. They also disclosed mixed reactions to senior operators' views on training and widespread dissatisfaction with the status quo. Because the situation was so volatile, the mill manager wanted to approach training carefully and to emphasize the importance of employee commitment at each step in the program. He suggested that the program begin in stock preparation because resistance to outside assistance was lower there than on the paper machines. Managers believed that a successful program in stock preparation would lessen resistance on the machines.

The mill management team believed that involving hourly workers in all stock preparation classifications on all shifts was essential to give the program credibility. Managers realized that they were attempting to do more than improve training. They sought to use OJL, combined with an employee involvement strategy, to boost organization effectiveness. The mill superintendent asked operators who appeared interested in learning and training to participate in a training development group. The group's stated purpose was to help guide the development of a training program and to communicate progress to hourly workers. Operators from all classifications responded, and the group was formed.

To begin the improvement process, a consultant interviewed all of the hourly workers in stock preparation. Interviews focused on what previous training had worked well, what hadn't worked so well, what changes were needed, and what performance needs should be addressed first, next, and so on. Workers offered their opinions freely, and several said that they were glad their opinions were asked. Interview results showed that senior operators saw junior operators as uninterested in learning and wanting to "slide by." Junior operators saw senior operators as unwilling to share their knowledge, impatient, and often hostile. Senior operators believed that they needed no training but stated that younger operators needed it badly. Both groups said that some operators in all classifications needed to know how the stock preparation systems worked, said that management had appeared indifferent to training, and said that the classroom training sessions had been too long and had presented unnecessary information.

The consultant shared and discussed interview results with the training development group in a two-hour meeting. In an environment that became more positive as the meeting progressed, he suggested that they use an improvement approach which structured OJT and supplemented it with off-the-job training when needed. The approach gave most of the responsibility for training to operators. Group members stated that they wanted to try it and spent the last half of the meeting prioritizing training needs and discussing next steps. A high-classification group member, an assistant head stock operator who had helped develop and present the previous training, was asked to partner with the consultant in this approach.

A few operators volunteered to write task lists for their own jobs and list the steps performed to complete each task. Stock preparation checklists in this mill were different from those in Paper Mill South because the mill produced such different paper. Operators in the lowest stock preparation classification, bailer room operator, listed 17 different tasks containing from 7 to 20 steps. Additive room operators listed 23 tasks. One task contained 64 steps that had to be performed strictly in sequence. If the sequence was not strictly followed, scrap paper resulted. Each successively higher job classification tended to have more tasks with more steps. Control room operators listed 35 tasks, each containing from 5 to 70 steps.

As checklists were developed, they were reviewed and discussed by one of two methods. The first was the semiformal review process used in Paper Mill South. In the second, the head stock operator on each of the four crews was asked to distribute the task guidelines and discuss them with his crew. During this process, the mill's most senior head stock operator, John, began criticizing the entire training program. A discussion with John revealed that he was angry and hurt that he hadn't been asked to participate in the training development group. The paper mill superintendent quickly realized that this had been an error that could jeopardize the program. He apologized and invited John to participate.

Supervisors and operators recognized checklists as tools for reducing daily operator errors. So instead of waiting until all materials were completed to begin training, some checklists were introduced on the floor immediately after they were reviewed and approved. The operator who developed the list used it to review the tasks with a junior operator. This tested the operator's comfort in using the checklist and the checklist's effectiveness as a training tool.

The consultant observed several of these review sessions and noted practices which blocked learning. Frequently the trainer's explanation was too fast to follow and couldn't be heard above the noise on the floor. Occasionally the trainer unintentionally hid the material he was trying to demonstrate. Often trainers showed impatience with trainees.

Production demands and hunting season made scheduling a train-the-trainers workshop for four trainers impossible. So the consultant individually coached OJT trainers to help them unlearn habits which blocked learning and learn behaviors which facilitated learning.

The 22 stock preparation systems required special attention. The training group suggested that John, the head stock operator, conduct field trips to familiarize operators with the systems and explain how they work. At first the tours were well received, but complaints showed limitations. People on the trips complained of forgetting what they had learned. Neither John nor the trainees were sure that necessary learning was occurring. Improvements in the learning process were obviously needed.

The training group considered John to be *the* subject matter expert on stock preparation systems. When asked, "What do new operators in each classification have to know about each system to do the job?" and "How will you know when they know each system?" John responded with specific answers. He described what operators needed to know and how they could demonstrate that they knew it. For example, additive room operators must be able to show where the hardwood system begins, where it ends, what pumps move the material, how the pumps can be bypassed, and the location of the valves the computerized controllers manipulate.

These descriptions were the foundation for learning objectives that were written for the field trip on each system. The ability to complete statements about systems and equipment became the criterion for demonstrating the ability to use them. To further facilitate learning, John learned to use a computer and used it to draw diagrams that enabled interested trainees to take their own follow-up field trips.

Improving training required dealing with the hourly workers' perceptions. It was essential to change their perception of management's indifference to training, junior operators' indifference to learning, and senior operators' indifference to helping. Learning contracts were introduced to make the changes. Before OJT began, the department supervisor held structured discussions with trainers and operators. He stated his expectations of both trainer and trainee and asked each to tell the other what he or she hoped for and what each was willing to give in order to get the help. This discussion produced an explicit, unwritten learning contract between trainer and trainee. The contract affirmed the trainees' responsibility for their own learning. It also affirmed that they could expect sincere help from their trainers. At the conclusion of the contract meeting, trainers gave trainees copies of learning/training checklists and tips for learning.

The training development group met for a year to monitor progress, to modify priorities, and to discuss emerging needs. The group finally disbanded after operational improvements were linked to the training intervention.

Success in stock preparation diminished resistance to change on the paper machines enough so that a back tender and third hand from each of the paper machines volunteered to work as training development partners with the consultant. These four worked to develop checklists for five jobs on each machine. They identified the need for off-the-job training on these topics: the steam system (the system which dries the wood pulp after it has been formed), threading the paper machine, adjusting the draws (mechanisms which tighten and loosen the sheet of paper on the machine), and the calender stacks (the last mechanism, which affects the paper's surface qualities). As this chapter is being written, the training development partners are in a workshop and learning to develop and present off-the-job training. Stock preparation trainers are learning to use a procedure that officially certifies operators.

9.4.1 Results

By January 1994, the paper mill superintendent reported that hourly workers in stock preparation showed increased interest in process improvement and increased cooperation. He said they had "assumed responsibility for the training system and are developing materials, training on and off the job, and evaluating results."

9.5 Envelope Co.: Machine Adjuster's Methods Reverse Plant Results

Envelope Co. is a secondary processor in the paper industry. The company makes envelopes to customer specifications 24 hours a day, 6 days a week in plants in the South, the West Coast, the Midwest, and the East Coast. In each plant, machines are set up to run specific envelopes until the order has been completed. The machine is then changed over and set up to make another envelope. Some machines make 25 different types of envelopes. Each different envelope requires a changeover and a new setup. The number of changeovers made in a day depends on customer orders; sometimes a machine is changed over and set up twice in the same day. Two people, an operator and a machine adjuster, tend each machine. The operator keeps the envelopes flowing (up to 1,000 per minute) and packs them in boxes. The adjuster sets up the machine and troubleshoots it when problems occur.

Operators are hired off the street and are immediately teamed with an old hand for OJT. New operators have usually learned the job and begun performing to standard in a week. Machine adjusters are promoted from the operator job. When they are promoted, they are familiar with the machine and how it makes envelopes. They don't know the major tasks of setup, changeover, and troubleshooting or the less difficult routine tasks. Sometimes an operator from one machine is promoted to the adjuster's job on another. Adjusters have also traditionally learned their jobs through OJT. The adjuster they replaced has usually worked with them for two or three weeks, and then they sank or swam.

Adjusters are expected to eventually be able to adjust all machines in the plant. Plants have up to seven different types of machines. The newer machines are more complex, faster, and potentially more profitable than older machines. When they aren't running, they are far less profitable because they are so expensive.

Operating results at Envelope Co.'s West Coast plant were below standard on two types of newer machines. The plant manager had concluded that inadequate training was a part of the problem, contributing to excessive changeover and downtime. In December 1992, he assigned his best adjuster, Gil, to train all new adjusters and to retrain incumbent adjusters on the two fastest machines. A training consultant was brought in as project manager. The project had two primary objectives: to develop structured training materials, and to train Gil for adjusters' on-the-job training.

Gil was enthusiastic about developing work instructions which described the steps in adjusters' tasks in simple formats. He realized that much of the plant's downtime resulted from adjusters' bad habits. He recognized the checklist as a tool for establishing standard practices and helping adjusters to learn them. He identified seven tasks: startup, shutdown, changeover, beginning of shift, during shift, ending shift, and troubleshooting. The steps for completing some tasks differed completely from one machine to another, although the task names were identical.

As checklists were developed, Gil distributed them to adjusters and asked for comments and suggestions. He and the consultant worked with a group leader whose job was to organize the tools and machine parts for changeovers according to factory setup sheets. The training program also provided an opportunity to formalize previously recommended improvements in factory setup procedures. The suggestion was discussed with the plant supervisor, who supported it. Nearly a quarter of the setup procedures were improved as a result of the changes.

After having completed two checklists, Gil felt confident in his ability to develop them for the remaining machines in the plant. Before he was promoted to the training job, he had trained adjusters to make changeovers and had also helped them troubleshoot machine problems. He acknowledged that he tended to "jump in and solve the problem" rather than coach adjusters to solve the problems themselves. He learned to ask, "Did you set up the machine according to the checklist?" and "Are you troubleshooting the machine according to the checklist?" When adjusters hadn't followed the setup steps, he demonstrated the procedure and then asked the adjuster to perform the same steps. He learned to let adjusters struggle a bit instead of solving problems himself.

The plant manager and his staff recognized that behavioral changes were required if the new OJT approach was to succeed. They believed that teaching new adjusters to use checklists would be easier than retraining incumbents. Retraining required unlearning old habits, learning new skills, and practicing the new skills until they became habits. Supervisors and adjusters had to feel the need to change, and the supervisor's role was critical in the improvement process. Two-hour sessions were held with supervisors to discuss the need for change, the use of checklists, and Gil's training approach. Gil explained that he would work individually with adjusters to review their work practices and help change them when change meant improvement. He and the plant manager emphasized the importance of supervisor follow-up and reinforcement. When operating problems occurred, supervisors were to ask the same questions Gil would be asking: "Did you set up the machine according to the checklist? Are you troubleshooting according to the checklist?" This routine would reinforce the importance of the single accepted way of setting up and adjusting machines.

Gil scheduled a series of plantwide meetings led by the plant manager. In the meetings he openly shared plant operating and financial results with hourly employees. These results showed that if operations didn't improve, the plant would be forced to close in a year. The importance of productivity improvement (productivity was defined as envelopes meeting quality standards and shipped to customers) was discussed. Training's potential contribution to operating improvement was also discussed. The plant manager stated that he realized that changing habits was difficult, and that success wasn't expected overnight, but that individual change and improvement were essential to overall improvement. These meetings were followed by small group meetings in which the shift supervisors and Gil discussed the checklist and how it was to be used with adjusters. At the conclusion of the meeting, checklists were given to adjusters along with tips for learning.

In January 1994, Envelope Co. decided to apply for ISO 9000 certification. This decision meant that learning/training checklists would become the mandated tool for conducting OJT in all plants. They had to be written for four more machines in two locations. Certification required that operators in all plant locations be uniformly trained.

Uniform training required that all tasks on all machines be documented in a user-friendly style.

The consultant was teamed with an adjuster and an in-house trainer in the Southwest plant. The team was asked to develop a checklist for the most versatile new machine in the company. The trainer could operate and train adjusters on all machines but this one. The chosen adjuster, Jerry, made changeovers more quickly and produced less scrap than any of the other adjusters. The machine had a bad reputation with adjusters because the same features that made it fast and versatile made it hard to change. Jerry had attempted to train other adjusters with his methods but had become frustrated by their inability to learn.

During the task analysis, Jerry showed his team members how he had modified the manufacturer's setup sequence to reduce travel up and down the machine. The modified sequence required that setup tools be reorganized on the plant floor around the new sequence. The team agreed that this change should be documented and taught to other adjusters. Jerry next explained a formula he had devised which identified the tools needed for each size envelope, eliminating the trial and error that other adjusters used. Using the formula, the training team devised a matrix as a job aid for all adjusters to use in selecting needed tools.

The team also created a "new adjuster orientation" showing the machine sections that were important to setup sequences. It referred to the L/T checklist that described the steps performed at each section during setup. Jerry drew a simple diagram illustrating how to complete the most difficult changes. The illustration was laminated and placed by the machine with the setup tools. After the checklist had been approved, the trainer used it to demonstrate the approach to the other adjusters, who quickly adopted it.

9.5.1 Results

A year after training began, the West Coast plant began to break even and show an occasional monthly profit. The plant manager credited OJL with helping to decrease changeover time and machine downtime and increase productivity. The company was granted ISO 9000 certification in 1994.

9.6 Unstructured OJT Deficiencies

These three cases illustrate deficiencies which are characteristic of the unstructured OJT practiced by many companies.

First, the "buddy system" is often the only training and employee involvement strategy used. When exceptional performers conduct the training, trainees learn the best established way to perform a job. But different trainers teach different ways of doing the same job, and sometimes they teach the job differently. Operator/trainers are not encouraged to change and improve the job and are rarely supported by an environment that promotes improvement. They teach the job the way it has always been done, and valuable information is lost as each successive generation of trainers passes on information.

Second, unstructured OJT doesn't make use of accepted learning principles to facilitate learning. Trainees are expected to learn solely from auditory input; there are no written materials. Training is unorganized, and trainees often learn unsafe and undesirable ways of performing. They may not learn all the steps or even all the tasks they need to know to perform the whole job.

Manufacturing environments are usually noisy, and it's hard for trainees to hear the information presented. When one step depends on another, trainees get lost early in the process and don't really understand the job. Some trainees learn the moves to produce a product but don't understand why they make the moves. Consequently, when unusual events occur, they are unable to respond and make needed adjustments.

Third, OJT trainers are often neither carefully selected nor trained. Trainees say, "You take what you get." Some trainers resent the training duties assigned to them, saying that they learned the job themselves and everyone else should learn it the same way. Outstanding performers often aren't good trainers. Many of them don't want to train. Even well-intentioned trainers inadvertently practice behaviors that block learning. Some experienced OJT trainers have learned to facilitate learning, however. These trainers say that they wish they had known what they have learned about learning when they started training.

Fourth, OJT trainers and trainees are usually expected to do at least two things at once. Trainers show trainees the ropes, but "you train while you work." Some managers believe that when trainees produce while they learn, training costs are reduced. But when trainees learn unsafe practices and techniques that detract from quality, OJT becomes a very expensive method of training. Most jobs require focus and concentration to do them well. Even top operators generally can't do the job well while they are teaching someone else to do it. Trainees' attempts to produce while they learn usually increase rework and scrap.

Fifth, unstructured OJT isn't linked to management policy and strategy. Managers have shown little interest in OJT until recently. Because OJT has been largely ignored and allowed to take care of itself, hourly workers have perceived a lack of management interest in training that is extended to performance. Incomplete communication on procedure leads to product inconsistency. Managers in the same organization have different notions of how training should be conducted. Some schedule OJT on overtime, some don't. Some continue training until the trainer says the trainee is ready, and some just ask the trainee to certify his or her own readiness. When there is doubt about training adequacy and related job performance, there are sure to be perceptions of unfairness and favoritism.

Sixth, there is no conceptual foundation for improvement. Operating results bury training ineffectiveness. Numerous variables are blamed for poor performance, but the potential of training to positively affect operations is largely overlooked.

9.7 Seven Building Blocks of OJL

The three examples we have reviewed demonstrate OJL's potential for boosting productivity and improving organization effectiveness. This potential becomes a reality when seven building blocks are used to structure OJT and fashion effective OJL. The seven building blocks are

1. Analyze needs
2. Consciously involve employees
3. Develop structured exercises and written materials
4. Select and train trainers
5. Implement an effective training process
6. Establish OJT policy and procedures
7. Evaluate results and reinforce success

9.7.1 Analyze needs

The importance of employee commitment to the new training system is a lesson we can learn from each case cited. The first block in building employee commitment is a needs analysis.

A needs analysis openly and actively involves a majority of employees in examining the way in which they learn and perform their work. It offers managers who are still looking for ways to involve workers in improvement a ready solution. The needs analysis builds commitment to change because people usually support what they help to create. The analysis demonstrates the need for change and begins building the commitment to make change happen.

A needs analysis also determines whether a genuine need for training exists. It identifies performance competencies. It identifies the skills required to perform the work, actual skill levels, and the gaps between what now exists and what is needed. It identifies which training has worked and which hasn't. Finally, the analysis differentiates between training needs and the need to improve equipment or to change motivation and reward systems.

The needs analysis helps ensure that recommended training will be used. Many training professionals have developed programs which remained on the shelf after they were developed. Often, lack of use is due to inadequate user involvement in program development. Implementation of training works best when users are involved at the outset of program development, the needs analysis.

9.7.2 Consciously involve employees

The second building block is an employee involvement strategy. This block derives from the needs analysis. It may require some managers and training professionals to change their perspectives about involvement and training. The question, "How do we get them to buy in?" is recast to, "How do we (all of us) best serve our customers?" The question, "What training do we give them?" is recast to, "How do we learn what we need to serve our customers?" These perspectives incorporate what we know about quality management and adult learning. We know that operators at every point in a work process can learn to relate to serving customers. We also know that most learning takes place on the job, that adults learn best while doing, and that much adult learning is self-directed. The new perspectives emphasize the importance of OJT but vest the major responsibility for learning with trainees. They emphasize performance, not subject matter.

The employee involvement strategy recognizes that much learning and improvement occurs when workers reflect on their jobs as they prepare to help others learn. The reflection, in turn, leads to changes and improvements in the work itself.

When learning and performance are emphasized, training ceases to be important as an end in itself. Subject matter experts don't create agendas to use classroom time, they look for alternative ways of helping trainees acquire the knowledge and skills needed for performance. This learning focus results in shorter, less formal off-the-job training sessions to supplement on-the-job learning.

A conscious employee involvement training strategy lets managers choose the degree to which they will involve employees and how much training responsibility to give them. The strategy recognizes the benefits of involvement and balances the benefits against the increased up-front time that it requires. Envelope Co. consciously involved only a few key workers in each plant, whereas Paper Mill South involved the entire hourly paper mill workforce in two-hour train-the-trainer workshops. Paper Mill North gave the stock preparation training development group more responsibility for training, and more freedom in guiding the training program, than it had ever given a group of hourly employees for any program in the past.

9.7.3 Develop structured exercises and written materials

Structured exercises and written materials that are developed by operators and subject matter experts are essential for effective OJT. We saw three types of written materials in the cases: work instructions, learning and training guides, and job aids.

Work instructions were called Learning/Training Checklists or L/T Checklists. Trainers organize information for on-the-job presentation to trainees, beginning with a short summary of the job's purpose and how the operator accomplishes it. They present critical information in a logical, user-friendly style, including all major tasks performed in a job. For example, a checklist for a machine operator includes the tasks of machine startup, changeover, boilout, shutdown, beginning of shift routines, during shift routines, and end of shift routines, and troubleshooting steps for each task. Operators decide what steps to include, and the level of detail for each. They always include steps that refer to operating parameters, limits, and tolerances and steps that are important to product quality and safe operating practices.

Some tasks require close team cooperation. For example, the tasks of threading the paper machine after breaks and threading the winder require that the entire winder team work in concert. The tasks are included in the learning/training checklists for the third hand, fourth hand, fifth hand, and sixth hand. Some task checklists outline the series of activities regularly performed for preventive maintenance. These *basic care checklists* are also included in the complete L/T checklist.

Each operator has his or her own checklist. A library of checklists is maintained on the manufacturing floor for easy reference. Filing checklists in expandable binders like those in a parts store permits hundreds of laminated pages of checklists to be laid flat for easy reference and reading.

Learning guides are just what their name suggests: guides for learning. These brief handouts describe how trainees can use L/T checklists, offer tips for "partnering" with trainers, and provide information that facilitates learning and remembering. *Training guides* are guides for training which serve as memory joggers. They contain the training dos and don'ts discussed in train-the-trainer workshops.

Operators in most manufacturing facilities have written memory joggers on machinery and in personal notebooks to ensure that they do things right. These are, in fact, operator-produced job aids that typically include operating parameters, illustrations, and diagrams showing connections and relationships. Often an individual operator's job aids are so personalized that they mean little to other operators. They refer to machine setups that deviate from standard. Informal personalized job aids are often hard to read and out of date. Formal job aids also help operators perform. They may contain important operating information that is difficult to remember, especially if it is seldom used. Formal job aids are current, accurate, and standardized. The best examples are written for operators in a simple, friendly format. Most off-the-job training sessions are enhanced when trainees are presented with a job aid as a reference or memory jogger.

All on- and off-the-job training materials work best when they are written in a nontechnical, user-friendly style in the operators' own language. Materials should be formatted with adequate white space around words. Whether the work instructions are called L/T checklists, manuals, or guides, space is provided for both trainers and trainees to mark and track progress, and for review and improvement. Written materials highlight steps associated with hazardous materials and conditions, and steps important to product quality.

Structured exercises in the cases included the self-paced interactive videotaped orientation for the winder crew, the stock preparation tours, and the new machine adjuster orientation. The supplemental off-the-job training in each case was closely tied to OJT and designed to help trainees meet specific performance-based learning objectives.

9.7.4 Select and train trainers

The fourth building block is a cadre of trainers who are coached in a train-the-trainer session after being selected on the basis of criteria such as the following. Effective OJT trainers must have credibility with hourly workers coming from demonstrable job knowledge. Effective facilitation also requires humility, patience, and a genuine interest in trainees and their progress. These qualities can be demonstrated and observed. Individuals having these qualities are often described or identified in needs analysis interviews. The characteristics are objective criteria for the selection of trainers and have been used successfully to help operators match their own interests and abilities with the demands of a trainer's job.

Preparing for OJL requires training for in-house people, even those who have shown that they can successfully facilitate learning. The training agenda is obviously linked to the task at hand. In our three examples, in-house people worked as partners with an outside consultant in conducting the task analysis, writing L/T checklists, and developing job aids. Training development partners helped consultants train OJT trainers to use training materials. Both TDPs and on-the-job trainers conducted initial training, certified trainees, and sustained continuing coaching. Developing a training agenda for TDPs and on-the-job trainers begins with writing their learning/training checklist.

Here is an example of a learning/training checklist for training development partners listing all their tasks and describing the activities performed in the three cases.

Learning/Training Checklist
Organization: Paper mill
Job Title: Training Coordinator
Date: January 1995

Summary. The training coordinator works as a partner with the external consultant. He or she learns to organize, structure, and conduct effective on-the-job learning for stock preparation and machine room operators. Key activities include preparing on- and off-the-job learning and training materials, training OJT trainers, conducting on- and off-the-job training, continuing coaching, certifying trainers, and administering training.

Task analysis. Conducts a structured task analysis on jobs for which training will be conducted. The analysis is used to write work instructions, determine if off-the-job training is needed, and develop job aids.

Work instructions

   Develops work instructions called learning/training checklists from personal work experience and task analyses. Checklists follow standard format and are used for on- and off-the-job training.

   Conducts L/T checklist reviews during development.

   Develops new task descriptions as needed on a continuing basis.

Job aids

   Develops job aids to assist operators in performing their activities accurately and safely.

   Documents job aids in L/T checklists.

   Works with supervisors and operators to update job aids and work instructions.

Off-the-job presentations

> Writes learning objectives for off-the-job presentations to be made individually or to small groups.
>
> Develops materials to facilitate attainment of learning objectives, including lesson plans, visual aids, and reference materials.
>
> Assists in selecting and developing information presentation media: print, slide/tape, and videotape.
>
> Conducts off-the-job presentations to enable operators to meet learning objectives.
>
> Checks trainees' abilities to perform against objectives.

On-the-job training (OJT)

> Uses L/T checklists and learning guides to present OJT for paper mill people.
>
> Certifies performance competency using the certification procedure. (As this is being written, the union has not agreed to a certification process. The procedure is being used, but operators are not officially pronounced certified.)
>
> Conducts ongoing coaching as needed to maintain operator competency.
>
> Trains OJT trainers to conduct OJT.

Training administration

> Maintains a master copy of each L/T checklist.
>
> Schedules training and maintains records of on- and off-the-job training by individual and department.
>
> Maintains records of task and job certification for each stock preparation and paper mill person.
>
> Maintains records of training and training needs by individual worker.
>
> Keeps training materials current.

Training for TDPs and OJT trainers can be conducted individually or in small groups. Trainers need to get in touch with the feelings of confusion, anxiety, and frustration that new trainees feel. Operators selected as TDPs and trainers have usually demonstrated expertise in their jobs over time. Consequently, they perform so quickly and effortlessly that their actions are nearly automatic. Actions requiring deliberation don't appear deliberate to the observer. Experienced operators have forgotten that they had to learn each individual step of the task they now automatically perform so easily. They have forgotten the anxiety and the fear of looking foolish that they felt when they first learned their job. Getting in touch with the emotions they experienced as new learners helps them empathize with trainees and work with the deliberation and patience which is required for learning facilitation. (Union officials have agreed that seniority is only *one* of the criteria for trainer selection. The membership has been very vocal in insisting on criteria like these.)

Most training development partners and trainers need to learn how to conduct OJT, how to present and demonstrate tasks, and how to coach trainees while they practice a task. Here is a sample list of workshop learning objectives for a train-the-trainer workshop for TDPs.

Learning objectives for TDPs and OJT trainers. After a workshop or individual training, the participant will be able to

- Use the training cycle visual aid to explain how the training process works.
- Use a task analysis checklist to conduct a task analysis.
- Use "Guidelines for Writing an L/T Checklist" to write a checklist.
- Use "Guidelines for Reviewing an L/T Checklist" to review a learning/training checklist with job incumbents and reach agreement on the checklist.
- Explain when off-the-job training is needed to supplement OJT and describe a specific need for off-the-job training from his or her own experience.
- Use "Guidelines for Learning Objectives" to write learning objectives for an off-the-job training session.
- Use these learning objectives to design an off-the-job training session.
- Use the learning objectives and design to conduct an off-the-job training session and verify learning against the objectives.
- Demonstrate four training dos and avoid all training don'ts while conducting OJT.
- Use an L/T checklist to conduct OJT for a task he or she can perform.
- Verify learning of the task presented, and, given a training completion checklist, complete it as prescribed in the guidelines.
- Describe how to use the "Procedure for New and Revised Tasks and OJT."

- Describe OJT from the perspective of a new trainee.
- Describe a learning/training contract and, in a role play, lead a trainee through the process of developing an L/T contract.

9.7.5 Implement an effective training process

An effective training process begins with a contract between trainer and trainee similar to the contract used in Paper Mill North. The contract explicitly states and clarifies the expectations of supervisor, trainer, and trainee. An effective process uses a variety of prepared training tools: work instructions, job aids, tips for learning and training, structured exercises, and off-the-job presentations designed to meet learning objectives.

The stated objective of the training and certification process is to qualify trainees, not to disqualify them. Learner needs and performance standards drive the process. Trainers adjust their presentation and demonstration pace to the trainees' ability to absorb information. They create a climate of mutual respect and exchange information with trainees as equals. Trainees have a large measure of control over their own qualification because they know up front the criteria by which they will be evaluated, and have open access to the material they need to learn.

Managers and trainers schedule the OJT process, taking fatigue, production demands, and other considerations into account. For example, it is easier to teach and to learn before working an eight-hour shift than it is after the shift; top-performing crews provide a better learning environment than poorer-performing crews; some days of the week and month are less hectic and better for training than others; approval may be required for overtime; some tasks will require off-the-job explanation and discussion. Experienced trainers factor all these aspects into their OJT schedule.

9.7.6 Establish OJT policy and procedures

Local OJT policy and procedures describe the operation's position on training. The Paper Mill South example included a description of a procedure that was implemented there. Here is another example of a policy statement.

Training policy

> We recognize that effective training is necessary for satisfactory performance. While we believe that continued learning is each employee's career-long responsibility, we intend to meet our responsibility in facili-

tating that learning. We will provide resources for learning including OJT and other training, written materials, scheduled time, competent trainers, and adequate facilities and equipment.

The Paper Mill North management team

Here is an example of a procedure that specifies how ongoing changes in work will be documented and how training is to be conducted on the changes.

Procedure: revising learning/training checklists and OJT

1. Learning/training checklists define the tasks qualified operators must be able to perform.
2. When tasks change, the task list in the learning/training checklist is revised to reflect the change.
3. When new instructions or procedures are required to perform a task, a task list detailing the steps is written, approved, dated, and added to the learning/training checklist.
4. When task lists are revised, and when new task lists are written, they are discussed with two job incumbents, who are asked for suggestions on performing the new tasks.
5. After a new or revised task list has been approved, the writer reviews it with all job incumbents and, if needed, conducts training on the task.
6. The person who writes the task list discusses it with shift supervisors as it is written and immediately after approval.

9.7.7 Evaluate results and reinforce success

If you don't identify the variables when you are tracking improvement, then you won't know when improvement occurs. Get agreement with operating managers on the operating results that training will influence. Agree on an estimate of the percent improvement attributable to training and to other variables if you can't agree on a more precise measurement. Baseline data already in the accounting system can probably be used to evaluate improvement. In our examples, improvement measurement centered on machine utilization, machine downtime, specific definitions of scrap and production, and the time required for new operators to reach competency. All of these variables were being tracked before training began.

Publicize and discuss improvements and success stories as they appear. Recognition and publicity reinforce new behaviors and habit patterns and help make continuing improvement a way of life.

9.8 Conclusion

OJL corrects the training deficiencies which are usually associated with unstructured OJT and offers a natural, comfortable method of employee involvement. The approach has helped several organizations improve their work team collaboration and operating results, and earn ISO 9000 certification.

OJL is not a quick fix. Among the cases cited, Paper Mill South is continuing to modify materials and improve its process six years after the needs analysis was first conducted there. Paper Mill North is continuing to develop materials and train paper machine operators in various classifications. Envelope Co. recognizes the need to train new trainers who will modify materials and train new adjusters.

Improved operating results can be expected to pay for improvements in OJT. Sometimes dramatic improvements appear immediately, but usually they begin to emerge six months to a year after training starts. OJL requires an investment of planning, patience, and continual attention. It offers a tangible and continuing return on investment that usually begins 12 to 18 months from the start of training.

9.9 References

Marsh, P. J., "Turning a New Page in OJT," *Technical & Skills Training,* May/June 1992.

Marsh, P. J., "On-the-Job Learning," *Technical & Skills Training,* August/September 1994.

Chapter

10

Putting Some Fun in Your Technical Training

Annie S. W. Phoon

Annie S. W. Phoon is a consultant at Learning Management International and an adjunct teaching fellow at the National University of Singapore. She received her B.A. from the University of Singapore and her B.Soc.Sc. (Honors) and postgraduate Diploma in Education from the National University of Singapore. While at the National Productivity Board, she was involved in the ASEAN Human Resource Development project in Singapore, a U.S.$40 million effort aimed at developing the Productivity Movement in Singapore. She was formerly Vice President (Human Resources) at the United Overseas Bank Group. She was a member of the National Trainers' Skills Standards Setting Committee in 1990 and the Professional Development of Trainers Task Force in 1989. She was also a member of the National Video Awards Committee in 1988 and 1989 and served on the Singapore Training and Development Association Executive Committee for three terms, from 1988 to 1990. She received the Singapore President's Commendation Award in recognition of her contribution to training the Scout Movement in 1991. Her interests are in the creative design and delivery of training programs, training of trainers, and organizational development.

10.1 Introduction

In our first five or six years of life, we were astounding in our capacity to learn—we learned an entire language, gained control of our bodies, and discovered much about the world in those short years. Between the ages of two and five, the human child learns proportionately more per day than during any other time of life. I believe that much of this is due to the difference in the learning and "teaching" methodologies used before and after the age of five.

Learning methodologies used before the age of five were

- Lots of emotion and celebration
- Multisensory experiences
- Lots of play
- Relaxation and restful periods
- Humor
- Use of music and singing
- Fantasy and imagination
- A rich, visually stimulating environment
- Positive suggestive language
- Supportive group dynamics
- Games and physical activity
- Tireless support, love, and adulation (Jensen, 1988)

However, these extremely powerful elements of effective learning seem to disappear when we attend formal schooling. And when we enter the workplace, learning becomes even more removed from the creative, exploratory play that we experienced as little children. Learning becomes serious, even stressful, and one has to learn predetermined amounts of information at a prescribed pace; it also tends to preclude cooperation and teamplay and becomes more an individual, sometimes solitary activity. Teachers and trainers teach in a linear and inductive way, putting learners in a passive mode rather than allowing them to explore and deduce through active participation, and learners quickly become afraid of trying and failing. In other words, learning is stripped of those same elements of fun, exploration, and participation that made it possible for us to absorb and retain remarkable amounts of knowledge.

The purpose of this chapter is to suggest some techniques that trainers could use to recapture and recreate the joy of learning in their learners. This may mean a radical departure from the traditional and conventional and a stepping out of our comfort zones. The basic underlying assumption is that as trainers, our main role is not so much to teach as to create conditions conducive for our participants to learn.

The techniques described here have worked well for me over the years, as well as for technical and other trainers whom I have trained. I hope that they will stimulate you to innovate and create other techniques that will also inject fun and enjoyment into your participants' learning, making them learn more effectively and efficiently.

This chapter has four parts:

1. Techniques to create a stimulating learning environment
2. Techniques to open the training session
3. Techniques to replace or modify the lecture
4. Techniques to review learning

10.2 Techniques to Create a Stimulating Learning Environment

The training environment is a very powerful and perhaps underexploited learning strategy. The environment comprises the physical setting and the atmosphere and surroundings. People learn best in an atmosphere that is positive, emotionally safe, relaxed, and joyous, and one where they may explore without fear or constraints. People also learn best if the environment matches their personal learning style.

Dunn and Dunn found that individuals learn in one of two broad styles: global and analytic. These are opposite ends of a continuum and represent quite different learning needs. In setting up the physical environment, we need to bear in mind that our audience will include people with both learning styles. Section 10.7 gives a brief description of the two learning styles.

Dr. Marian Diamond, in her research on the brain, found that at any age, from birth to death, we can increase our mental ability by environmental stimulation. Mark Rosenzweig and colleagues at the University of Berkeley found that an enriched environment led to enhanced performance and learning ability. As trainers, we can enhance our participants' learning capacity and their retention of learning by consciously creating a rich, visually stimulating learning environment. Here are some suggestions:

- *Furniture:* Arrange furniture in such a way that each person is able to see and interact with as many of the others as possible. A recommended arrangement is to put chairs in a three-quarter circle, so that everyone faces everyone else. Where possible, avoid using tables, as they inhibit movement and form a physical and psychological barrier between trainers and participants, as well as among the participants themselves. With a circular arrangement, participants very quickly "unfreeze" and are more willing to participate in group and other activities. This arrangement is also informal, and creates a positive, cooperative group feeling and a sense of equality between participants and the trainer, who is also part of the circle.

Some people (global learners) prefer easy chairs and informal furniture with cushions, whereas others (analytic learners) prefer to have a more formal setting. Where possible, use a mix of the two, allowing participants to choose where to sit.

- *Lighting:* Control the lighting so that some parts of the room are a little brighter than other parts. Global learners prefer more dimly lit environments, whereas analytic learners learn best under bright light. If a room's lighting cannot be controlled, use small table or stand lamps to create variable lighting.

- *Music:* Research shows that music has a great effect on our ability to learn and retain what we have learned. Dr. Georgi Lozanov, a pioneer of accelerated learning, found that relaxation induced by baroque music leaves the mind alert and able to concentrate. Such music also awakens the intuitive, creative right brain so that its input can also be integrated into the learning process.

  Use baroque music when participants are involved in learning activities where they need to concentrate, such as solving a problem or doing a case study, and faster-beat music during breaks and in activities that require physical movement and lots of quick interaction. Analytic learners prefer not to have a noisy environment when they are getting inputs. This noise refers to people talking loudly, chattering, etc. Baroque music is quite different from noise—it is soothing, and analytic learners generally *do not* have any difficulty learning with Baroque music background. Global learners, in contrast, can be quite happy reading in the marketplace, bus stop, etc., where it is really noisy. Section 10.8 is a list of baroque music you can use.

- *Visuals:* Mount posters and pictures around the walls of the room. You can create your own posters, making them colorful and interesting. Being homemade gives them a special charm and warmth, although commercially produced ones can be attractive, too. The posters could contain inspirational or thought-provoking statements or quotes. These create a positive frame of mind in the participants and generate attitudes that are favorable to learning.

  The posters could also reflect the content of the training session, drawn or written in an interesting way. For example, in safety training, pictorial representations of safety guidelines could be mounted. When training tellers, a huge specimen of a check could be mounted, highlighting the "seven material parts of a check." These posters will enable participants to experience peripheral learning, that is, unconscious learning from the environment. Participants who are early can begin their learning without waiting for the training session to start. These posters often stimulate participants' interest in learning about the subject matter, and often the participants end up learning more than the proposed course coverage, as the posters stimulate them to discuss the material and ask questions which might not have occurred to them otherwise.

As the training progresses, participants' work on flipcharts can also be mounted on the walls. This gives them ownership of the learning environment and serves as a positive acknowledgment of their contribution to the group's learning.

- *Temperature:* Research shows that the best temperature for the brain is about 65 degrees Fahrenheit—at this temperature, we have maximum clarity of mind. This is cooler than most people may be accustomed to, so ask participants to bring sweaters.
- *Plants:* All human beings have a natural positive response to nature, whether they are conscious of it or not. Try to bring nature into the training environment by having many potted plants around the room or, if this is not possible, some natural, fresh flowers or bouquets.

Nobel Prize winner Buckminster Fuller said, "If you change the environment, you change the people." This is what a positive, enriched, and stimulating environment will do:

- It creates a positive relationship between the learners and the subject matter. When participants arrive for a course on safety regulations or teller training or other technical training, many may not come with the most positive expectations of the course. When they step into a training room which welcomes them with visuals and music, and a cheerful trainer is on hand to greet them, their feelings about the subject matter are likely to become very much more favorable.
- A positive environment also creates rapport between trainer and participants. In the subconscious minds of the learners, the environment is reflective of the trainer. The warm, friendly environment becomes in the minds of the learners an extension of the trainer, and they will likewise warm up to the trainer.
- An innovatively arranged environment also gives participants a sense of exploration and adventure. It invites them to be different,

to try the unknown, to move outside of themselves. When the subject being taught is something considered "difficult" by the target audience, like accounting or financial statement analysis for clerks, the environment can give them the assurance that they will explore together and need not be afraid of failure.

- When introducing new techniques of training, having a new environment that is different from what participants are used to is more likely to make them game to try rather than fold their arms and wait to see whether the trainer succeeds or fails.

10.3 Techniques to Open the Training Session

The first few minutes of a training session are the most important. Having an appropriate opening activity accomplishes three important goals (Silberman, 1990):

1. *Group building.* It enables participants to get to know one another and creates a spirit of cooperation and mutual support that will last throughout the course, and often even after it has ended.
2. *On-the-spot assessment.* It provides some feedback to the trainer and the participants about the attitudes, knowledge, and experience of the participants.
3. *Immediate learning involvement.* It creates some initial interest in the topic and serves as a springboard for a fuller discussion or treatment of the subject matter.

Opening activities should be designed to achieve all three goals mentioned above. As there are many books on opening activities and icebreakers, this chapter will describe only two opening activities here. A training favorite is Human Jigsaw Puzzle. This is how it goes:

1. Prepare jigsaw puzzles from square colored paper, with about four or five pieces to each jigsaw puzzle. Use one color for every three jigsaw puzzles. The total number of jigsaw puzzle pieces should correspond to the number of participants in the class. Paste double-sided Scotch tape on the reverse side of each jigsaw puzzle piece.
2. As participants enter the room, give each a piece of the puzzle and ask the person to stick it to any part of his or her clothing where it is visible to others.
3. When all the participants have arrived, give this instruction: "Each of you has been given a jigsaw puzzle piece. You need to find three or four others in this room whose jigsaw puzzle pieces

correspond with yours so that together your pieces form a perfect square. But you are not allowed to remove the jigsaw puzzle piece from your clothing. You have three minutes to find your team, and the first team that forms a perfect square will win a prize."
4. Participants then search out their team members.
5. When the participants have formed their teams, ask each team to give itself a name. Then ask each team to come up in turn to paste its jigsaw puzzle pieces onto a blank flipchart page to see if they indeed form a square. This is usually very hilarious, because some teams will have very unusual shapes! Write the name of each team below its assembled jigsaw shapes so that everyone can see the teams' names. Give the promised prize to the winning team—buy something that they can then share around the class, such as a box of chocolates or cookies with enough pieces for everyone.
6. While participants are still in their teams, ask them to find answers to the following within their teams:
   a. Three things they have in common apart from attributes that can be seen, such as height, color, clothing, etc.
   b. One word or phrase to describe how they feel about the topic and why, or a shared experience related to the topic
   c. What they would like to get out of the course
7. Tell participants that they need to present these to the class on a flipchart without using words. Give them crayons or magic pens and a piece of flipchart paper.
8. Item 6a gives participants an opportunity to self-disclose and find out about one another and continues the group building started earlier. Item 6b provides some data about their attitudes and experience pertaining to the topic. Item 6c enables us to know their expectations of both the content and the process.
9. Asking participants to present without using written words gets them out of their comfort zone and forces them to express themselves using drawings or symbols. They usually enjoy it! Giving them crayons and magic pens evokes memories of their childhood, and adds to the fun of the exercise.
10. After participants have presented (one minute per group), give them a questionnaire related to the topic and ask them to fill it out individually, then agree on the answers as a group. The questionnaire could be of a fill-in-the-blanks type or a true-false type, covering the main aspects of the course content.
11. Getting participants to fill out the questionnaire individually gives them time to ponder or think through the issues. Getting them to discuss their answers provides an opportunity for them to check their responses against those of the group in a relatively

safe way. It also gets them involved in the actual subject matter early in the course.
12. Instead of a questionnaire, you could give a scenario and get them to respond to it. For example, when teaching Law Relating to Banking and Finance, I would give an actual case and ask participants for their verdict if they were the judge—just from a common-sense viewpoint. Later, when covering the legal principles, participants would be better able to relate these principles to the case.
13. Go through the answers to the questionnaire and explain that the rest of the course will provide more details on some of the items there.

This activity has three parts—forming a group, sharing with one another, and assessing participants' current level of knowledge about the subject matter. You could also design your own version of an opening activity, using ideas and suggestions from other trainers or books. The last part of an opening activity should allow the main content of the training to be phased in, so that the training process becomes seamless.

Another recommended opening activity is the Human Treasure Hunt (some trainers call it People Scavenger Hunt):

1. Give participants a copy of the Human Treasure Hunt sheet.
2. Here is a sample Human Treasure Hunt sheet for bank credit officers:

    "For each item below, find someone who fits the description. Write that person's name down and get him or her to sign against it. You may not use anyone's name more than once.
    Find someone in the room who

    - Has the same size thumb as you
    - Has opened a current account for a corporate customer
    - Is the newest member of this company
    - Specializes in accounts receivable financing
    - Has the same number of siblings as you
    - Thinks that we should revise house rules on loan approval
    - Has never had a bad loan while in this bank
    - Was born in the same month as you
    - Has served bankruptcy proceedings against customers
    - Has seen the same movie as you, more than once

3. Tell participants to complete their sheets within three to five minutes, depending on the class size and the number of items in the

Treasure Hunt sheet. To make it more fun, mention that a prize will be given to the first five participants who complete the sheet.

4. When the winners have been declared, survey the class about the items and, where appropriate, generate short discussions around some of the items.

10.4 Techniques to Replace or Modify the Lecture

The lecture is one of the most commonly used training methods. It is efficient and, when delivered by a skillful, well-prepared presenter, can be an interesting learning experience. The lecture method's main drawback is that information is presented to the learners, who remain passive. As the saying goes, "I hear and I forget, I see and I remember, I do and I understand." With the lecture method, people tend to forget much of what they hear. We therefore need to modify our lectures so that our participants "do and understand."

Here are some techniques for modifying or replacing the lecture method that have produced high learner enjoyment and led to enhanced learning retention for my trainees.

10.4.1 Teaching pairs

1. Instead of giving a lecture, convert your lecture into a handout that has two main parts. Distribute this handout to participants.
2. Divide the class into two equal parts, say A and B. Assign the first part of the handout to the As and the second part of the handout to the Bs. Tell the class that they have 10 minutes to read their part of the handout, at the end of which they have to teach it without referring to the handout.
3. When participants have completed reading and preparing to teach, get each of them to find a partner who has read the other part of the handout. Give them three to four minutes each to teach, after which they should swap roles.
4. Give participants a simple test or quiz which covers the entire handout to provide some feedback on how much they have learned. Where necessary, discuss areas that require further elaboration.

This activity makes participants responsible for their own learning as well as for that of their partner. Because they have to teach the material, they concentrate on it in a far deeper way than they would if they were just listening to a lecture. They are likely to translate the material into a form that they understand more readily in order to teach it, and this reordering of information causes them to decode the information and store it in long-term memory. Most of us can recall things that we have taught far more readily than things that were taught to us.

Teaching each other also creates a bond between the pairs. Learning becomes not just a solitary experience of listening to a lecture, but a more enjoyable social exchange. This is important for global learners, who need to relate to someone else to learn better.

10.4.2 Fill in the blanks

1. Instead of giving a straight lecture, convert the lecture material into a questionnaire with a fill-in-the-blanks format.
2. Give the questionnaire to the participants and organize them into trios to find the answers.
3. After most of the participants have attempted the questionnaire, give them the answers, arranged in random order. Ask them to fit the answers into the blanks.
4. Go through the questionnaire and elaborate on and explain the learning point of each item. Invite questions and challenges to your answers.

The main purpose of this activity is to create cognitive dissonance in the participants. When we give a straight lecture, participants are spoon-fed with information, and often are not motivated to think beyond what is told to them. By giving them a questionnaire with blanks to fill in, we are asking participants to think and seek reasonable answers—we are getting them into the learning material as a mental challenge. Items with which they have the most difficulty will create the greatest cognitive dissonance. When the participants finally find the answers, they are far more likely to retain the learning in long-term memory.

This activity also involves the participants in their own learning—they figure out the answers, generate questions, argue with their group members, and challenge the trainer, all of which put them in an active learning mode. Being in a group makes the learning more enjoyable and allows participants to share their answers safely without fear of public ridicule or shame should they be wrong.

10.4.3 Mind mapping

Instead of giving participants notes, or having participants take notes in the usual way, we could either mind-map our lecture or teach participants to mind-map their understanding of the lecture.

But first of all, what is a mind map? Mind mapping is a whole-brain approach to taking notes that allows us to fit the entire subject on one page. Developed by Tony Buzan, a recognized specialist on the brain, it is based on the way the brain actually works. Our brains recall information in the form of pictures, symbols, sounds, shapes, and feelings. A mind map uses these to capture information that is presented to us. It activates both sides of the brain and is much easier than traditional methods of note taking. It is also fun, relaxing, and creative!

How do we mind-map? It would be useful to turn a piece of paper sideways to provide more space and arm yourself with colored pens. Then follow these steps:

1. Write the main topic or idea in the middle of the page and draw a circle, square, or any other shape around it.
2. Draw a branch extending outward from the center shape for each key point or main idea. You should have as many branches as you have main ideas or segments. Use a different color for each branch—the brain remembers colors vividly, so this helps recall.
3. Write a key word or phrase on each branch, branching out to add details. Key words are those which capture the essence of the idea and therefore trigger your memory. Better still, draw a symbol or illustration of the key ideas for better recall.

Figure 10.1 is an example of a mind map. Imagine the colors for the main branches (practice your right brain!), since we do not have the privilege of color printing. Try drawing a mind map of your next lesson plan, or of a speech that you need to give. The more you practice it, the easier and more enjoyable you will find it to be. In fact, I mind-map all my lesson plans, every book I read, and every meeting I attend.

To make your notes even more memorable:

- Use bold letters. Underline words.
- Personalize your symbols. You don't have to use traditional symbols or notations; create your own!
- Be creative and outrageously so, because the brain remembers the unusual more easily.
- Use many colors and random shapes to highlight action or ideas.

When we present our lecture in a mind map, we are actually presenting information in a brain-compatible way. It makes it easier for participants to remember and recall the main points. When our participants mind-map our lecture in their own way, using their own

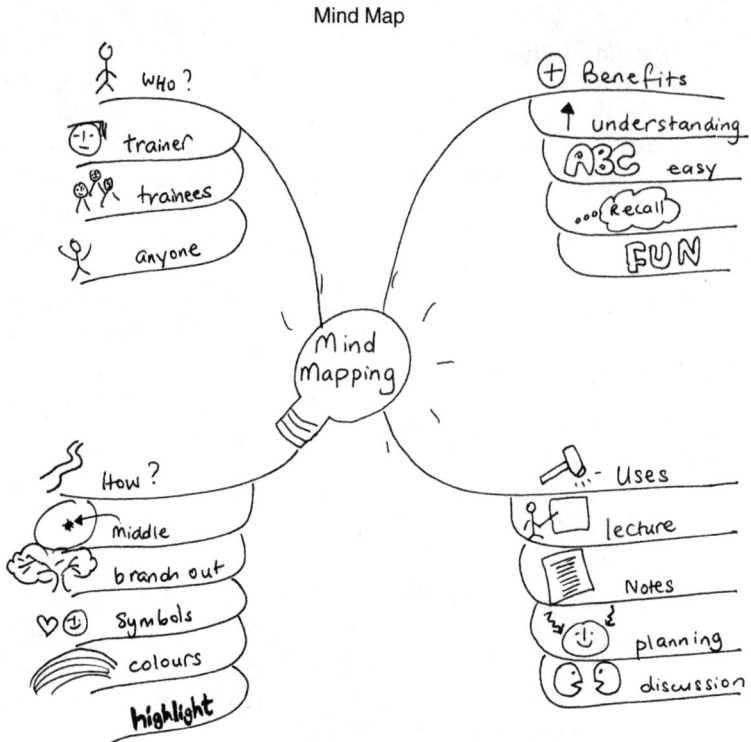

Figure 10.1 A mind map.

illustrations and symbols, they are actively involved in creating meaning from what we tell them. They are also far more likely to remember most if not all of the content of our lecture. And most important of all, they are actually enjoying themselves while listening to our lecture.

10.4.4 Placards parade

This is useful when teaching procedures, especially if there are many steps and it is critical that participants remember every step—for instance, procedures in a plant or refinery where any error can lead to a fatal accident. This activity involves the following:

1. Write each step of the procedure on an A3 size placard so that the words can be clearly read by others from a distance of 10 feet or so. Attach a rope or string to the two upper corners of the placard so that the placard can be hung around a person's neck.

2. Give each participant one placard. If there are more participants than steps, you could have two participants with the same placard.
3. Give participants one or two minutes to read and understand their step of the procedure and to clarify with you if they do not understand it. Then tell them to think of an action that describes their step. If two participants have the same placard, they need to agree on the action.
4. When all the participants have thought of an action for their step, ask them to hang their placards from their necks and stand in a circle. The person with step 1 says and acts out his or her step. Everyone repeats it after him or her, doing the same action. The person with step 2 does the same for his or her step. Everyone then says and acts out step 1, *and then* says and acts out step 2. The same applies for step 3. After the person says and acts out his or her step, everyone says and acts out steps 1 and 2 *and then* step 3. And so on, until all the steps are completed.

Usually, participants will come up with some very funny actions, which add to the fun. This activity makes use of the visual (words on the placards), auditory (hearing each person say his or her step), oral (repeating steps as a group), and kinesthetic (acting out the steps) senses. It makes procedures which are usually quite dry come alive. Doing this activity makes everyone a child again, playing *and* learning.

10.4.5 Machine parts

Very often, in technical training, participants need to understand how a certain piece of equipment or machine works. Instead of *telling* them, we could have them discover the various parts and functions themselves:

1. Write names of the different parts of the equipment or machine and their functions on strips of paper, with the name of each part and its function on a separate slip of paper.
2. Group participants into teams of three or four. Give each team a complete set of the slips of paper naming the equipment parts.
3. If the physical equipment is available, assign one piece to each team. If it is not available, give the teams a large drawing of the equipment. Each team is then given three to four minutes to label the equipment.
4. The trainer then labels the equipment, explaining each part and its function. As the trainer explains each part, participants are encouraged to reposition their labels so that they are correct.

5. After explaining the equipment, have each team take turns labeling the equipment and explaining the function of each part to the rest of the class.

This activity is suitable where participants need to understand the workings of a fairly complex machine or piece of equipment, and where safety is tied to a correct understanding of how a machine works. Participants remember what they themselves figure out better than they remember what is told to them. They also have a chance to correct themselves when the trainer gives the correct answer. This, together with the final team demonstration/explanation to the class, reinforces their learning.

10.5 Techniques to Review Learning

Our memory mechanism is divided into short-term and long-term memory. Short-term memory holds information for a few seconds to a few hours. Long-term memory is our main storage—once information reaches long-term memory, it stays there indefinitely. The challenge to trainers is to help our participants transfer information learned in class from short-term to long-term memory. This takes place through a process called *consolidation*. Studies done by German psychologist Hermann Ebbinghaus found that most forgetting occurs immediately after learning: Within one hour, more than half the original material is forgotten; nine hours later, about 60 percent is lost; and within a month, 80 percent is lost. However, if material is reviewed frequently, retention can be almost perfect (McCarthy, 1991).

What this means for us trainers is that we need to build in frequent reviews of information learned in class. There are many ways to have participants review what they have learned. Here are some techniques which participants have reported to be both fun and effective.

10.5.1 Circle of knowledge

This may be used after one or two days, when participants have learned a fairly large amount of information.

1. Divide participants into two large groups.
2. Ask participants to go through the material that has been covered so far and write the key words or phrases that remind them of what they have learned. This is done individually.
3. Tell participants that they will compete to see which group can remember the most material, in terms of key words or phrases

related to the material covered. Give the groups about five minutes to share and consolidate their strategy.

4. Tell participants the rules of the game:
   - Each group has two seconds to come up with a word or phrase.
   - The word or phrase will be written down by the trainer on the flipchart or transparency for all to see.
   - If a group repeats a word that has already been given, one mark will be deducted.
   - If a group cannot produce a word or phrase within two seconds, it has to pass and the other group takes its turn.
   - The winning group is the one with the most marks (one mark per acceptable word or phrase).
   - A token prize will be awarded to the winning group.

This activity brings out a friendly competitive spirit between groups and a high level of cooperation and team play within each group. The entire game usually lasts not more than eight to ten minutes, and within this short period, participants will have covered many if not most of the key learning points. It is also fun and sometimes hilarious, as participants try to find ways of scoring points by rephrasing and paraphrasing (both allowed) items that have already been listed.

10.5.2 Seven-Up

This activity is taken from a TV show, and somehow the name Seven-Up has stuck, although it is unclear why it is called that.

1. Before the class starts, write down 10 to 15 key learning points on a flipchart. Cover each with a different piece of paper, using 3M spray glue for easy removal.
2. Divide participants into two groups and give them ten minutes to review their learning in their respective groups.
3. Explain that each group is to take turns guessing what the 10 to 15 learning points are. Each group gets two marks for guessing one of the words or phrases.
4. Each time participants guess a word or phrase on the flipchart, uncover that word or phrase. Repeat until all 10 to 15 points have been uncovered.

This activity gets participants to review their learning in a group, which is more enjoyable and interactive than doing it alone. In guessing the 10 to 15 words or phrases, the participants need to shout or state a lot more learning points—that is a form of review in itself.

10.5.3 Do-it-yourself quiz

This activity gets participants to create their own quiz.

1. Organize participants into pairs and assign each pair a topic. Each pair is to think of two questions related to its topic and write them on 4" by 6" cards, with the questions on one side and the answers on the other.
2. Collect the cards and place them in a box or bowl.
3. Divide the class into two teams and use the collected cards to conduct the quiz.

This activity gets participants to review the material covered in the training in three ways: First of all, in order to generate the questions and answers, participants need to review the content of the topic assigned to them; second, in order to do well in the quiz, participants are motivated to review the content of other topics that they were not assigned; and third, as the quiz is conducted, the questions asked and the answers given provide a refresher to them, another form of review.

Getting participants to generate the review or quiz questions also makes the review less threatening, and certainly a lot more fun, than if the trainer had thought of the questions. My experience is that participants often ask far more difficult questions (and many tricky ones, too) than do trainers. There is also an element of trying to outdo one another in the questions asked, albeit in a friendly way, that makes the quiz more enjoyable.

10.5.4 Three-person teaching

In three-person teaching, participants review the material three times: when they review it individually, when they discuss with their partner how to present the material, and when they present it and listen to others giving their presentations.

This is something I picked up from a Stephen Covey course. Instead of reviewing or summarizing the content of a previous day in a three- or four-day course, the trainer invites the participants to do so.

1. At the end of the first day, get participants to pair up. Each pair then selects a topic from a list of topics covered during that day. The pairs then work on preparing to present their topics the next morning.
2. The next day, participants take turns presenting their topics to the class. Participants can be encouraged to use a different approach in presenting than was used in the actual training itself. This will

give variety to the session and encourage participants to innovate and create other approaches.

As a variation, the trainer could divide the material to be reviewed into three parts. Participants are divided into three groups, with the people in each group preparing to teach one of the three parts. The next day, participants get into trios (each teaching a different part), in which each person takes turns teaching the other two his or her part of the material. This variation would be useful in situations where participants feel very uncomfortable in presenting to a large group.

10.6 Conclusion

There are many other techniques and activities that can replace the traditional way of designing and delivering technical training. You can probably think of several by now, adapting childhood games or activities or TV game shows or just innovating from whatever method you currently use. The whole purpose of these activities is not to be innovative and different for its own sake, but to design a learning experience that is both effective and fun.

In Singapore, where I come from, training is becoming more and more important, and companies are being pressured to provide even more training for their employees. As a trainer, I feel that it is not enough to just train people—we need to ensure that the people who have come for the training have learned. And the only way to do this is to involve them in their own learning, so that they are not mere receptacles for someone else's undigested output.

10.7 Learning Styles

Dunn and Dunn studied the characteristics of successful students and found that people learn in a global, "simultaneous" way or in an analytic or "successive" way. Each learning style represents different needs, as can be seen from the following:

Analytic learners

    Prefer working in bright light

    Like to work alone

    Do not like to snack while concentrating

    Cannot concentrate with noise or extraneous sounds

    Take lots of notes in a lecture

    Are auditory learners

Think best sitting up, preferably in a straight-backed chair
Always finish tasks that they start

Global learners

Prefer a less brightly lit environment
Like to work with others
Like to snack when they concentrate or think
Can concentrate with background noise
Like to draw or use diagrams when they work
Are visual learners
Think best lying or sitting in a soft chair or couch
Are multiple starters, making many attempts at a job before completing it

10.8 List of Baroque Music

Bach

Aria from The Goldberg Variations
Largo from Harpsichord Concerto in F Minor
Adagio from Concerto in D Minor for Two Violins

Corelli

Largo from Concerto no. 7 in D Minor, op. 5
Any largo movement from 12 Concerti Grossi, op. 6

Handel

Largo from Concerto no 1 in B flat Major, op. 3

Pachelbel

Canon in D, op. 1

Scarlatti

Adagio from Concerto no 8

Vivaldi

Largo from "Winter" from *The Four Seasons*

Largo from Concerto in D Major for Guitar and D strings

Largo from Concerto in C Major for Mandolin, Strings, and Harpsichord

Andante molto from Concerto for Two Mandolins, RV 558

10.9 References

Diamond, M., *Heredity: The Impact of Environment on the Brain.* New York, Free Press, 1988.

Dunn, R., and Dunn, K., *Teaching Students Through Their Individual Learning Style: A Practical Approach.* Reston, VA: Reston Publishing Co., 1978.

Jensen, Eric P., *Super-Teaching,* Dubuque, Iowa: Kendall Hunt Publishing Company, 1988.

Lozanov, Dr. Georgi, *Suggestology and Outlines Suggestology.* New York: Gordon and Breach, 1978.

McCarthy, Michael, *Mastering the Information Age.* Los Angeles: Jeremy P. Tarcher, 1991.

Silberman, Mel, *Active Training,* New York: Macmillan, 1990.

Index

Advanced signaling systems, 3
Alliances (*see* Regional Quality Network)
Alternative workplaces, 8–9
Ambiguity, tolerance for, 11
Ambulatory care training initiative, at University of Chicago Hospitals, 79–80
Analytic learners, 207–208
Anderson Consulting, 21
Aptitude tests, 158–159
Artifacts, culture and, 47, 48
Assessment:
   in competency-based training, 96
   (*See also* Evaluation; Needs asessment; Test development)
Assumptions, culture and, 47–49
Automotive industry, computer-aided manufacturing in, 4–5

Basic care checklists for on-the-job learning, 183
Behavior, cultural change and, 47
BHIS (Burroughs Hospital Information Systems), 72
Business, relationship to educational community, 7–8

Cadence system, 72–73
CAM (computer-aided manufacturing), 4–5
CBT [*see* Competency-based training (CBT); Computer-based training (CBT)]
CD-ROM for interactive desktop learning, 21

CEDEO certification, 122–123
Central Michigan University, 21
Certification programs in Netherlands, 122–129
Circle of knowledge, 204–205
Clinical management at University of Chicago Hospitals, 75–76
Collins, James, 49–55
Communications equipment for information superhighway, 3–4
Communication skills, employee need for, 11
Compensation, impact of information superhighway on, 9–10
Competency, definition of, 93
Competency-based training (CBT):
   advantages and limitations of, 94–96
   characteristics of, 94
   definition of, 93–94
   delivery and evaluation activities for, 105–106
   design activities for, 101–105
   evaluation and assessment in, 96
   international (*see* International competency-based training)
   models and simulations in, 96
   transfer of training and, 107–108
Computer-aided manufacturing (CAM), 4–5
Computer-based training (CBT), 21
Computer skills, employee need for, 11–12
Construct validation approach, 157
Contamination of test criteria, 156
Content validation approach, 156
Continuing education in Netherlands, 117
Contract management at University of Chicago Hospitals, 77–78

212 Index

Controlling organizations, learning organizations distinguished from, 57–58
Copper wiring, 3
Cost savings from Regional Quality Network, 33–34
Creativity, employee need for, 11
Criteria for test development, 155
Criterion-related validation approach, 156–157, 163–164
Critical thinking skills, employee need for, 11
Cultural change, Schein's work on, 46–49
Cultural differences, competency-based training and, 97

Database management skills, employee need for, 12
Data entry, 5
Decision making skills, employee need for, 12
Decision support systems, 6
Desktop learning, interactive, 21
Discrimination, testing and, 163
Distance learning, 20–21
Distractors in multiple-choice test item, 159, 160
Documentation of test development, 162
Do-it-yourself quizzes, 206

Education:
  in Netherlands (see Netherlands)
  at University of Chicago Hospitals, 76–77
Educational community, relationship of business to, 7–8
Electronic performance support systems (EPSS), 6, 20
Employees:
  alternative workplaces for, 8–9
  certifying competency of, 86–87
  impact of information superhighway on, 6–10
  involvement in on-the-job learning, 182–183
  as on-the-job learning trainers, 172–176
  skill development of (see Skill development)
  skills needed by, 10–13
Entrepreneurial education in Netherlands, 120–121

EPSS (electronic performance support systems), 6, 20
EQFM (European Foundation for Quality Management), 122
Essay tests, 160
European Foundation for Quality Management (EQFM), 122
Evaluation:
  in competency-based training, 96
  of on-the-job learning, 189
  (See also Assessment; Test development)

Fairness of tests, 163–164
Fiber-optic cable, 3–4
Filling in the blanks, 200
Fill-in test items, 159
Flexibility, employee need for, 11
Ford Motor Company, 21
Funding for Regional Quality Network, 33
Furniture for stimulating learning environments, 193–194

Gap analysis for information superhighway, 13–14
General Motors Corporation, merging of total quality with cultural change and learning organization concepts at, 43–66
Global learners, 208
Government of Netherlands, 114
Group building, 196

Hardware for information superhighway, 3–4
Higher education in Netherlands, 116–117
High-tech environments, merging of total quality with cultural change and learning organization concepts in, 43–66
Human resources management, training for, 132–135

Immediate learning environments, 196
Independence, employee need for, 12
Information-based systems, 8
Information-gathering interviews at University of Chicago Hospitals, 80

Index

Information superhighway, 1–25
  definition of, 2
  employee skill development related to, 14–21
  employee skill needs related to, 10–13
  hardware and software for, 3–4
  impact on employees, 6–10
  impact on workplace, 4–6
  initial access to, 2
  needs assessment and gap analysis related to, 13–14
  universal access to, 3
Innovation, employee need for, 11
Insurance coverage, impact on University of Chicago Hospitals, 73–74
Integrated Services Digital Network (ISDN), 3
Interactive desktop learning, 21
International competency-based training, 96–101
  cultural differences and, 97
  delivery of, 100–101
  preparing to conduct, 98–100
  understanding of audience for, 97
Internet, 2
Inventory control, 5
ISDN (Integrated Services Digital Network), 3
ISO 9000, 122
ISO 9000 committee of Regional Quality Network, 35–36
Item analysis for test development, 161

JHPIEGO Corporation, competency-based training by, 91–109
Job analysis for test development, 154–155
Job knowledge tests, 158
Just-in-time environment, skill development for, 19–20

Knowledge maturity curve, 8

Learning:
  framework for, 19
  techniques for reviewing, 204
Learning environment, stimulating, creating, 193–196
Learning guides for on-the-job learning, 183

Learning objectives for on-the-job learning, 187–188
Learning organizations, 19–20
  controlling organizations distinguished from, 57–58
  merging of total quality with cultural change and learning organization concepts in high-tech environments and, 43–66
Learning styles, 207–208
Lecture, techniques to replace or modify, 199–204
Liability, 131–146
  adventure-based training and, 136–139
  framework for identifying high-liability tasks and, 140–145
  for negligent training in retail store, 139–140
  sex discrimination, technical training, and human resources management and, 132–135
  strategies for preventing, 145
Lighting for stimulating learning environments, 194

Machine parts exercise, 203–204
Managed care, University of Chicago Hospitals move toward, 67–90
Managed Care Working Group at University of Chicago Hospitals, 74–78
Martha Hood v. Sears, Roebuck & Company, 139–140
Matching test items, 159
Media-oriented approaches, self-study, 20
Mental models in learning organizations, 57
Mind mapping, 200–202
Models:
  in competency-based training, 96
  mental, in learning organizations, 57
Motivation of self, employee need for, 13
Multiple-choice test items, 159–160
Music for stimulating learning environments, 194, 208–209
Myths, making organizations poor learners, 58

Needs assessment:
  for information superhighway, 13–14
  for on-the-job learning, 181–182

Netherlands, 111–130
  adult continuing education in, 117
  certification programs in, 122–129
  outside educational opportunities in, 119–120
  entrepreneurial education in, 120–121
  government of, 114
  higher education in, 116–117
  higher vocational education in, 121
  primary education in, 114, 116
  secondary education in, 116
  technical training in, 117–119
Network Administrator of Regional Quality Network, 30
Network Consultant of Regional Quality Network, 30
Networking committee of Regional Quality Network, 36
Nominal group technique (NGT), 144

On-the-job learning (OJL), 165–190
  developing training checklists for, 167–172
  development and delivery by hourly workers, 172–176
  employee involvement in, 182–183
  evaluation of results of, 189
  implementation of, 188
  needs analysis for, 181–182
  plant results and, 176–179
  policy and procedures for, 188–189
  reinforcement of success in, 189
  structured exercises and written materials for, 183–184
  trainer selection and training for, 184–188
  unstructured, deficiencies of, 179–181
On-the-spot assessment, 196
Opening training sessions, 196–199
Operating committee of Regional Quality Network, 29
Organizing skills, employee need for, 12

Papermaking industry, 166–167
  on-the-job learning in [see On-the-job learning (OJL)]
Passing score development for tests, 162
Pay for knowledge, 9–10
Pay for learning, 10
Performance tests, 160–161

Personal growth skills, employee need for, 10–13
Personal mastery in learning organizations, 57
Pilot sessions at University of Chicago Hospitals, 84–86
Pilot sites at University of Chicago Hospitals, 83
Placards parade, 202–203
Planning skills, employee need for, 12
Plants for stimulating learning environments, 195
Policy and procedures for on-the-job learning, 188–189
Porras, Jerry, 49–55
Practicality of test criteria, 156
Pretraining assessment at University of Chicago Hospitals, 83
Primary education in Netherlands, 114, 116
Problem solving skills, employee need for, 12
Product-process development, 6
Professional guidelines for test development, 153–154, 163–164
Program services committee of Regional Quality Network, 36
Project management skills, employee need for, 11

Quality programs, offered by Regional Quality Network, 38
Questionnaires for competency-based training, 105–106
Quizzes, do-it-yourself, 206

Referral at University of Chicago Hospitals, 75–76
Regional Quality Network:
  benefits of, 33–35
  by-laws of, 39–42
  committees of, 35–37
  funding for, 33
  goals of, 30
  historical background of, 28–30
  membership in, 32–33
  objectives of, 31
  operating criteria of, 31–32
  quality programs offered by, 38
  technical programs offered by, 38–39

Registration aids at University of Chicago Hospitals, 76
Reinforcement for on-the-job learning, 189
Relevance of test criteria, 156
Reliability of test criteria, 156
Resources, available through Regional Quality Network, 34
Response bias in multiple-choice test items, 159–160
Retailing, negligent technical training and, 139–140
Review techniques, 204
RQN expansion committee of Regional Quality Network, 35, 37

Schein, Edgar, 46–49
Secondary education in Netherlands, 116
Security of tests, 162–163
Self-management skills, employee need for, 12–13
Self-monitoring skills, employee need for, 11
Self-motivation, employee need for, 13
Self-study media-oriented approaches, 20
Senge, Peter, 55–59
Sensitivity of test criteria, 156
Services assessment committee of Regional Quality Network, 35, 36–37
Seven-Up exercise, 205
Sex discrimination, 132–135
Shared vision in learning organizations, 57
Simulations in competency-based training, 96
Skill development:
    distance learning for, 20–21
    for information superhighway, 14–21
    learning organizations and, 19–20
Skills:
    definition of, 93
    needed by employees, 10–13
    transfer of, measurement of, 83–84
SKO certification, 123, 126
Socialization, cultural change and, 47
Sponsorship for training at University of Chicago Hospitals, 80
Staffing, impact of information superhighway on, 7–9
Steering committee of Regional Quality Network, 30, 37
Stem of multiple-choice test item, 159

Structured exercises for on-the-job learning, 183–184
Synergy from Regional Quality Network, 34
Systems thinking in learning organizations, 57

Task analysis for on-the-job learning, 185
Teaching pairs, 199–200
Team learning in learning organizations, 58
Technical programs, offered by Regional Quality Network, 38–39
Technical skills, information superhighway and, 4–6
Technical training:
    competency-based [see Competency-based training (CBT)]
    liability and (see Liability)
    in Netherlands, 117–119
Telecommunications, adventure-based training in, 136–137
Teleconferencing, 20–21
Television networks, 20–21
Temperature for stimulating learning environments, 195
Test development, 149–164
    alternative tests and, 164
    case studies of, 150–153
    criteria for, 155
    documentation of, 162
    evidence of discrimination and, 163
    fairness and, 163–164
    guidelines for, 153–154
    item analysis for, 161
    job analysis for, 154–155
    passing score determination in, 162
    test administration and, 162
    test security and, 162–163
    types of tests and, 158–161
    validation approach and, 163–164
    validation approach for, 155–158
Three-person teaching, 206–207
Total quality management (TQM), 43–66
    Collins and Porras' impact on, 49–55
    Schein's impact on, 46–49
    Senge's impact on, 55–59
Trainers, for on-the-job learning, 172–176, 184–188
Training checklistsTemperature for stimulating learning environments, for on-the-job learning, 167–172

Training guidesTraining checklistsTemperature for stimulating learning environments, for on-the-job learning, 183
Training planTraining guidesTraining checklistsTemperature for stimulating learning environments, for University of Chicago Hospitals, 81–83
Transfer of training, competency-based training and, 107–108
Trustworthiness, employee need for, 12

Uniform Guidelines on Employee Selection procedures, 153–154, 163–164
Universal access to information superhighway, 3
University of Chicago Hospitals:
  anticipated technology in ambulatory care clinics of, 72–73
  certification of employee competency at, 86–87
  current and future status of training at, 87–88
  current technology in ambulatory care clinics of, 71–72
  focus on ambulatory care training initiative at, 79–80
  historical background of, 68–69
  impact of new kinds of insurance coverage on, 73–74
  information gathering at, 80

University of Chicago Hospitals (*Cont.*):
  Managed Care Systems and Operations Committee of, 79
  Managed Care Working Group of, 74–78
  move toward managed care environment and, 67–90
  organizational structure of, 70–71
  pilot sessions at, 84–86
  pilot site selection for, 83
  pretraining assessment and, 83
  provision of care to community by, 69–70
  short- and long-term goals of, 78
  skill transfer measurement and, 83–84
  sponsorship for training at, 80
  training plan development for, 81–83

Validation approach for test development, 155–158
Validity generalization, 157
Values, culture and, 47, 48
Virtual workplaces, 8–9
Visuals for stimulating learning environments, 194–195
Vocational education in Netherlands, 121

Word processing skills, employee need for, 12
Workplaces, alternative, 8–9
Written materials for on-the-job learning, 183–184

ABOUT THE AUTHOR

Leslie Kelly is president of Kelly & Associates, Ltd., an eighteen-year-old human resource development firm specializing in technical training and small business personnel work. Her background includes more than 25 years of experience working with scientists, engineers, and technicians in a variety of business and industry settings. Ms. Kelly is Editor in Chief of *The ASTD Technical and Skills Training Handbook*, published by McGraw-Hill.